Historical Problems:
Studies and Documents

Edited by
PROFESSOR G. R. ELTON
University of Cambridge

25

NOBLES AND THE NOBLE LIFE
1295–1500

NOBLES AND THE NOBLE LIFE 1295–1500

Joel T. Rosenthal

Professor of History, State University of New York at Stony Brook

LONDON: GEORGE ALLEN & UNWIN LTD

NEW YORK: BARNES & NOBLE BOOKS

(a division of Harper & Row Publishers, Inc.)

First published in 1976

UK ISBN 0 04 942139 5

Published in the USA 1976 by
HARPER & ROW PUBLISHERS, INC.
BARNES & NOBLE IMPORT DIVISION

US ISBN 0-06-495985-6

Printed in Great Britain
in 10 on 11 pt Plantin type
by The Aldine Press, Letchworth

PREFACE

This book is meant to offer an introduction to the manifold activities of the secular peerage in the fourteenth and fifteenth centuries. It only treats the parliamentary peerage, the men summoned by individual writs of summons to sessions of the king's parliament (plus members of their families). The great gentry, the professional captains, and the spiritual lords – the bishops and the mitred abbots – are not included. But there are peers aplenty, and if many of them have been deemed worthy of individual treatment, where the data permit, it seems self-evident that as a group they also merit our attention.

I am not concerned here to explain any particular event or single phenomenon. The Introduction, as well as the documents I have selected, is designed to survey many facets of aristocratic life and behaviour. If the political is the most striking and familiar, it must share the stage with economic, familial and personal concerns. Though I am an historian, and I write for an audience of historians, it may be that my frame of reference as well as some of my terminology will strike some readers as tainted by sociology. I apologise for unintentional insults. I do believe that we can best understand the medieval nobility if we view it as an articulate elite, the topmost segment of the upper class. The nobles expressed a considerable degree of class-consciousness and a concern with class privilege: *they* worried about class and status, and we should also.

This book is written under strict censures regarding length. This means that some substantive material has been jettisoned: the role of the peers in the council and their activity as builders are but two casualties, and there are many others. My debt to many scholars, living and dead, at best is summarily indicated; in too many instances it is not explicitly mentioned. Suffice it to say that I could not have written this small piece but for the labours of others. Most of the documents which make it possible to illustrate aristocratic life have already been printed, so for the most part all I had to do was to translate or modernise. A few manuscripts have been included, to give a sample of the large storehouse which is still undisturbed. I have included extracts from the various calendars of documents published by the Public Record Office. While calendared excerpts are not primary documents, they were done carefully to catch the substance of the extended original, and their brevity constitutes a compelling virtue. I have transcribed several such pieces in full (Documents 3, 26(b), 30(b) (c) (d), 36(b), 47, 68) to show the full wording. In the interests of comprehensibility I have also taken some liberties with the spelling, and occasionally with the actual wording, of English documents.

I wish to thank the general editor of this series for his encouragement. The library (and librarians) at the Institute of Historical Research and at the University of Sussex were generous with time and advice. I also wish to thank the archivists and staff at the repositories where I worked on documents. Mr Francis Steer at Arundel Castle was very helpful, in conditions more befitting a medieval castle, probably under siege, than a modern library. V. Lebovics and D. S. Petrey helped with translations. Lastly, many academic authors speak fulsomely of the help received from wife and children. I may love my family as much as the next, but they have little to do with my books.

CONTENTS

CONTENTS

ACKNOWLEDGEMENTS

I wish to acknowledge the kindness of many parties for permission to reprint these documents: Oxford University Press for documents 16a, 71, 75 and 76; David McKay Co. Inc. for document 17; Cambridge University Press for document 18; Eyre & Spottiswoode Ltd for documents 27 and 73; the Controller of HM Stationery Office for the use of printed documents 30a, 31b, 31c, 54a and 54b, and for permission to use manuscripts within the Crown Copyright kept in the Public Record Office, documents 30b, 30c, 30d, 36b, 40, 58a, 58b, 59 and 68; Sydney University Press for document 37; the Dean and Chapter of Westminster for their courteous permission to use document 38; the Sussex Record Society for document 39; the Royal Historical Society for documents 41, 42, 43 and 48; the County Record Office of the East Sussex County Council for document 44; the British Library Board for documents 45 and 46; the Director of the Institute of Historical Research for document 47 (which I have translated); and Archon Books, Shoestring Press, Inc. for documents 49 and 50.

ABBREVIATIONS

CCR	*Calendar of the Close Rolls.*
CChR	*Calendar of the Chartered Rolls.*
CFR	*Calendar of the Fine Rolls.*
CPL	*Calendar of Papal Letters.*
CPR	*Calendar of the Patent Rolls.*
Chichele	E. F. Jacob (ed.), *The Register of Henry Chichele, Archbishop of Canterbury,* 1414–1443 (Oxford, 1938), vol. II (Wills).
McFarlane, *Nobility*	K. B. McFarlane, *The Nobility of Later Medieval England* (Oxford, 1973).
PCC	Wills of the Prerogative Court of Canterbury, now preserved in the Public Record Office.
PL	James Gairdner (ed.), *The Paston Letters* (London, 1895), 3 volumes.
PPC	N. H. Nicolas (ed.), *Proceedings of the Privy Council of England* (London, 1834), 6 volumes.
PRO	Public Record Office (London).
RDP	*Reports from the Lords Committees Touching the Dignity of a Peer of the Realm* (London, 1829), 5 volumes.
Rot. Parl.	*Rotuli Parliamentorum* (London, 1767–77), 6 volumes.
Rymer	Thomas Rymer, *Foedera, conventiones, literae, . . .* (London, 2nd edn, 1704–32).
SR	*Statutes of the Realm* (London, 1810–28), 12 volumes.
TV	N. H. Nicolas, *Testamenta Vetusta* (London, 1826), 2 volumes.

INTRODUCTION

INTRODUCTION

Every human society is hierarchical. There are always one or more elite groups. Some people are always more equal than others, and through most of recorded history the overwhelming majority of people have not been equal at all. The pre-eminence of the few may be a result of many attributes: physical strength, wealth, age, knowledge of lore or of technological processes, blood relationship, intimacy with the gods, or any combination of these and other factors. The superiority can either be ascribed or achieved. It might be held from birth, or after a certain milestone has been reached and proper public ceremonies performed. It can be held for life or for a lesser duration, either a set term or until a superior rival topples his predecessor. But regardless of all the different possibilities that come to mind, there are invariably some who are set apart as the leaders of their society.

When we investigate a specific society – in this case late medieval England – with institutions and mores in large part designed to protect private property and to regulate its transmission, we can expect that the political and social elite will possess and control the bulk of the wealth as well as of the power. Sometimes strength and status precede and lead to wealth. Sometimes wealth precedes status, and only afterwards does the political and social structure bend to accommodate the new reality. But regardless of which is cause and which effect – and the interaction is usually so close as to be inextricable – the phenomena of wealth and power tend to stand together. Though there are qualifications and anomalies, generally neither institutional checks nor individual austerity are designed to impoverish the ruling classes or to remove the wealthy from the centre of public life. The aristocracy of fourteenth- and fifteenth-century England profited from this indissoluble union, and woe unto him who questioned the rightness of the marriage.

In this introduction I wish to state some points that are obvious but worth noting at the outset. Why is a brief study of the medieval lay nobility simultaneously 'about' wealth and power, land and family, control of the Church and cultural patronage, status and feud, marriage, local government, liveried retainers, etc.? The fabric of life is indeed sewn of many pieces, but in the garment of society they are not readily distinguishable. An aristocracy bestrides its world, and it continues to do this through time by means of the hereditary transmission of status, wealth and power. Present eminence grows in part from past eminence, and the knowledge that today's greatness helps to lead to tomorrow's is

17

a powerful weapon in both law and the public mind. Few other groups can match this combination of *synchronic* and *diachronic* power. As the greatest modern medievalist tells us:[1]

'Not every dominant class is a nobility. To deserve this name such a class must evidently combine two characteristics. First, it must have a legal status of its own, which confirms and makes effectual the superiority to which it lays claim. In the second place, this status must be hereditary – with the qualification, however, that a limited number of new families must be admitted to it, in accordance with formally established rules. In other words, actual power is not enough . . . It is necessary in addition, that social privileges as well as hereditary succession should be recognised by law.'

Much of this book is a case study of what the peculiar English variations of this theme meant in a political and social framework. The story is neither simple nor straightforward (in the sense of a linear development). Classes and institutions are concepts as much as or more than they are tangible entities. We deem them important in our effort to make order of the past, and so we are sensitive to their origins and evolution. Accordingly we isolate the elements which enable us to create the desired compound, but we must remember the arbitrary nature of the order we impose. England never had a noble caste or a wholly separate order of *nobilis*.[2] Some of Bloch's criteria were never fully grown, while others were present in insular variations.[3] Indeed, it is in this combination of the typical and the peculiar that much of the fascination of this inquiry lies.

This book has two points of focus, both in the introductory essay and in the selection of documents. One is the nobles as a group of elite leaders: laymen, males, deeply involved in national and local affairs. This is the parliamentary peerage.[4] The other point of interest is the aristocratic family, seen perhaps through several generations as the centre of the web around which so much of the activity revolved. In reality the two subjects – the peers as political leaders and the peers as heads of a social aristocracy – were never distinct. The lord did not forget his own connections; the family knew who its leader was. In these pages I hope to convey an idea of the complexities and diversities of aristocratic existence. No single attitude or activity was the key note, the unique characteristic of the nobility. The peer and his family played many roles, in both time and space. They were a force in government at all levels. They had economic fortunes to maintain and transmit. Their economic successes were tied in part to political success at court and in war, both civil and foreign, but they were also linked to the state of agriculture, the land market, and the quality of estate management.

And if the family was never an end wholly unto itself, it did have, in some of its activities, an almost organic drive towards self-preservation. There was a Darwinian element in medieval life, and via the control of marriages and wardships, the creation of enfeoffments, and the contracts for private arms and liveried retainers, each separate lineal unit sustained and nourished itself until ultimately it came to an end and its heirs bore different surnames (if not always a different title). Many of the most basic human motives can be expressed through truisms and tautologies; success brought status and ennoblement, status helped to guarantee continuing success.

We can learn more about the aristocrats of the fourteenth and fifteenth centuries than we can about any other large groups among the contemporary laity. To what extent do data about the upper class allow us to generalise from known to unknown people? If a peer married two or three times, and always another peer's daughter, does this permit the generalisation that like married like? The demographic realities of birth, copulation and death were not too different at various social levels, or were they? [5] And if the baronial answer to the question of what to do with surplus children was different from the bourgeois or proletarian one, was it a dilemma encountered more or less often? Reflection shows how two-edged all these inquiries can be, and answers should not casually be offered. If all historical comparisons must be advanced with caution, those about medieval society are even more tentative. But the nobles were human animals, and by continually pushing at the frontiers of our knowledge about them we might get some idea of what other, less exalted, less documented lives were like.

On the other hand, this book is not a concerted effort at 'debunking'. Social history is not anti-political, and while we strive to see the barons as people we should also remember that part of their power derived from an ancient mythology which linked birth and political weight and innate virtue. The aristocrats of medieval society were not just ordinary people writ large. They were 'the best'. Since the dawn of history men have lied about their ancestors and exaggerated the attributes of their rulers. Those with a disproportionately large slice of power take pains to separate themselves from ordinary mortals; the political fable and the iron boot are both useful tools in this process. Furthermore, all too often those denied a share of power have rationalised their servitude by accepting the idea that they were under the sway of superior creatures. That noblemen and women were set apart, from birth onwards, is a venerable and persistent concept. When Ulysses returns from his wanderings his natural nobility – and the word 'natural' has a literal force in this usage – is so great that neither rags nor a decade's misfortune can be allowed to hide his true stature: [6]

> Athenà lent a hand, making him seem
> taller, and massive too, with crisping hair
> in curls like petals of wild hyacinth,
> but all red-golden. Think of gold infused
> on silver by a craftsman . . .

This is similar in thrust to the wish-fulfilment passages of fairy tales and peasant folk-hero literature; the wisdom, beauty and virtuous prowess of princes and princesses can be temporarily disguised by adversity but never extinguished.[7] Blue blood always comes out, no matter how long hidden in the guise of the chimney sweep or kitchen menial. The medieval nobility revelled in and profited from this kind of fatuous exaltation. Given their unfair share of protein-rich food, of warm clothing and fuel, of freedom to flee from the plague and other such advantages, they may really have had some genetic and physical advantages which helped to support the literary propaganda.

Whatever nature did for them, the arts and sciences of social control more than reinforced. A special training for a special life was the ordained role for the upper classes, the medieval counterpart to the ancient 'free mind in a strong body'. War and the chase were their special pastimes, and theirs alone. In England the draconic law of the forest kept lesser men away from the red deer, and the chase offers a prime example of an area where law reinforced if it did not create class privilege. In chivalric literature a man revealed his high birth through a knowledge of the arcane mysteries of venery, and young Tristan uncloaked his noble lineage through his demonstration of meat carving.[8] The specialised literature centring upon the hunt and falconry was the province of noblemen, and the select company of authors included the Emperor Frederick II along with Edward III's grandson, the duke of York. While we can dismiss all this hunting rigmarole as a complicated rationalisation designed to deprive the poor of a supplementary supply of protein, we must also recognise the complexity of the social structure erected for this simple if vicious purpose.

The chase was the training camp, and war the race in which a man's worth was tested. In economic and social terms war was the *raison d'être* of the whole system which elevated a specially trained and exploitative aristocracy; and, as the original needs for feudal organisation diminished, the nobles worked to fasten the idea of their essential value upon their world. The clash of the highly trained parasites was a noble thing, with its own virtues:[9]

> How I like the gay time of spring
> That makes leaves and flowers grow . . .
> I tell you: no pleasure's so large

(Not eating, or drinking or sleep)
As when I hear the cry: 'Charge!' . . .

This joyous masculine cry from creative literature is not very different from the competitive if mannered blood-lust that Froissart was still detailing, presumably to an eager audience, in the late fourteenth century. The chivalry of Chaucer's knight was not meant facetiously, and even a cynical modern audience is stirred by the passions which course through the dream that Hotspur's wife reminds him of.[10] That the military heroes were also diplomats, administrators and the king's servants detracted neither from their manly dignity nor from the interest of their careers.

CHAPTER I

This chapter is concerned with the nobles as individuals of high status and privilege. It deals with the regularisation and isolation of social rank. It presents a case study of the way an elite group gets defined and delineated, and how in turn the rigidity of definition serves to close and to consolidate the ranks of those enclosed within.

There is no historical definition of a social or economic aristocracy in medieval England. No legal distinction served to separate some men (and their families) from others. The real but imprecise considerations of gentility or purity of birth applied to many people of some standing. These concepts covered most landholders of any significance but they had little to so with the formulation of a definition of peerage: that was a constitutional matter. In Thomas Dekker's *The Shoemaker's Holiday*, the speaker may be a good sociologist but he is of little help as a constitutional expert when he says: 'Are not these my brave men, brave shoemakers, all gentlemen of the gentle craft? Prince am I not, yet am I noble born, as being the sole son of a shoemaker . . .' Consequently it falls to the historian to enunciate who is covered by a study of the peerage, and who is excluded.

The most relevant contemporary distinction was that which singled out the recipients of individual writs of summons to sessions of the king's parliament and which gradually came to see these men as a distinct group, i.e. as a hereditary peerage.[1] Such men – there were about 740 of them between 1295 and 1500 – are the subject of this book, and this chapter deals with the way in which the issue and receipt of the individual summons evolved from a random indication of the king's will into a permanent component of the constitution. In the thirteenth century there had been a large reserve of men who were, at least potentially, considered as 'worthy' of the summons, if the royal pleasure was extended towards them. But change came in time, and eventually the summons ran along more and more defined lines: the element of choosing anew fell out of use, and traditional names and recipients came to dominate, if not quite to monopolise, the composition of the 'Lords'.[2] Behind this bland statement lies a great transition in both government and in social stratification: the gap between the peers and the rest of the 'upper class' opened, and those at the top assumed a special role in the world. If the separate stones on this path were often unnoticed, the general direction was clear, and by the fifteenth century when one said he was 'not usid to meddel with Lordes maters

22

meche forther than me nedith', he was referring to the parliamentary peers.[3]

Between Edward I's 'model parliament' of 1295 and 1500 the 740 peers came before their king from all parts of the realm, from a variety of backgrounds, and with different skills and fortunes to make and preserve. They ranged from royal dukes to relative parvenus, enriched through friendship, the fruits of war, and the plums of patronage and office-holding. Many of them simply followed fathers or other relatives into the elite. Others – almost one-third of the group – were new men, i.e. the first of the immediate family to receive the royal summons. The peers ranged as much in importance as in ability. Collectively they were not simply a baronage of fighters or of landlords, and they well knew that 'it was an esssential feature of the life of the upper ranks of lay society . . . that the road to success lay in the service of the crown'.[4] Sessions of the 'House of Lords' were simultaneously an aggregation of the realm's greatest laymen and of the king's greatest servants.

The history of the nobility between 1295 and 1500 is a tale of definition and contraction.[5] What began as a large and loose group of great men gradually became a relatively fixed estate. The number of peers shrank and the distinctions between noble and non-noble became sharper (though not necessarily harder to bridge). Such a line of development was clearly not contrary to the royal interests: Stubbs saw it as a compromise between the king's freedom to issue summonses and the need to equate tenure with stability of rank.[6] Though the kings varied in their attitudes towards the policy of creating new titles, the truth probably is that they were hostile or receptive to individuals rather than to a course of constitutional development, and to speak of the parsimonious Henry VII as one who 'repelled this invasion' of new peers is to impose a modern and politic view.[7] Good friends were advantageous, while enemies could be over-awed but usually had to be borne.

Edward I kept a very tight hold on the earldoms, but with his lesser barons, not yet able or concerned to press a claim for continuous summons, the policy was very liberal. Edward II ennobled men to build a royal party, Edward III to assert his identification with aristocratic life and military glory. Richard II followed Edward II's motive, and his five new dukes of 1397 were derisively referred to as 'duketti' by a public which presumably took vicarious pride in the narrowness of the highest ranks. The first two Lancastrians were conservative, but Henry VI made fifteen new creations in the year after 1447, and Edward IV, also in need of well-placed friends, made thirteen creations in his first decade. The mid-fourteenth-century lay peerage usually numbered in the fifties; well down from the large assemblies of Edward I and II, that number remained about the norm through the period. However, the number of peers could be academic, for between minorities,

incapacity and service elsewhere the size of the group free to attend
might have little relationship to the number of hereditary barons. In the
1360s Edward III sometimes had a bare two dozen men because of the
demands of the French wars. Spokesmen, supporters and well-rewarded
friends, not votes, was what the monarch had to have available.[8]

In the process of the contraction and definition of the peerage several
factors are particularly important. Once it became accepted that regular
receipt of an individual writ carried a peculiar distinction, the logical
(and almost inevitable) progression was to make the receipt of the writ
into an hereditary privilege (though this was not recognised in law until
the seventeenth century). Once it became accepted, even though
implicitly, that when a man was summoned so his heir would continue
to be, we have a peerage. The actual writs or summonses issued after
1295 differed but little from earlier calls to council or military service,
and they never carried any indication of continuity, let alone hereditability. But their regularity, if not their phraseology, was the critical
point. After 1295 they became an ordinary instrument of government,
just as parliament itself (following the model forms of 1264 and 1295)
gradually became a regular organ or occasion of public business. Even
had no other factors been operative, the very frequency of the writs
would have served to distinguish their recipients from otherwise
similar colleagues who were now passed over. In the 190 years after
Edward I's model parliament there were 161 separate instances of
summons: 10 in Edward's remaining years, 21 in Edward II's time, 54
in Edward III's, 24 in Richard II's, 10 in Henry IV's, 11 in Henry V's,
22 in Henry VI's, 8 in Edward IV's, and 1 in the short reign of Richard
III.[9] And out of a body of about 2,000 tenants-in-chief, all potentially
eligible for summons, never more than about 100 laymen were summoned at one time. So without any constitutional or legal landmarks,
without any notable precedents to serve as guideposts, an institution was
born and a distinction gradually drawn between a call to parliament and
any and all other forms of royal notice.

This explanation sees the growth of lords from the aristocratic
vantage point. From the royal the advantages of continuity and heredity
must have outweighed the dangers posed by permanently entrenching
the barons in the machinery of government. The disadvantages of
simply allowing an unending stream of lay councillors to come and go
were pretty obvious.[10] And if regularity of personnel was to become the
practice, it had to follow some principle. In a world of property and
inheritance, the rules actually adopted, *de facto*, were so natural as to be
almost fore-ordained. Wealth and stature went together. The peers were
already men of importance, and most were related to if not always the
heirs of other peers. In effect the king was merely rationalising and regu-
larising the realities of service, wealth and power. No baron was likely to

rebel just to gain a seat or to avoid his obligation, and no king was likely
to follow a practice which cast any cloud upon the principle of heredity.
Richard II paid the price for appearing to do this, and no one had any
trouble remembering his fate.[11]

The watershed between the casual issuing of summons and the
creation of a semi-continuous and hereditary peerage lies around 1350.
Before then many men were summoned but once or twice, and sometimes not even to consecutive parliaments.[12] Many others among the
early recipients were called regularly but were not succeeded by their
sons (let alone by other male heirs). After 1350 the story differs considerably. Men no longer drop in and out in this casual way. With fewer
and fewer exceptions, the peerage comes to consist of a regular group,
all of whom are almost always summoned. And not only does the male
heir (whoever that is) usually take over the peerage – title and right to a
writ are now seen to accompany the inheritance of the patrimony, or
even of a large share of it – but a new tendency is appearing. There is a
reluctance to let titles go into abeyance. By the end of the fourteenth
century the husband or male heir of the heiress-daughter of a peer is,
almost as a matter of course, receiving the summons which had previously gone to the woman's father or brother. She can now transmit if
not hold a title (Doc. 31). The result of the sharper definition within the
ruling class may mean more difficulty in ascending the social ladder, but
there is also a great reluctance to see the elite ranks diminished or
depleted. From the nobility of service have come the seeds of the idea of
a nobility of blood.

The transition from a random to a regular peerage is illustrated by a
comparison of an early fourteenth-century and an early fifteenth-
century writ of summons. That of 6 Edward II (1313) went to ninety-
nine laymen (Doc. 1). There were ten earls on the list. Of these two were
close relatives of the lord king: his half-brother, Thomas of Brotherton,
and his cousin, Thomas of Lancaster (as was his brother, Lord Henry of
Lancaster). Of the other eight all but Aymar de Valence had succeeded
a father or grandfather. But such was the turnover rate of blood lines in
the Middle Ages that only Arundel, Hereford and Warwick of the ten
were succeeded in turn by their own sons. Richmond's heir was his
nephew, as was Oxford's. Gilbert de Clare died, childless, at Bannock-
burn in 1314, and his honours reverted to the crown. Aymar de Valence
(d. 1324) was eventually succeeded, in 1339, by Laurence Hastings, his
great-nephew, the grandson of his sister and co-heiress Isabel (who had
married John, Lord Hastings). Thomas of Brotherton's daughter became
duchess of Norfolk in her own right, thanks to an anomalous creation in
1397, but there was no male lord of Norfolk between Thomas's death in
1338 and the elevation of Thomas Mowbray to the dukedom in 1397.
The earl of Surrey was the last of the ancient Warenne line, and after his

death in 1347 the title and estates went to his sister's son, Richard FitzAlan, when the Surrey honours were permanently merged with those of Arundel.

This picture of shaky and unstable family lines is typical of all the ninety-nine men summoned. Table I analyses the continuity or succession pattern for them and it compares their dynastic or breeding fortunes with the men summoned to Henry IV's parliament of 1401. In Edward's time 61 per cent of those summoned were eventually followed to parliament by a male heir. But no less than twenty of the peers had a male heir – a son in seventeen of the cases – who was never summoned. Some of the non-successors were of little import, and the marginal hold their fathers had had upon nobility was insufficient to sweep them along. Robert Bayard had been summoned twice in 1313 and never again before his death in 1330, so his son's omission is hardly striking. Maruce Brun was called between 1313 and 1322, but he lived until 1355 and it would not seem as though his son William had ever been a likely candidate for a summons.[13] But quite a few men on the list of sons not summoned were of some importance, and the omission of the next generation is only explicable in terms of the inconsistency of royal directives. The fathers were neither more nor less prominent than others whose sons were subsequently summoned, and no policy determined who belonged. Robert Felton's unsummoned son John became keeper of the castle at Newcastle; John of St John's son was a keeper of Hampshire and a king's yeoman; and others rose to similar positions of trust without attendance among the lords. This also shows that parliament was still something less than the premier form of governmental participation.

Beyond the twenty men of the 1313 parliament who left unsummoned heirs nine more left only heiresses, and in none of these instances were the women ever seen as transmitters of a peerage (though they did transmit the relevant estates). Whether we look at John Giffard of Brymsfield, leaving four half-sisters after his death at Boroughbridge, or at Alan de Zouche, with three daughters as his co-heiresses, or at John de la Mare, with his daughter Florence as his survivor, the tale is the same.[14] Only the earldoms were transmitted through female blood in the early fourteenth century, even sometimes in defiance of the common law. The one exception among the barons to the prevalent form of male chauvinism was the case of Edward Burnell. He died, *sine prole*, in 1315 and his sister's son Nicholas Haudlo was summoned in right of his uncle's peerage. But since Nicholas was not summoned until 1350 the line of descent was pretty tortuous, and the new man's own distinction as much as his inheritance played a part.

Even among the more successful dynasts of the 1313 parliament the line might be rather wavy. John Northwood was followed to parliament

Table I.—*Succession and Non-Succession of Title*

| | Succeeded by: | | | Not directly succeeded | | |
	son	other male heir	through female	son not summoned	left heiress only	title extinct or in abeyance
1313 parliament 99 peers	44 44%	17 17%	0 0%	20 20%	9 9%	9 9%
1401 parliament 46 peers	21 47%	10 22%	7 16%	1 2%	0 0%	7 14%

by his grandson Roger, but the old man died in 1319 and the young one did not receive a summons until 1360, when he was about fifty-three. Piers Mauley was not summoned for the last twelve years of his life but then his son followed immediately upon his death. The same pattern is found for Philip Kyme. Robert FitzPayn's son, of age already when his father died in 1315, was first summoned by Edward II in 1326. Adam Everingham, summoned from 1309 through 1315, died in 1341 and was then succeeded by his son, summoned for the first time in 1371.[15] Again, no policy explains these anomalous practices, beyond that large and vague one of royal freedom to summon or not to summon. Consistency was neither expected nor demanded.

A comparison between the men of 1313 and those summoned in 2 Henry IV indicates changes in the nature of the peerage. The later list had but half the names of the earlier one – forty-six as against the ninety-nine laymen of 1313.[16] This, as we have said, was about typical for the respective periods. The fifteenth-century list is more stratified or hierarchical; there are now two dukes (the king's son and his uncle) as well as ten earls. And whereas the ten earls of Edward II's day represented but 10 per cent of the lay peers, now the higher nobles comprise 25 per cent of those summoned. Two of the earls, Rutland and Somerset, were royal kin through the male line. Of the others only Warwick, Devon and Arundel were from families whose comital rank went as far back as the mid-fourteenth century.

By the turn of the fifteenth century the nobles were almost completely self-perpetuating, at least in terms of normal succession: this change derived from legal, not biological, developments since 1313. Of Henry IV's peers 69 per cent were eventually to be succeeded in their station by a male heir, and 16 per cent by a man either married to or descended from an heiress: an 85 per cent succession rate, as against 61 per cent for 1313. The new factor, of course, was the succession of title via the woman. Some of the new transmissions were but temporary, as was John Oldcastle's claim to be Lord Cobham because of his childless union with Cobham's daughter Joan, or the right of Hugh Stafford and then of Lewis Robessart to a peerage because of their successive marriages with Elizabeth, Bartholomew Bourchier's daughter and heiress. But the old de la Warre title became the permanent possession of the West family when Reynold West succeeded to both the lands and title of his mother's brother, Thomas de la Warre, in 1426. Some lines were transmitted only to be subsumed when marriage and elevation brought about further consolidation. Edmund Grey became Lord Ferrers through marriage with the daughter of William, Lord Ferrers (though Grey went on to the earldom of Kent and ceased to use the Ferrers title). Similarly the title of Lord Furnival was borne at one time by John Talbot because of his marriage with the Furnival heiress, but when he became an earl he dropped the lesser title (though he hung on to the tangible benefits of the marriage). Marriages to a peer's heiress in the fourteenth century carried, for the heir of the union if not for the husband, the lands which she had inherited. In the fifteenth century the marriage was likely to bring along her father's title as well.

Two other changes are also brought out. One was the very low number of legitimate claimants to titles who by the fifteenth century were to go unsummoned. Philip Despenser had a son and heir who never received a summons after his father died in 1401. In no other case was there a male heir of the peers of 2 Henry IV who was untainted by treason and who was ignored in future summonses. The baronies of Burnell, Darcy, Mauley, Heron and Camoys all became extinct or went into abeyance, but all were minor peerages with quite complicated and divided lines of succession. Thomas Percy, earl of Worcester, was attainted and his honours forfeited after his double-dealing caught him up in 1403, but Thomas was unmarried anyway and so the windfall to the crown was premature but wholly likely. Another change since 1313 was the disappearance of the irregular issue of writs to a given individual. Generally, 'ever summoned, always summoned' was the rule by the time of Richard II, and most peers were now called to every session of parliament held between their majority and their ultimate removal. There was now a fixity which may look logical and even inevitable when we compare 1401 with 1313, but the process is nowhere recognised nor analysed by contemporary observation. This is a prime example of the historian identifying change or evolution which escaped the eyes of those concerned with the process.

An examination of the two summons lists shows us how a *de facto* process came to govern subsequent situations. Edward I never meant to create a peerage of his great lords and vassals – an estate or assemblage with its own dynamic, rules, and continuity of personnel. Though it was widely understood that the descent of an earldom could be restricted or governed, e.g. to male heirs, or only in conjunction with the comital estates etc., this was very different from the formulation of laws or policies which established the hereditary composition of an estate of government. Once it became accepted that many lay councillors, rather than just earls, were born as well as made, the royal prerogative was greatly circumscribed, at least potentially. Kings were saddled, for better or for worse, with a group of men over whose membership they had but limited control. As they could not deprive an heir of his property, so they lost the power to exclude an heir from his unique constitutional role (with its accompanying status).[17] This conflict was sometimes a latent one, but at other times kings smarted under the obligation to hear men who were wholly repugnant and yet could not be dismissed or ignored.

For several generations after 1295 new peers were 'created' simply by being added to the summons lists: a *de facto* process and nothing else. Writs of creation in the form of charters or letters patent were used only to elevate men to higher ranks within the peerage, rather than from without to within. The exception was Piers Gaveston who jumped from the common ranks to the earldom of Cornwall in 1307. He was the first earl unrelated to the royal family in almost a century, and 'the majority of the barons of the land did not concur [in his elevation], both because Peter was a foreigner from Gascony, and also because of envy'.[18] There was also some controversy as to whether the title, and its estates, could be separated from the crown by simple royal fiat. Andrew Harcla was also raised directly to an earldom, that of Carlisle in 1322, 'for good and laudable service . . . lately rendered to us in conquering Thomas, then earl of Lancaster'.[19] But both these men came to bad (that is violent) ends, and the practice of creating earls in a single leap was ended.

Because 'this realm has long suffered a serious decline in names, honours and ranks of dignity', Edward III was moved on 16 March 1337 'to increase the number of earldoms and illustrious personages in our realm'.[20] He did this by creating six new earls, all men already in the ranks of the baronage, and mostly young men who had been his companions in Mortimer's overthrow and/or in the early victories of the French wars.[21] There was truth in the comment about declining numbers, thanks largely to the king's grandfather, and Edward wanted a peerage that was young, sympathetic, and coupled with his interests. Ancient ideas held the earl to be a quasi-territorial ruler, not just a royal baron, and in the fourteenth century new earls were still invested with the 'third-penny' of their counties, girded with a sword upon accession, and frequently enriched by the king 'to maintain more honourably and better the state and honour of an earl and so that he may more easily support the burden incumbent on so great an honour'.[22] In the protests against Gaveston in 1308 the earls had already spoken of themselves as an estate within the realm. While they were subjected to an uncomfortable amount of royal concern, and while their inheritances were regulated in their patents of creation, they still preserved an aura of independence far beyond that of the ordinary peers. The creations of 1337 were made with explicit parliamentary support, an indication that these created 'offices' were not just private business between grantor and recipient.

We can look in some detail at one of the new creations, William Montague, now elevated to the earldom of Salisbury (Doc. 2). He had been born around 1303, son and heir of William, second Lord Montague, and Elizabeth de Montfort. He succeeded his father in 1319 and began his royal service on an overseas venture with prince Edward in 1325. William was knighted in 1326, summoned for service in Scotland in 1327, and became a prime mover in the palace coup of 1330 which toppled Mortimer and gave Edward his independence. The king recognised him as Lord Montague in 1331. He received the third-penny of Wiltshire upon his elevation in 1337, this being now standardised at £20 per annum. The grant of £1,000, in land or money, was to support him and the male heirs of his body in the honour of an earldom. Beyond these official emoluments, Montague profited immensely as one of the king's closest friends, and in subsequent years he gathered in the reversion of the Montalt inheritance, land in Somerset, Lundy Isle, land in Berkshire, etc.[23] Friendship and service, not elevation, were the causal factors in the enrichment, but we should not fail to note that at a certain point it became advisable to elevate a peer lest his wealth seem disproportionate to his status (Doc. 6).

Simple creations of peerage were not done by charter or letters patent, i.e. in a *de jure* fashion, until John Beauchamp became Lord Beauchamp of Kidderminster in 1387. Richard raised an old and trusted 'civil servant' to the peerage in his need for friends, and the sixty-eight-year-old Beauchamp moved up from the office of steward of the king's household (Doc. 3). Unfortunately for the old man, he was impeached and executed the following spring without ever having attended a meeting of the Lords. But the precedent was set, and many – by the mid-fifteenth century virtually all – new creations in the baronage were effected by solemn instruments of government rather than by simple issue of a writ of summons. In 1432 Henry VI's government made Lord Fanhope out of John Cornwall, acting on the principle that 'merits should receive the worthy reward which flows from the throne'.[24] This wording puts the grant of a peerage squarely in the context of patronage: an appropriate and candid assessment. After Fanhope's creation the new peerages were generally created in this formal fashion: Sudeley in 1441, Milbroke in 1442, Lisle of Kingston Lisle in 1444, Say and Sele in 1447, Beauchamp of Powicke in 1447, Hoo in 1448, Rivers in 1448, Stourton in 1448, Richemount Grey in 1449, Egremont in 1449, etc. Most of these peerages were to descend to the male heir of the body of the grantee, though the earlier patent to Kingston Lisle had limited the descent to the heir while in possession of the territorial barony. The use of these formal instruments of government to elevate new men reflects the great distinction now accepted between hereditary peers and ordinary mortals, for the path of inheritance in the patent could be contrary to that normally followed at common law.

In terms of status and privilege even the lowest baron was a great man, and even as ordinary a baron as Lord Botreaux was commended for his 'talent, maturity in counsel, valour in arms, honesty, faithfulness and industry'.[25] But when we look at the peerage as an entity we see that their internal stratification became more pronounced through time. An

unceasing competitive drive was partially satisfied through the creation
of gradations within the peerage, and the royal desire to emulate the
elaborate French court and to differentiate within the in-group led to the
existence of a peerage with dukes, marquises, earls and viscounts as well
as plain old English barons. The Black Prince became the first duke (of
Cornwall) in 1337, but by the time of Edward III's death there had been
four more creations (within the royal family) and the process was not
about to end.[26] By 1500 there had been forty-five ducal creations. They
mostly went to royal princes: twenty were for the kings' sons (including
people like Richard II before his accession, and Henry VI's son Edward
who never reached his majority or a seat in the Lords). Other dukedoms
went to quasi-royal relatives, like Richard II's half-brothers, four of the
Beauforts, and, in 1485, Jasper Tudor. Few went very far from the
royal family in the male line, though the Staffords got the dukedom of
Buckingham, and the Mowbrays and then the Howards got Norfolk.
Because of grants to royal infants, duplications, and the surrender of
titles, there were never very many functioning dukes at any given time.
By reigns the creations were five by Edward III, nine by Richard II,
three by Henry IV, four by Henry V, ten by Henry VI, seven by
Edward IV, and two by Richard III and then five by Henry VII (all
made before 1500).

The other ranks of higher peers were looked on as being a little
peculiar and they never became very popular. Robert de Vere, Richard
II's favourite, became the first English marquis in 1385 when he was
created marquis of Dublin. But his unpopularity, plus his fate, were
such that when John Beaufort was asked by the Commons in November
1399 to resume the title of marquis of Dorset, which he had held in 1397,
he declined and said that 'as the title of marquess was a strange title in
this realm, not to confer it on him, because by the king's leave, he would
by no means bear or take on himself such a title'.[27] The title was only
used five more times before 1500: Edmund Beaufort became marquis of
Dorset in 1443, William de la Pole of Suffolk in 1444, John Neville of
Montague in 1470, Thomas Grey of Dorset in 1475, and William
Berkeley of Berkeley in 1489. All these men were earls when raised in
rank, though Neville and Grey went through the curious formality
of resigning their earldoms (of Northumberland and Huntingdon
respectively) when accepting the new position. But it was always
an alien and unattractive rank, and the unpleasant air of France hung
about it.

The title of viscount was used even less than that of marquis. It was
first bestowed upon John Beaumont in January 1440 (Doc. 4). Again, it
was used for someone already in the peerage. In fact Beaumont was the
sixth baron of his line, being a direct descendant of the John who had
come to parliament in 1309 as the king's second cousin. Viscount

Beaumont was set 'above all viscounts then created or to be created, and above the heirs and sons of all earls, with seat and honour immediately after the earls'.[28] He also received twenty marks annually, from the revenues of the county of Lincoln. But again, this was an exotic title, and it was but rarely used: Bourchier, already count of Eu in Normandy, became Viscount Bourchier in 1445-6, and Lord Lovel was promoted by Richard III.

Rivalry for position, however, was not confined to a quest for a higher nominal rank within the peerage. Those safely and permanently seated could still contend with one another for precedence within any given rank: there was no logical end to the competitive urge, and upward mobility could be an insatiable itch (as the careers of Henry Bolingbroke and Richard of York show). Honour indicated greater royal favour or love, greater antiquity of one's house, and perhaps ancestors of more prowess. When Richard II made de Vere a marquis he 'commanded him, with a glad countenance, to sit in a higher place among the peers of parliament, between the dukes and earls, and the marquis at once gratefully did this'.[29] In 1405 there were various disputes – between the Beaumonts and Grey, the earls of Warwick and Norfolk, etc. – as to precedence in seating, and various of the old families began to think their antiquity should give them some pride of place. Family histories, real or imaginary, were produced to support the claims (Docs. 8, 64).

The Arundel-Courtenay (Devon) quarrel of 23 Henry VI was but one of many such disputes which were enacted before parliaments in the fifteenth century. Families contended with each other over their respective seniority, disputed estates, seating arrangements, lineages, etc. In 1425 the earl marshal, disputing with Warwick, asserted that 'he had sprung from royal stock, and was entitled for this reason to the royal arms of England, and sought and claimed, by his counsel, for this reason to have his seat in parliaments of this kind above Richard, Earl of Warwick . . .'[30] But Warwick eventually won the contest, for a royal charter of 22 Henry VI gave him precedence over other earls. When he became a duke his position was next to that of Norfolk, above the duke of Buckingham. Exeter, as of royal descent, was likewise put into a preferred position, immediately below York. Henry VI also gave Lords Bourchier, Lisle, and Pembroke primacy within their ranks, as did Edward IV for Lord Dacre of Gillesland. It is worth noting that these quarrels were not generally over the right *per se* to be in the Lords, but over *where* in the Lords one was. A century earlier they would have been utterly meaningless, for it was only when the peers had become a self-perpetuating estate that such arguments could take on a political or constitutional context, rather than merely a social one. What men consider worth contending and litigating about is an indication of what is important and where they think they have to assert themselves to preserve their status. Social demotion, in a relative sense, must have constantly stared these men in the face.

Another example of the way peers were set off from all others is provided by the legitimation of the Beaufort children in 1397. That old John of Gaunt decided to marry his mistress of many years, Katherine Swynford, can perhaps be considered as the pleasant sentimentality of the elderly. But to legitimate their four children so that they could assume their proper place within the peerage was a political decision which, implicitly, accepted the gap between the genuine legal nobility and those merely of noble birth. Gone was the casual style in which Norman and Plantagenet bastards had been inserted into earldoms or bishoprics at the royal will. If entry into the peerage was primarily the king's business, its membership was a public affair. Formal legal processes, backed by both Rome (for the legitimation of the children and the marriage of the parents) and by parliament were now needed. Parliament accepted that the Beauforts were not to be in line for the throne – which seemed unlikely in 1397 anyway, and Henry IV ironically re-emphasised the bar in 1407 – but otherwise they were fully-fledged nobles. The daughter Joan married the earl of Westmorland, while the two sons who remained laymen rose high (to the dukedoms of Somerset and Exeter) and Henry became bishop of Winchester and a cardinal. But it is noteworthy that Richard II paid some of his debt to his uncle John by elevating the children, the 'kin of our beloved uncle'.

For some men the quest for eminence was direct, for others more tortuous. We have referred to the practice of allowing titles, along with the estates, to pass through heiress-transmitters to their husbands or children. This was yet another *de facto* addition to the constitution. Neither legislation, nor case law, nor royal edict ever signalled the adoption of the practice, though it eventually became the normal route for a peerage when direct male heirs failed. In 1297 Ralph Monthermer (Monte Hermerii) made a clandestine marriage with Joan of Acre, Edward I's daughter and the recent widow of Gilbert de Clare, earl of Gloucester and Hertford. When the king's anger cooled he summoned Monthermer to parliament, from May 1298 to January 1307, as the earl of Gloucester. Joan died in April 1307, and for the remaining eighteen years of his life Monthermer was summoned simply as 'Radulph de Monte Hermerii', while Joan's son Gilbert was now recognised, though still under age, as the earl. This was a case of a title being granted to the husband almost as a courtesy to the wife.

The later norm is illustrated by a brief look at the meanderings, via marriage, of the Furnival title (see Table II). The second Lord Thomas was summoned to parliament from 1318 to 1338, and his son (Thomas III) from 1348 to 1364. Then William Furnival succeeded his childless brother from 1366 until his death in 1383. At that point (Doc. 31) his son-in-law, Thomas Neville was recognised, as the heiress's husband, as the heir to the peerage and he was summoned in 1383 as 'Thome de Nevill de Halumshire' in the parliamentary writs, and as 'Le Sire de Furnivall' in the Rolls of Parliament. In turn Neville's son-in-law, John Talbot, was summoned as 'Johannes Talbot, Dominus de Furnivall' and as 'Johannes Talbot de Furnivall' until he became earl of Shrewsbury in 1442 and stopped using his lesser appellations. In the fifteenth century numerous other men were summoned in right of their wives: Henry Percy as Lord Poynings, William Lovel as Lord Morley, George Stanley as Lord Le Straunge, Edward Hastings as Lord Hungerford, Robert Hastings as Lord Welles, Edward Grey as Lord Welles, etc.

Table II

Thomas, I Lord Furnivall
|
Thomas, II Lord Furnivall
|

Thomas, III Lord   *William, IV Lord*
|
Joan = *Thomas Neville*
|
Maud = *John Talbot,* Earl
of Shrewsbury

Between 1438 and 1504 some twenty-one peerages were continued via heiress-wives. Many of the men who made the nobility in this fashion were younger sons of peers, and so the desire for continuity within the peerage could offer a better ladder of upward mobility for relatives of noblemen than it did for genuine outsiders and new men. The five Neville brothers who sat simultaneously, the numerous Bourchiers, Greys and Hastings, among others, all crowded in because of this practice.

We have been concerned with how men entered the peerage. We can also consider how they left it. Except for the failure of an heir – an eventuality which the flexibility of succession customs made less and less likely – only treason and a sentence of attainder served to cut people down from the heights after the mid-fourteenth century. Though about a dozen men resigned or surrendered peerages, these were not demotions or the loss of rank: [31] the earldoms that were given up when a marquisate was assumed have been mentioned, and John of Gaunt's resignation of the earldom of Richmond to the king in 1372 had little to do with a diminution of status. Only the degradation of young George Neville from the dukedom of Bedford in 1477 was real, unqualified and un-

reversed (Doc. 9). Neville was the 'Kingmaker's' nephew, and after his
uncle fell no one had much interest in the earlier schemes to push him
up the peerage ladder and into a royal marriage. This case was also of
interest because the document asserts that wealth was a concomitant of
high title rather than a coincidental factor: poverty, it would follow, was
more properly associated with common status. No precedent was
created by Neville's fall, for the circumstances were too anomalous, but
modern historians if not contemporary observers have noted that some
of Thomas of Woodstock's instability and rapacity may have stemmed
from his lack of a secure patrimony rather than his psychological
disposition.[32]

The treason statute of 1352 was deliberately designed to cause the
felon's family a loss of status and wealth. It became a lever of social
control, often threatened or even used in haste and then remedied,
perhaps for a price, at leisure and in a calmer climate. But the punishment was draconic enough, and between 1350 and 1500 several dozen
peers suffered the law's extreme teeth. Life at the top was certainly risky
enough. Of the forty-five ducal creations fifteen ended with attainder or
a related proscription, and where even royal blood failed to protect York
(in 1459) or Clarence (in 1478), high office alone was of little comfort.
Through the centuries about 20 per cent of the peers died from some
form of violence, much of it of a direct political nature – and such great
treason-trimmings as that centring upon the battle of Boroughbridge
in 1322 contributed a fair share. Of the magnates who had opposed the
king, eight either died in battle or immediately afterwards, and three
more died in imprisonment. Long after, the Coventry parliament of
1459 attainted York and his two sons, March and Rutland, the earl of
Salisbury and three of his sons, Lord Clinton, John and Edward
Bourchier, 'nevues to the seid duc of York', plus thirteen others, not all
of them noble. The coups and counter-coups of Richard II's time, the
turbulence surrounding Henry IV's accession, the battles of the 1450s
and 1460s, and the decimations of Yorkist kings and of Henry VII all
took a heavy and almost regular toll.

The proceedings which led to sentences of treason offer a glimpse of
the way the law, political opportunism and privilege were all juxtaposed.
Sometimes, as with Thomas of Lancaster in 1322 or Andrew Harcla,
earl of Carlisle, in 1323, or Scrope of Masham in 1415, the king was the
motive force behind the execution. At other times, as when Gaveston died
in 1313 or the Despensers in 1326, he was disposed against the proceedings but either could not or dared not arrest them. The charges against
the nobles were about as convincing as those levied against Edward II
and Richard II at their respective depositions: political crimes, whether
committed in ancient Athens or in modern Latin America, have a
similar and unconvincing ring. They show how little scope there has

been through most of history for a 'loyal opposition': if you were wrong you were probably disloyal, and vice versa. At least Edward IV, when moving to outlaw his enemies in 1471, had the candour to state that he was condemning a queen, a royal prince, two dukes, two earls, and one viscount,[33]

'not only by reason and authority but also by divers victories in battles, the truth, right, and will of God evidently appearing to every wise, indifferent and well disposed man [to be] for our party, considering namely that in such division and controversy moved betwixt princes about the high soverain royal power, more evident proof or declaration of rightful truth and God's will may not be had than by the said means, that is, reason, authority, and victory in battles'.

For a specific case study we can look at the charges brought against the duke of Suffolk in 1450. Though the constitution of England may have been more affected by his grandfather's trial in 1386, his own probably took the award for (hostile) public interest (Doc. 7). Though he was the fourth de la Pole to sit as a peer, the animus against him still partially stemmed from his jumped-up origins. Following the precedent of the 'Good Parliament' of 1376, the Commons in 1450 became the *vox populi* and charged the king's closest adviser with 'divers great [and] heinous treasons'. Vengeance was to come, appropriately, through the application of 'the laws of this your land', against which Suffolk could offer 'no answer sufficient'. Though Suffolk was allowed to leave the realm, this was a grim business and it was being played for keeps. Though most peers adjudged guilty of treason were tried by their fellow peers, rather than by the king's common subjects, stone dead knew few legal niceties, and this impeachment process charged the duke with treason.

But if death was irreversible, political misfortune was not. Many a man or family that seemingly had taken a fatal plunge was soon restored to the high station of the *ante bellum* days. It was almost as hard to get out of the peerage as to get in. The king might find the threat of treason and attainder a more useful lever of social control than the actual penalties; and financial bonds for good behaviour, rather than dead peers, helped to keep the countryside orderly and supported the king's writ. Of the thirty-four nobles punished by attainder and forfeiture between Henry VI's accession and Henry VII's death, twenty-nine (or 84 per cent of them) were eventually restored to land and status. Nor was this propensity to kiss and make up (with guarantees exacted to ensure future loyalty) one we should only associate with the end of the period. Of the thirty-three nobles who lined up against Edward II at Boroughbridge, only the eight mentioned above were executed; twelve were pardoned after being fined, Roger Bavent forfeited but eventually recovered his estates, and seven men escaped and ultimately were reaccepted into high society.

Even a blatant sinner like the earl of Cambridge, guilty of plotting against Henry V in 1415 and about to die, could seek mercy: 'take me into the hands of your merciful and piteous grace, thinking you well of your great goodness'.[34] His birth and his abject pleas did at least serve to keep his son, the future duke of York, unstained by the parental treason and free to inherit the estates of his uncles, Edward of York and the earl of March. Many others who had been dragged down found the second rise much easier to negotiate than the first had been. Such condign villains as the Despensers were widely hated, but by 1357 the younger Edward's grandson, advantageously married to the daughter and heiress of Bartholomew Burghersh, was back in the Lords. When the earl of March was executed in 1330 for his role in Edward II's fall, who would have predicted that the king's wrath would so cool that the heir would be summoned to parliament in 1348? The Percys came back from their devastating quarrel with Henry IV within a decade, though it took a generation or two to reclaim all the dispersed estates. Though a marginal noble family like the Lumleys needed two-thirds of a century to see their restoration carried through and their name cleared (Doc. 10), the truth is that while few families escaped setbacks, fewer yet, as long as they produced heirs who could petition, pay, and be humble, were permanently brought down just because of political errors and treasons.

The peers were not just the ruling political elite. They were the great men, the best of the realm. Their splendour shone on the lesser folk – their retainers, their tenants, and those who merely gloried to see their retinues pass. Their deaths were a sharp reminder of the mutability of all earthly things. 'In the midst of life we are in death' and 'the turn of fortune's wheel' were considered profound observations at the time; they were also accurate ones (Doc. 11). It is no wonder that monastic and urban chroniclers, balladeers and local gossip-mongers, all followed the demise of the nobles, and that the surviving literature is full of transparently cryptic comments like 'Thereward asked no question why/But on the dogges he set full round;/They there made the dogs to cry,/The game was done in a little stand,/The buck was slain, and borne away . . .'[35] The peers themselves, through vast funeral processions, tombs and chantries, gifts and distributions for prayers and such like, made their own deaths into major public spectacles. The preservation of their memories meant prayers for the soul in purgatory and a hold on enduring fame on earth. The dead were a very big business. When a peer was brought to his grave, usually within a major ecclesiastical establishment, he went with the trappings of a state funeral. A funeral like that of Salisbury was a social, familial and political affair of importance: partisans wanted to be seen to be present, opponents kept well away (Doc. 13). Such funerals, with their liveried mourners and mass charities, show us how medieval religious observance could be interwoven with the institutions of bastard feudalism. The great chantry tombs reinforced the idea that God's world was designed to be run by aristocratic families.

But nothing was quite as dramatic as sudden death, and when it came at the hands of social inferiors, divine retribution and public indignation were simultaneously appeased. We have looked at the Commons' proceedings against Suffolk. The duke fled, but his murder soon after by lynch law received the sort of public attention reserved today for natural disasters and international soccer matches. The different accounts of Suffolk's end reflect the glee it aroused, and they reveal that no one purporting to cover public events was content to let it pass without some comment (Doc. 12). The replication of the entries also shows, despite the generalisation about lack of freedom of expression, that one could frankly judge one's superiors. From the harsh obituary of William the Conqueror in the *Anglo-Saxon Chronicle* onwards many a peer had to take his lumps. Gaveston's death had been hailed with unmixed relief by the author who said, 'the bad tree is cut down, when Peter is struck in the neck: – Blessed be the weapon . . . Celebrate, my tongue, the death of Peter who disturbed England. . . .'[36]

Public interest in the great did not even end with death and burial. While every medieval man and woman could, in theory, aspire to canonisation, the highborn also had a chance of becoming heroes of popular political hagiolatry. Tales regularly grew up around the 'martyred' leader of the opposition. Dreams and disenchantment led men of the thirteenth century to see Simon de Montfort as a saintly leader of the public weal, and the *Song of Lewes* presented him as the medieval version of a Whig statesman. Stubbs might put him down as a 'buccaneering old Gladstone' but it was a fourteenth-century monk who spoke rather of 'that noble man' who, as an example to others, 'laid down his life in the cause of justice'.[37] Miracles at Simon's tomb, pilgrimages, and finally royal efforts to suppress the cult were almost part of a ritualised game.

Simon may have been the outstanding member of this group of popular saints, but he was hardly alone. Archbishop Scrope of York posthumously enjoyed such adulation after Henry IV had him executed for treason in 1405. He had supposedly forgiven his actual executioner and asked to be dispatched in five strokes, one for each of Christ's wounds. It is no wonder that in this atmosphere political casualties like the earl of Arundel, in Richard II's time, or the duke of York in Henry VI's, became objects of sanguine eulogies and memories.[38] Only a partisan could say of York that 'God and his saints guard him from injury, This noble duke died at Wakefield,/Treating for sweet peace, force upon him rushed.' [39]

A final example of the exalted reputation of the departed noble is provided by 'The office of earl Thomas' (Doc. 14). No one, from his wife on, has ever liked Thomas of Lancaster.[40] The emergence of a cult in his honour is a sign of Edward II's unpopularity and of the need for a safety valve or fantasy world. But if the miracles of Edward the Confessor and of Henry VI were taken with full seriousness, at least Thomas could pose as having died for some cause. The poem goes beyond mere romanticism, and in making Thomas a Christ figure the author hovers in a literary limbo which is somewhere between blasphemy and the proper tribute to the second peer of the realm and a grandson of Edward I.

CHAPTER II

This chapter covers in brief two different aspects of the public face of the nobility. One centres upon the peers as a functioning elite within the House of Lords and looks at the way they developed a sense of class consciousness and came to formulate and to hold a high opinion of their special role within the constitution. The self-consciousness was largely but not wholly a product of the institutional development of the House of Lords itself. The attempt we make here to present an historical case study of group privilege is one that has to be put together from different types of documents, reflecting different activities and divergent ideologies. Vague though it may seem at times, the sense of status and political privilege was a real phenomenon. In times of social or constitutional crisis, their exalted role was seen by the peers to be their cherished birth-right, well worth fighting for. Also in times of crisis the peers might express themselves with clarity as to their special position. From these considerations we can point a political moral: when collective activity becomes an ordinary part of government, and when the participants are set apart from others, and when they intensively interact in personal and in public business, *then* the evolution of an elitist or exclusivist ideology can be expected. The House of Lords came to have a special role because its members were important individuals, but to a lesser extent the members of the Lords were exalted because they were part of a privileged body. This reciprocity was not necessarily balanced, nor did all contribute equally, but the forces making for class solidarity could be very strong in the face of external threats.

The other topic we will touch, though very superficially, is service. The nobles actively participated in almost all levels of lay government and they bore a disproportionate share of high offices. We must not posit a tight, self-conscious lay elite pitting itself against the king above and the gentry and bourgeoisie below. The lay peerage *v.* the monarchy, or *v.* the prelates, or *v.* the third estate is an accurate reflection of neither the medieval polity nor the social structure. In the course of their labours the nobles worked with those above and below them, as well as with their equals and with churchmen of all ranks and positions. In the world of action, social barriers were constantly crossed in all directions. If the hatred between Henry III and Simon de Montfort, or between Edward II and Thomas of Lancaster, can be explained only in personal and psychological terms, we should also remember how often the wolf lay down with the lamb. Co-operation, as well as competition, was a feature of public life. Nor were the peers just a military caste. Their services were wide-ranging, sometimes fairly technical, and often skilfully rendered. Nobles were officials, civil servants, generals, local deputies, representatives, commissioners, judges, parliamentarians, wardens of the marches, diplomats and admirals. As a group there was little they could not be expected to perform.

In a discussion of medieval class distinctions the king was in many ways a member of the lay aristocracy. About half of the younger royal children, between Edward I and Edward IV, married into the ranks of English nobility. The king's social world-view was not antithetic to that of his nobles, regardless of how divergent the political course might run. Medieval aristocrats were not republicans, perhaps least so when plotting rebellion or even regicide.[1] Neither were kings democrats, no matter how disgusted they might become with baronial counsel and self-assertion. A new nobility of royal favourites and courtiers, rather than no nobility at all, was the response generated by exasperation or desperation. Equality was for the next world, if at all. In this one the mighty had too much in common, even in their bitterest moments: attacks could be on persons and families, but rarely on status *per se*. This view of the need for class solidarity helps to explain the willingness to re-elevate the heirs of fallen traitors, just as do the speeches in the Lords or their marital preferences. Dependency and ambivalence, if not harmony, are the keynotes to baronial relations with the crown and within the nobility itself.

There is no single source which relates the full tale of baronial class consciousness. Sometimes the complexities of the narrative lie buried beneath mountains of thwarted ambitions and obscure phraseology. The concept of class is more than just an abstraction, however, and this is particularly true when applied to the ruling class. Those within the elite usually have some awareness of their position, though the propensity to discuss or defend it may vary. Ideas about status and hierarchy do not descend from heaven in a cloud of unknowing good fortune. It is in someone's interest to develop and to propagate the beliefs. If the ruling classes do not necessarily create the ideology which gives them support, they at least have the wit to embrace those ideas.

The specific form of elitist ideology relevant here is that which holds that an aristocracy has a 'natural' position in public matters, i.e. at the top. There are two forms in which this idea was expressed by the barons and their apologists. One was in its positive version. This emphasised order and hierarchy and guaranteed a preferred place for the peerage. In this form the ideas were part of the 'descending' view of the order of power and authority on earth.[2] Then there was a negative side which took the form of an attack upon those who usurped that natural position;

this was often linked to an attack upon the king who allowed this monstrous set of events to occur.

The positive aspects of hierarchical thought are familiar. They were the stock in trade response of the Middle Ages to questions about the organisation of human society. They run, with little change, from the political thought of the early church fathers (and before) to modern conservatives who draw their sustenance from Edmund Burke. The ideas are meant as a large dose of social narcotic, mostly administered by the upper classes to the lower. Different variations on the theme that society has a logical and requisite order are expressed in Aesop's fables, by Cromwell and Ireton at the Putney debates, by the *Book of Common Prayer*, and by the duke of Wellington to all who would listen. The passages in Shakespeare which bespeak such a view are well known, and there is little reason to suppose that fourteenth- and fifteenth-century men of property would have found anything (except the diction) objectionable in Ulysses' words:[3]

> . . . O, when degree is shak'd,
> Which is the ladder to all high designs,
> Then enterprise is sick! . . .
> Take but degree away, untune that string,
> And hark what discord follows! Each thing meets
> In mere oppugnancy . . .

These views were serious bits of conceptual baggage. When we accept other assumptions made about society – the basis of authority in property, the role of divine and natural law, the imminence of Antichrist and/or a second coming, the intercessions of the Virgin and the Saints in the struggle for souls, etc. – we can see how the need for a static social hierarchy was neither unreasonable nor peripheral. Reactionary guardians of vested interests are not paranoids. Both the ravings of the sixteenth-century anabaptist sects and the millenarian doctrines of the 1640s indicate that the medieval fear of how a broken thread could unseam the whole fabric were well grounded. And, needless to say, high among the desiderata for stability were the views on the proper rank of hereditary aristocrats.

But neither the king's government nor the general welfare could be expected to function without the proper contribution of the peers. The *Modus Tenendi Parliamentum* (Doc. 17) is an anonymous tract from the late fourteenth century.[4] It urges a 'liberal' view of the constitution, i.e. it argues for a balanced or mixed composition to government. 'The author . . . appears to have had a clearer view of what was happening – or of what he hoped was going to happen – than most of his contemporaries.'[5] But even he has to take as given that the great (and wealthy) would take their place in the king's parliaments and councils, summoned because of their 'tenure' rather than as representatives of others. 'Each and every earl, barons, and their peers' was to be summoned, and income from property was positively correlated with rank. The natural pre-eminence of the peers was so woven into the social fabric that it could merely be alluded to in passing, rather than explained in full exposition.

Fortescue wrote his *Governance* in the 1470s. He was a disappointed Lancastrian, now pardoned by Edward IV for his many political sins. Fortescue was an early exponent of the view that 'bastard feudalism' was responsible for the civil disorder of his day, and he was hardly likely to be sympathetic to the over-mighty nobles. Their unholy alliances and battles had toppled his king, and the son of the greatest (or worst) of their number was now seated on the throne. But even so he wanted his *Governance* to be a realistic rather than a utopian treatise. Accordingly, the most he could hope to offer as a cure was a demotion of the baronial role. More than that, i.e. a real trimming of their power, was not credible, and his tepid enthusiasm must be read against the complacent support which Bishop Russell lent to the peers as a matter of course. A parliamentary sermon was obviously not the occasion for iconoclastic social criticism, and it was the consistency with which the peerage was accepted, rather than the enthusiasm, that makes this form of official propaganda worth noting.[6] (Docs. 18, 19.)

Taken *en bloc* these miscellaneous political sentiments indicate the naturalness of the peerage's status and special position. Nobles came and went, and the peerage not only remained but all were generally agreed it should remain. These acknowledgements represent the political face of a social role, otherwise expressed in the books of manners which spoke of special seating arrangements, in the books on hunting, hawking and fighting which told common people not to mix with their betters, in the books on degree, etiquette and upbringing.[7] Men were unequal, and as the body social reflected this, so did the body politic.

There was also a negative side to the articulation of class consciousness. It was the resentment, expressed by the peers and their spokesmen, against those 'wicked advisers' who excluded them from their rightful place in government.[8] Kings, new men among the peers, privileged clerics and old courtier-companions might all become the butt of the venom. The word 'natural' when used to describe a baron's position, at least as he saw it, was used in a wholly literal fashion. As a peer of the realm he had been designated in God's plan as a royal intimate. The attacks upon wicked advisers antedated Edward I's model parliament, and in one form or other such plaints were part of almost every baronial rebellion between that which culminated in Magna Carta and that which used the doggerel, 'The Cat, the Rat, and Lovel the Dog/Rule all England under the Hog', to ridicule Richard III.[9] It was a necessary fiction, for an attack on wicked advisers left the institution of monarchy, if not the king, in a revered position, and yet it allowed an open attack upon the Gavestons, the de la Poles, the Wydvilles and the many lesser favourites who never reached the peerage.

The charges against evil favourites which emanate from the struggles of Edward II's time were only unusual for the frequency of iteration. The chronicles and record sources contain abundant evidence of aristocratic grievances for what they believed to be an affront to social tranquillity and a threat to their unique place (Doc. 16). From the hostility of 1309, reported in the *Vita Edwardi*, to the final charges in the articles of deposition, feelings ran strongly against a king who 'has been badly advised and guided by evil councillors'. It was not a mere coincidence that the first expression of the Lords as a separate estate came from these years, nor that only a few years later the knights were permanently separated from the peers in parliamentary deliberations. The medieval genius for translating ideas into their institutional form was in evidence here: a new, elitist concept of rank, and the creation of an upper house in what was becoming a bicameral, conciliar and legislative body.

It was in the House of Lords that the regular expression of baronial self-assertion became embodied. Therefore it is in the story of that branch of government that we should seek evidences of the self-awareness. Like the process of ennoblement, or the formulation of the common law, the evolution of the Lords was hardly a deliberate affair. It happened. A peculiar combination of individual and institutional forces worked in a certain fashion. As 'counter-factual' history tries to say, that which came to pass was neither inevitable nor the only possible or even likely alternative. Parliament in the form we know did not have to emerge or evolve. Though constitutionalism and representation were in the air of western Europe in this period, practice and theory could diverge considerably and institutional development could follow many paths. In both France and the Spanish kingdoms the bloom of fourteenth-century participation faded into fifteenth-century autocracy, and in other areas forms of representation other than the English came to life.[10]

This is a caveat against any (Whig) tendency to take the development of parliamentary government for granted, let alone in its specific English form, with peers and prelates in one chamber, and knights and burgesses in the other. No one could have foreseen how the legal dictate, *ut quod omnes similiter tangit, ab omnibus comprobetur*, would become institutionalised. But despite all the possible combinations and permutations, by the late thirteenth century there were the roots of a *de facto*

House of Lords, and by the mid-fourteenth century it had become a distinct and regular part of government.

One root of the House of Lords is found in the king's ancient and undoubted right to summon his tenants in chief for a variety of traditional purposes. This power was inherent in the whole set of political and economic exchanges that we simply sum up as feudalism, and the direct antecedents of Edward I's call to military duty run, via William the Conqueror, back to the Carolingians if not to the chieftains described by Tacitus in the *Germania*. The summons to military service was sent to any tenants whom the king chose, but the logic of military and economic planning meant that some nationally prominent barons, plus some locally active ones, would be summoned for the Welsh or Scottish frontier. Pragmatic consideration pushed some names forward, but the military summons lists always varied from each other a good deal, just as did the very early lists of parliamentary summonses. The summons to the feudal host, used to raise the king's forces into the late fourteenth century, bore no institutional fruit but it reminds us that different royal needs were not neatly compartmentalised into army, council, parliament, etc. The king's freedom of action was considerable, though as he acted he created traditions and customs which partially bound his future choices.

The military summons of 1276 was typical of those Edward I used to muster his barons for wars on the borders of England (Doc. 15). This document, antedating the model parliament by nineteen years, is comparable to the parliamentary summons of 1313 in several ways: the long list of recipients, the fixing of time and place for the rendezvous, the pious comments on faithful and loving service, and the laconic statement of the major purpose of the business. The writ served to launch the business in hand and to get the men there – little more had to be done in advance. The summons of 1276 went to no less than 179 men, 13 earls and 166 different barons or tenants in chief, which was a typical number to be individually called at the time.

If the House of Lords did not grow directly from the military host, at least the latter collection reinforced the idea of an *esprit de corps* for men singled out for individual summonses. Once they began to meet regularly in parliament their special status leaped to the eye. As early as Edward I's crisis of 1297 and the Gaveston affair in 1308, the earls, and to some extent the other barons, were referring to themselves as having a collective interest as a special 'estate' of the realm. Their exemption from service on juries or royal assizes was a tangible mark of privilege. But in Edward II's time the peers began to push for privilege on two bases: their special right to be tried by their peers (or their fellow peers, to be precise), and their peculiar right to be 'judges of parliament' (as they said in the charges against the earl of March in 1330). The king's

failure to have Thomas of Lancaster judged by his peers was alleged to
be one of the errors in the proceedings, and therefore was one of the
grounds for Lancaster's posthumous vindication in 1327. But their
collective identity, as well as their special individual position, was a
product of the conflict of the 1320s, and terms like 'peers of the realm'
emanate from this decade.[11]

In 1341 the concept of a trial of a peer by other peers was asserted and
accepted, and it was rarely questioned again. In fact the doctrine became
so solidly established that the legal process of impeachment was largely
devised so that the Commons could get at members of the aristocracy,
admittedly for political reasons. The test case of 1341 centred upon
Edward III's quarrel with Archbishop John Stratford (Doc. 20), and it
provided the constitution with an aristocratic gloss on article 21 of
Magna Carta which said that 'Earls and Barons shall only be fined by
their peers, and only in proportion to their offence'. Stratford appealed
his case to the judgement of his peers, for he knew that, little though the
lay peers loved him, they could not afford to question the justice of his
claim to be tried by them alone. To go against him would be 'to the
manifest prejudice of all the peers and a most dangerous precedent'.[12]

The insistence upon special privilege was more than merely useful.
Lord Latimer's rapid return to grace, after impeachment by the 'Good
Parliament' of 1376, was based in part upon the fact that they had not
accorded him the special privilege his rank entitled him to claim. The
aristocratic assertion of 11 Richard II was but an attempt to further the
boundaries of elite status (Doc. 21), and the act of 1442 concerning the
trial of peeresses brought the husband's protected position over to the
wife (Doc. 22). Magna Carta had been silent regarding women's rights,
and the peeresses now gained because of the reaction against the harsh
(and relatively unprivileged) way the duchess of Gloucester had been
treated after she was accused of witchcraft which bordered on treason.[13]
A further reason to extend the aegis of peerage-privilege to women was
that, with the growing practice of seeing titles transmitted through
women, they had to be accorded some special (if recessive) nobility of
blood in their own right.

So much for the special position of those within the nobility. In
aggregate, i.e. as a peerage or an estate within the realm, the nobles
came to have a regular role in the wheels of the state. The advice and
assent of the peers – by which was meant the temporal and as many
of the spiritual peers as were present – became an accepted part
of the constitution. The special areas reserved to the Lords were the
trial of peers for treason and felony, hearing appeals on writs of error
from common law courts which grew from the concept of the peers as
an extension of the council and therefore a court, and to proceed in
impeachment cases. The actual scope of their contribution was un-

spectacular enough in normal times – advice, consultations with the Commons, etc. – and perhaps very critical in times of crisis when they chose to assert themselves. If much of the scholarly attention focused on parliament has understandably been concerned with the growth of the Commons, it is now generally held that the Lords often provided much of the initiative and that factions and partnerships embracing men in both houses, rather than class strife, offer a key to a balanced understanding.

If entry into the peerage and the House of Lords was the great quest for a tenant-in-chief or important soldier, from the king's point of view the problem often was to get such a man to show up when actually summoned. The writs we have looked at were summonses, invitation lists of a sort, rather than attendance lists which tell anything about who really was present. Non-attendance was a chronic medieval problem, in municipal councils and at ecumenical councils designed to heal the Great Schism, as well as at royal assemblies. But at all levels it was more than a curious or whimsical phenomenon. It weakened the value of collective decisions and it robbed deliberative bodies of badly needed voices (and torsos). If we look at an important affair we can see the problem. When the sentence of treason was recorded in the parliament of 2 Henry IV against Thomas Holand, formerly earl of Kent, and against four of his colleagues, twenty-five lords were named as being present. And yet the summonses to the early parliaments of Henry IV went out to considerably more people than that: the numbers ranged from thirty-five to fifty.[14] And this was a transaction that one *should* agree to in so far as the new monarch's favour was of interest. Many men simply found it convenient to keep out of things as much as possible.

The fragment of the Lords' journals from the 1461 session that has been preserved gives an idea of the attendance problem early in Edward IV's reign.[15] Between 28 November and 11 December 1461 there were seven sittings of the Lords. At these forty-one different peers were variously present. Some of the men were not tallied as either present or absent at some of the meetings, and if we only count where we are sure, the tally comes to a possible 257 'man days' of attendance. The checks for present come to only 176 of the possible 257, or but 68 per cent attendance. And since the whole span between the first and last sittings hardly permitted much travel, at least once a peer came to Westminster and attended his first session, and since the absences were between attendances as well as before or after, the conclusion seems to be that even great men preferred to stay at home or in their London lodgings some of the time.

This tale shows that while on the one hand parliament was the king's greatest council, and attendance was a social and political privilege, on the other it was still the time when the monarch wore his crown to check up on and awe his subjects. There were many reasons why his scrutiny might be unwelcome, just as his summons might be unwelcome for physical reasons as well as political. There was no simple correlation between absence and disloyalty. The Scrope-Grey-Cambridge plot of 1415 was hatched by men who were regular companions of the king, and enemies might come to parliament to keep abreast of news while friends might be busy elsewhere. If Lancaster really feared for his life in Edward II's presence, or Richard of York did before Suffolk and then Somerset around 1450, it still seems likely that poor attendance was generally caused as much by human as by a political disinclination to travel along muddy roads to spend a few weeks at Westminster or York or Coventry.

But the efficacy of royal counsel could be seriously diminished if the great men were not present. An individual who was reluctant to appear might be reminded of his obligations in a style considerably less haughty that that used by Henry II to call men before the exchequer: 'See that, as you love yourself and all that you have, you be at the Exchequer at such a place . . .' [16] The typical letter to Lord Cobham, meant to draw him to his proper duty, contains a distinct touch of supplication (Doc. 25). Clearly, more drastic efforts had to be made, and in 1454 the Duke of York, while Protector, sought to enforce a more 'thorough' approach to the problems of Lancastrian England (Doc. 24). The law to enforce attendance may also indicate that men who were inextricably enmeshed in affairs of state may have taken a dim view of peers who tried to keep out of the heat. But harsh fines probably did little to solve the real woes, and the chances are that few of them were ever collected. Furthermore, the general inefficiency of public affairs played a role, and after Lord Say was fined £40 for non-attendance the king (or his agents) intervened on his behalf, 'as we have recalled to our remembrance that the said Lord Say was not so absent but within the said time was with us, and with other lords of our Parliament present in the same, as it is also proved . . .' [17] This obvious hanky-panky was presumably enough to save Say's money. We are often told that medieval legislation is a guide to the legislator's intentions and to little else. Even after the session excuses could be sent which would lead to exoneration: 'our said council has taken just and indifferent examination of their said sickness and feebleness, and by the said examination found that it was so truth'.[18]

But there could be absence with a prior excuse as well as with a posterior one. Many men, on the king's business elsewhere, were simply omitted from the list of those summoned, and the fluctuations in the number of men called reflect foreign wars, death and minorities, and miscellaneous incapacity as well as a royal desire to contract or expand the size of the peerage. Men like the duke of Bedford or the earl of Shrewsbury, in the fifteenth century, spent the better part of one to three decades on military and governmental service in France, and their English presence was often sorely missed.[19] The demands of the Scottish border could be even more ceaseless, and flexibility was a wise king's guide in his calls to his northern lords for their southern obligations. The royal letter of 1449 excused no less than an earl and six barons (and four knights, some of noble families) from attendance at Westminster, lest their collective absence engender 'the greter boldeness' on the part of the lowland marauders. The earl of Northumberland won an excused absence for his victory at Berwick in 1455: [20]

'And what pleasure our cousin the Earl of Northumberland, warden, whom you remember in your said letters, hath done unto us, putting him in his true devoir against our said enemies, he shall understand by such letters as we send unto him and we have so excused him for not coming to our Parliament that it shall not be to his grievance or hurt in any wise.'

Nor was any of this new, for as far back as 6 Edward II the king had excused Walter Fauconberge and nine other peers from attending upon him because of their labours against the 'Scottish enemies and rebels against us'.[21]

There were also individual exemptions issued for medical reasons. About 30 per cent of the peers summoned between 1350 and 1500 lived past sixty, and 10 per cent actually seem to have passed their seventieth birthday. Since most of these men were summoned throughout the course of their adult lives, at least once they became peers, many of the recipients of the writs must have long outlived the full use of their faculties (Doc. 26). The premature senility of Edward III and the dramatic waning of Henry IV's great vigour are testimony to the strain an endless round of business and responsibility could produce. Many a nobleman, forced to combine military service, political participation and private seigneurial administrative cares, found himself worn out, both physically and mentally, by the time he reached late middle age. The king's permission to withdraw from parliament was an honourable route away from the burdens that high status continued to impose. From the king's point of view it was a way of removing an embarrassing dotard from high circles without affronting him or his family, worried about the hereditary claim to a title. Human decay was neither politically useful nor personally pleasing.

The discussion of the attendance problem shows us the way the peers matched their individualised conceptions of self-interest against the royal desire or need for their collective counsel. Once a given baron had gained the security of hereditary status he might be a bit casual towards his obligations. On the other hand, to be too lackadaisical meant risking exclusion from offices, missing out on the distribution of news and the formation of cliques. One had to strike a balance. Some idea of how this was achieved comes from looking, very briefly, at what the Lords as a group sought to do while in session. We have mentioned the areas or problems which came to be reserved for their attention alone. They also acted as intermediaries between the commoners and the king, furthering the interests of friends and dependants while emphasising the proximity to the throne to which their birth entitled them. In a typical matter of little national concern the good word of the 'lords in Parliament' might lubricate the slow machinery of the law: petitions never moved slower if the 'upper house' cast a glance their way (Doc. 23). Consultation between the Lords and spokesmen of the Commons took place,[22] the latter asking 'that they might have the advice and communication with certain lords on matters done in parliament for the common good and profit of the kingdom'.[23] Though the passage of legislation was not the preoccupying task of a medieval parliament, knights and burgesses who came prepared to urge their private petitions and bills took care to keep their betters informed of their intentions (Doc. 28).

Within the Lords there developed a community of interest which helped to some degree to counter the animosities the great men naturally felt towards one another. Sharing the same privileges and working through the same procedures represented some kind of bond, though undoubtedly it was a weak one when other forces intervened. Records of debates have survived, though in fragmentary fashion, and they provide us with a homely picture of speeches in discussions. That the records often preserve moments of low drama, which drew only pedestrian rhetoric and opinions, is probably a tribute to their typicality. Men simply got up, spoke their piece, and sat down when finished. Opinions were expressed and sometimes someone may have been convinced to change his mind, but there is little feeling of rhetoric aimed at affecting a vote. Furthermore, as in modern representative bodies, each speaker felt but little obligation to deal with the issues raised by the preceding speaker (Doc. 27).

A discussion of the normal procedures and conciliatory or advisory nature of the Lords should not hide, beneath a prosaic exterior, the fact that in a crisis the peers could emerge as the highest court of the realm, the ultimate body of decision-making short of the crown itself, and in some emergencies they even became the crown's *factotum*. During the course of the fifteenth century they heard and decided cases arising from disputed elections to parliament.[24] The role of gentleman's club receded, and that of 'natural advisers' came to the fore. In the 1450s, when Henry VI's grasp on government wavered and York claimed the throne, it was to the peers that the ultimate decision, short of battle, was

passed. A matter 'so high that it passed the learning of the justices' now
transcended rational deliberation. They were the highest court, the
highest council, the collection of the greatest men. They were nearest
the king and his crown. And lastly, if political settlements broke down,
they would lead the armies (Doc. 29).

Participation in the Lords (and membership in the aristocracy)
served to foster class consciousness. Service to the monarch was more
individualised, but here also social status gave the peer a 'right' to
serve, just as it put the king under an obligation to use his nobleman.
The tradition of royal service might fit neatly into the scope of private
interest as well – the Percy-Neville hold on the northern marches is a
good example. It offered both financial opportunities and honour. Many
functions performed for the king were lucrative, with the emoluments
taking various forms: a direct cash payment, perhaps via the sheriff's
county revenues or from the customs fees at a designated port, was a
common method. Indirect payments, in the form of exemptions from
burdens and restraints, were also used. Then office holding, be it ancient,
medieval or modern, can open the door to perquisites which may not
appear on the record and which are often at or beyond the edge of the
law. The profit motive was present, or just around the corner. If few
nobles needed the salary they earned in order to meet their ordinary
expenses, they too had extraordinary burdens, sometimes actually
incurred through their service, and few men were indifferent to the
possibilities of enhancing their income. Furthermore, a salary earned in
royal service, and perhaps augmented by sharp practice, could be
inflated much more rapidly than an income which came from manorial
revenues. So royal service was both a means to an end and an end in
itself.

Money was not all that was involved. Firstly, the anticipation of cash
received could be an uncertain reed on which to build one's expectations.
Kings, like lesser men, did not always honour their obligations, certainly
not promptly. In fact, kings could prove harder to dun for bad debts
than lesser men, as both the Italian bankers of Edward III and the great
baronial captains of Henry VI learned, to their own costs. The greater
the financial pit, the harder it was to fill, and some of the tension
between the king and the marcher lords of both the west and the north
stemmed from the ever-growing pile of uncollectable writs for wages
that royal service returned in lieu of money.

Honour, or what we might invidiously call social competition, was
also a keen spur to service, along with greed. This motive is discernible
in public life as well as in private dignity. Every position for which a
peer competed was one that, if he failed in his quest, someone else would
get, with its rewards and opportunities. Royal neglect in the distribution of patronage – which is what office holding was – was a serious

affair. Complaints against such oversights, when the neglect was systematic or obviously personal, reflected more than just personal pique.
The omission from an honorific position was a form of denigration
which raised doubts about the candidate's rightful or natural position.
It demeaned him before his peers and his social inferiors. Government
service, seen in this fashion, represented another kind of social reciprocity, with the king needing the labours of his magnates and they, for
both financial and social reasons, needing the expected summonses and
commissions. He gained a class of lay servants who did not need
primary or full-time financial support. He could tap the talents of men
who shared his outlook and had had a common education in terms of
technical training and social outlook. A snubbed baron might withdraw
to his inheritance, scornful and aloof. Or he might charge like a wounded
bear, as did the duke of York when he came home from Ireland in 1451
and found himself excluded from what he considered to be his rightful
position. Exclusion from office could either be the cause or the effect of
a serious rupture, but it was usually a factor. And on the other hand,
from an honoured and well-rewarded baron the king might expect loyal
service for a generation or more. If few men in English history could
offer the years of service that William the Marshall gave to Henry II,
his two sons and then young Henry III, it was more because of the
Marshall's unusual longevity than because he was alone in his (profit-
able) dedication. The Montagues, the Nevilles, the Talbots, the
Cromwells and many others laboured for more than one lifetime.

The bonds between royal needs and baronial service can be illustrated
in several ways. There are two methods that, taken together, offer a
glimpse of the terrain with a minimum of effort. One way is to look at
some major government positions and to see how often they were filled
or exercised by peers. The other is to follow the career of a particular
peer and to note how much of his active life was spent in appointed
office. In the latter case we should temper our idealisation of this selfless
servant by noting that he was usually well paid.

Some offices of medieval government were usually reserved for
ecclesiastics. The chancellor's great position was, but even here a few
laymen served. Edward III used five lay chancellors and all were
commoners. But Richard II's two lay chancellors were Lord Scrope
and Michael de la Pole, earl of Suffolk, and Henry VI was served by the
earl of Salisbury. The treasury, from the late fourteenth century on-
ward, was mostly in noble hands: four of the five treasurers of Henry IV,
two of Henry V's four men, all ten of Henry VI's, and all five of Edward
IV's treasurers. The most famous of them all was Ralph, Lord Cromwell, who served from 1433 until 1443. From Edward III's accession to
Edward IV's death there were forty stewards of the household, and
thirty-one were peers. Most of the admirals in the fourteenth and

fifteenth centuries were also nobles: thirty of forty-six commanders of
the northern fleet between Edward I and Henry V; twenty of forty-one
admirals of the western fleet; and all fifteen holders of the office of
'Admiral of England' in the time of Henry V, Henry VI, Edward IV
and Richard III. A survey of the staff used on fifteenth-century diplomatic missions shows the nobles to have comprised a fair fraction of the
personnel, with their representation being greater on more important
business, as with France rather than with the Spanish kingdoms. This
sketchy treatment ignores the obvious areas of military service, but even
so it shows the close correlation between high status and heavy service
(at a high level).

As well as the major offices of state, the nobles served their kings in
the more pedestrian area of local commissions. Here, perhaps, even
more than in the realm of the great positions, an omission from service
was a visible demotion, for in this area all men of property could be
called and the great man who was ignored now saw high neighbours,
perhaps even his own tenants and retainers, summoned in his absence.
But for the most part the king did use his nobles: he too was hardly a
free agent, able to pick and choose without constraints and pressures. If
we look at some of the commissions of the peace summoned in the early
years of Edward IV we can see the level of aristocratic participation.[25]
For Cambridgeshire there were eight commissions. Thirty-four men
were employed, two of whom were bishops and seven lay peers. For the
East Riding of Yorkshire eight commissions meant twenty-seven men,
three of whom were bishops and six lay peers. And if we measure the
number of men serving on the different commissions we find the nobles
to have been present in a slightly higher proportion than their mere
numbers would indicate. They were 22 per cent of the Yorkshire personnel and comprised 29 per cent of the service. They did not, therefore, completely dominate affairs, but their constant presence helped
to guarantee their leadership and sway. They were the king's natural
agents.

In individual terms, the peers were also devoted servants, and
biographies of medieval nobles are largely personalised glosses on royal
concerns. Great nobles, like the earl of Salisbury and John of Gaunt,
led lives that were an indistinguishable compound of the public and the
private. But even lesser peers gave some value in return for the honour
received. In a short life William, third Lord Latimer (1301–35),
responded to various summonses to parliament and military expeditions.
He was authorised to choose archers for the Irish expedition of 1332,
and he was named custodian of the Yorkshire coasts. Thomas, the
eighth Lord Roos (1406–30), found time to appear in France with the
duke of Bedford and then with young Henry VI. He was also a commissioner to treat for peace with Scotland. William Fiennes, Lord Say and

Sele, was a commissioner of oyer and terminer, of sewers (for Sussex), of the peace, to inquire into extortion in Kent, of array in Kent and Hampshire, etc. He was constable of Porchester Castle, for life, and keeper of the New Forest. A privy councillor and vice-admiral under the earl of Warwick, he accompanied Edward IV on his flight in 1470, and then died fighting for the Yorkists at Barnet in 1471. Lives of great men were not just illustrious: they were filled with business.

CHAPTER III

When we looked at men entering and leaving the peerage we were concerned with social status. When we looked at political privilege and office-holding we were concerned with class consciousness. In this chapter we deal with the estates and landed incomes of the peers, and we can say that our subject here is wealth. Which of these is the 'real' key to understanding aristocratic lives, which point of departure offers the deepest cut into medieval life?

The answer is, all of them. Life was a unified affair, or a seamless garment, in the popular metaphor of the time. This interconnectedness of roles and functions, though true for all members of society, is most easily documented for those at the very top. There was no status without wealth (except for saints), as Bishop Russell had urged in his parliamentary sermons, no individual political voice without status, etc. But no element in the equation was indisputably the independent variable, the prime mover. Some men gained their wealth because they served their king, others were called upon to serve because they were already wealthy and could move naturally into a responsible position. 'In the fourteenth century, status was handled realistically; it corresponded to wealth and power.' [1] The king needed servants as well as money – witness not just his efforts to enforce attendance at parliament, but his efforts to collect fines in distraint of knighthood from the gentry – and his servants needed wealth to subsidise a service that might offer rewards but which usually used those men already possessed of considerable means.

For most men of the upper class, land was the way to realise a large income. The quest for land helps to explain the efforts to construct dynasties and great kinship-webs, running through time as well as across the landscape. The quest outstretched an individual and became a continuous process. Marriages, enfeoffments, alliances, liveries, indentures, benefactions, and even the choice of burial sites were made with an eye upon estates, present and future. A survey of a peer's assets would include the worth of his repute and the number of his kinfolk as well as an inventory of his tangible possessions. The drive to acquire land, like that to acquire status and privilege, had no logical terminal point.

The nobles were all very rich. The greatest of them vied in wealth – measured both by income and by expenditure – with the great ecclesiastical princes. Even the least of the peers could usually rival the great merchants and squires who, for a variety of reasons, never quite attained the peerage. Noble wealth was almost exclusively rural, landed wealth.[2] This was considered proper; only land carried the air of gravity that urban and mercantile fortunes could aspire to but rarely reach. Medieval peers, for all the talk about mobility and opportunity, were rarely direct descendants of the prosperous burghers of London or York or Bristol or Norwich. If these men followed the stereotype and invested their coin in land, it rarely served to boost their children and grandchildren over the highest wall of privilege. Two roads led a family to the aristocracy after 1295. One was simply descent from an older rural gentry, the county knights, if by dint of luck, marriage and survival the value of the estates and the personal presence earned one an individual summons. This truism is worth stating because people came from somewhere in Edward I's day. The other route upwards was by virtue of royal service – the Scropes and the Cromwells are good examples – and in time pecuniary rewards became commensurate with a higher social dignity. Both roads, of course, were intertwined, and most new peers had trodden both during their public lives.

Clearly, rich is a relative term. The actual annual income of a medieval peer, whether we mean gross or net, is not often an easy item to calculate. Neither medieval accounting methods nor medieval fiscal policy was based on the need for such a calculation. Fortunately for us, the peers assessed themselves on the basis of landed income for a tax in 1436, and the figures have been examined with some care.[3] Not unexpectedly, the modern verdict is that these fifteenth-century statements erred on the low side, i.e. the peers were worth a good deal more than they claimed. The annual incomes ranged from York's £3,430 and the earl of Warwick's £3,116 down to Lord Clifford's £250 or Lord Clinton's meagre claim of £112. The average for the fifty-one peers on the list was £768 (or £865 if we add in the annuities they supposedly were receiving from the exchequer), and sixteen of the fifty-one were above £1,000 per annum. To set these numbers in some perspective, only three commoners that year reported incomes in excess of £600, only ten were worth more than £400 annually. There were 171 wirh incomes of between £101 and £399 (with their average around £200) and only 1,200 men were in the £25 to £100 category, and another 1,600 above £10. Any idea that middle-class affluence was sufficient to support real political independence seems pretty unlikely when held against these figures. And if the duke of York's income was really closer to £7,000 than to the reported £3,430, we can understand how he and a few of the other great peers thought they could almost literally buy and sell their inferiors, if not the throne itself.

Even if we mentally raise the fifteenth-century estimates by 20–50 per cent the great fourteenth-century magnates did as well or better. Henry of Lancaster (Thomas's brother and heir in the earldom) realised perhaps £6,000 or better in the 1330s, and John of Gaunt may have doubled this figure half a century later. The great Clare estates were returning £3,000 in the mid-fourteenth century. Another way of comparing the aggregate sums is to remember that the archbishop of Canterbury's estates were also returning £3,015 in 1422 and £3,049 in 1446, or that the total realised in the fourteenth century from the parliamentary grant of a tenth and a fifteenth was only £37,000. And whatever the general condition of the economy in the fifteenth century, a new and politically astute baron like William Herbert could go from obscurity to a landed income of £2,400 per annum within the course of a single eventful decade like the 1460s, mostly from royal grants of other people's lands.[4] So for most peers the worth of their estates was a good deal more than nominal, and its gain or loss a matter of political life and death.

From an economic viewpoint the story of the peerage is a tale of multigenerational efforts to accumulate vast landed estates. Sooner or later the line of success, as measured by continuity and accretion, was checked for any given family when it experienced the failure of a single male heir. If some families, like the Staffords or Beauchamps or Zouches or Cliffords, went on for generations before they proved mortal, others, for example the Bohuns or the house of Clarence (Thomas, duke of Gloucester) or the Uffords, were singularly incapable of producing many heirs. Cadet lines were notoriously sterile, though biological explanations seem less likely than social ones, and the end result was a fairly rapid turnover of the great aggregations. If the law generally favoured primogeniture, out of the need to maintain the stability on which feudal tenure had been based, it now allowed heiresses to divide the estates and to pass their share on to their children, and old patrimonies were merged into new groupings. We have seen how the rich might get themselves summoned to parliament and consequently into the nobility. And rich men, provided they survived, would do well: 'Their landed incomes were rising, not steadily but, more accurately, by leaps. The cause is a simple and obvious one: wealth attracted wealth; land married land.'[5] Over half the peers married, as one of their wives, an heiress. As genuine escheats were becoming rare, the rapid recirculation and reaggregation of lands became the pattern, and most of the great families were consistent winners in the contest.

We will look at the landed estates in three different ways. The first is to examine the process or milestones of transmission – the way in which lands passed from lord to lord, from old to new tenant. The second deals with the problems of loss and gain, of acquisition and divestment (which was usually involuntary when carried out beyond the level of charitable benefaction). The last treats the management of the land, for once acquired it had to be exploited.

Though transmission is not really the beginning of the chain – for land had to be acquired in some fashion – it brings an element of normality or stability to our exposition. In over half the cases of peerage succession the heir was a son or grandson or brother, so the direct link of male to male was preserved. When the administrative process, designed to produce an inquisition post-mortem, was instituted after a land-holder's death, the identity and age of the heir would be determined and forwarded to the king. Then, if the local inquisitions reported the succession to be clear-cut and the heir of age, the new tenant pledged his fealty and assumed his inheritance. Local juries could be rather casual, and they heard a lot of evidence about age like that offered by Juliet's nurse: [6]

> . . . I remember it well.
> 'Tis since the earthquake now eleven years;
> And she was wean'd (I never shall forget it),
> Of all the days of the year, upon that day . . .

When the heir was obviously of age there was little pressure for precise information, and 'his son and nearest heir is aged thirty six and more' might suffice for the king though it is confusing to a modern demographer. When the heir was a minor, and a wardship called for, things were much trickier, but that will be dealt with later.

An examination of one family gives us a detailed view of simple transmission and of accretion. The case of William, second Lord Zouche, who died in 1381, is instructive. He was one of a family of peers that stretched from his grandfather's summons in 1308 as the first lord into the sixteenth century. Lord William had been summoned to parliament from 1348, when his grandfather had died and he had inherited the title and family lands. He was a relatively minor peer, one of a good number of such men who never rose high but who successfully held their own, produced male heirs, and kept away from the sort of horrendous blunders that led to treason and attainder. Zouche's inquisition post-mortem (IPM) shows impressive but hardly fabulous wealth (Doc. 30). The counting of manors is a difficult game but Zouche seems to have died in possession of forty-one manors, in nineteen counties, plus a tenement in the city of London. The way in which these holdings came to him can be analysed, in part at least, without undue effort.

The Zouche holdings had come to Lord William from numerous ancestors (as shown in Table IIIa for the genealogy, and IIIb for an analysis of the lands in the IPM). In each generation the new plums came from the wives, in the typical fashion. From his great-grandmother Milicent Cauntelo had come nine of his manors, plus several others by way of Milicent's brother George, lord of Abergavenny.

Table IIIa

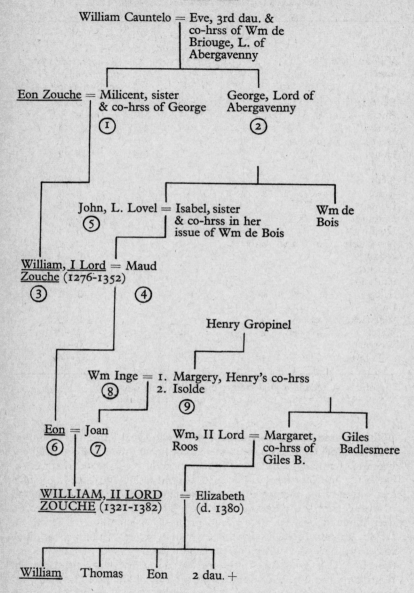

William Cauntelo = Eve, 3rd dau. &
co-hrss of Wm de
Briouge, L. of
Abergavenny

Eon Zouche = Milicent, sister
& co-hrss of George
①

George, Lord of
Abergavenny
②

John, L. Lovel = Isabel, sister
⑤ & co-hrss in her
issue of Wm de Bois

Wm de
Bois

William, I Lord = Maud
Zouche (1276-1352)
③ ④

Henry Gropinel

Wm Inge = 1. Margery, Henry's co-hrss
⑧ 2. Isolde
⑨

Eon = Joan
⑥ ⑦

Wm, II Lord = Margaret,
Roos co-hrss of
Giles B.

Giles
Badlesmere

WILLIAM, II LORD = Elizabeth
ZOUCHE (1321-1382) (d. 1380)

William Thomas Eon 2 dau. +

Table IIIb. *Manor listed on ancestors' IPM.*

Co. where William held land	Manor listed on IPM of person numbered in Genealogical Table IIIa									Comparison: no. of manors on old IPMs and on Lord's IPM
	Person number									
	1	2	3	4	5	6	7	8	9	
Bedford	a	a	ax			x	b		b	6 – 5
Bucks.	x									1 – 2
Derby										0 – 1
Devon	ab	ab								2 – 2
Hants							a	a	a	3 – 1
Herts.								xx		1 – 2
Kent								x		1 – 1
Leics.	a		a							2 – 2
Lincs.			xx							1 – 3
London										0 – 1
Norf.			a	a	a					3 – 1
Northants.	a	abc	xabc							3 – 4
Notts.										0 – 3
Oxford										0 – 1
Rutland			x							1 – 4
Salop		a	a							2 – 1
Suff.								x		1 – 1
Warwick.	xa		a							2 – 3
Wilts.	x	x	x							3 – 3
Worcs.										0 – 1
Totals	9	8	14	1	1	1	2	5	2	32 – 42

Note: x = manor in that county named on only one IPM.
a, b, c = same manor named on more than one IPM.

William's grandmother Maud brought land as well, inherited from her mother Isabel who had been co-heiress of her brother William de Bois. From his mother, Joan, Lord William picked up two manors named in her IPM, plus four more that came from her father, William Inge. The many lines of inheritance all converged upon William, and of the forty-two properties and possessions listed in his IPM only sixteen had not been mentioned in the inquisitions of his eight ancestors (plus that of Isolde, William Inge's second wife, who had held some land at the time of her death as part of her dower share of Inge's estate). Some properties, like Calstone and Calne in Wiltshire and Harringworth in Northamptonshire, can be traced from George Cauntelo through his sister Milicent and then through her son William down to the second Lord Zouche. The first William took livery of his mother's lands in

1298 or 1299, so the span of inheritance to Lord William's own heir covered almost a century.

The genealogical table reveals how many heiresses were involved in a successful family tapestry. William's paternal grandmother (through her mother) and his great-grandmother (through her brother) both received and transmitted some share of family lands. His mother-in-law was also an heiress, though her marriage with William, second Lord Roos, produced male heirs and the property never passed to the Zouches. Zouche's maternal grandmother was also a co-heiress, as was his great-grandmother's own mother, Eve de Briouge. So for a family that never married into a single great landed estate, as the Montagues did with the Beauchamps or the Nevilles with the Montagues, the Zouche clan was hardly dedicated to a succession of whimsical love-matches. The process of accretion was undramatic but steady.

Could they anticipate the continuation of such luck? The tale of the five lords who succeeded William, second Lord Zouche, takes us well into the sixteenth century, and it shows that the earlier success was emulated. From William, third lord and heir to our central figure down to John, second Lord Zouche (1459–1526), there was a straight chain of father-to-son inheritance, and seemingly it was always via the eldest son by the first marriage. The five peers after the second lord had eight wives. Two of the woman were heiresses and brought property to the Zouche family: Alice, first wife of William, fifth lord, was sister and co-heiress of Richard, fifth Lord St Maur, and then Joan, wife of John, seventh lord and sister and co-heiress of John, Lord Dinham. These two women, plus three more of the eight wives, had had mothers who had been heiresses as well (of the peerages of Burghersh, Grey of Codnor, and Beauchamp of Bletsoe, as well as of the landed families of Peyvre and Arches), though their holdings ultimately went elsewhere. So on a relatively minor scale the general point about the link between survival and the accretion of estates through marriages seems to be well vindicated.

Few families could boast of such a long series of smooth transitions. In something like one case out of four the heir was a minor male child, and then all the complications of a wardship – some political, some administrative – would arise. And when the estates passed into the hands of one or more heiresses the chances of litigation or violent contention were greatly increased. The great holdings of one generation were well worth the pains of the next, and sons-in-law, cousins, nephews and even more distant relatives were apt to go for each other's throats. The rivalry between Henry Bolingbroke and his uncle Thomas of Gloucester over the great Bohun estates of their wives was obviously based on a realistic financial estimate of the value of the prize, but many another family feud was more exacerbated and for far less. The dispute over the division of an inheritance could take on the characteristics of a blood feud, and Lady Berkeley was imprisoned by the Talbots until they got their way. The long contest between the Greys and the Hastings family was notable for its duration, but it was hardly peculiar.[7] Nor were such quarrels even foreseeable, for what seemed the prosaic marriage of a younger daughter might turn out to be, years later, the union with an heiress, now the only survivor of a great line. The union which eventually brought the Howards the dukedom of Norfolk was originally contracted when many other claimants, male and female, seemed more likely candidates for the great title than that East Anglian gentry family. A Bourchier marriage helped to fill the Stafford coffers, and 'once again a girl had become a great heiress after the wedding'.[8] All this underscores the luck of the Zouche family, and it indicates how success was far from inevitable.

When the heir was a minor, a wardship had to be countenanced. Wardship was the most lucrative feudal incident, so the king had economic as well as political interests to watch and the heir had to watch his (or her) lands go into and, hopefully, out of the hands of the temporary recipient.[9] Something like a quarter of the peers died leaving a minor heir. This meant that the crown could almost anticipate a regular annual income from the realisations and regranting of such windfalls. They could be doled out for cash, but mostly they went to political favourites or to those who were royal creditors and for whom ready cash was not available. Between these latter categories there was no shortage of candidates, and the promise of the next wardship to fall to the crown was as sure as, and likely to come sooner than, the promise of the next vacant bishopric. Though the growth of uses and enfeoffments to avoid the chances of a wardship cut into the crown's receipts, there is no question that short lives and young children had a great effect on the whole balance of political patronage.

An example of a typical transaction, though on the most exalted scale, is offered by the inheritance of Richard, duke of York (Doc. 32). He was the heir of his uncle, killed at Agincourt, as well as of his mother's brother, the earl of March, who died in 1425. The bulk of the vast complex of honours and receiverships was bestowed upon Ralph Neville, first early of Westmorland, and the *Fine Roll* indicates that Westmorland was to pay a very considerable sum within two years to repay the king for his generosity. Since York would not come of age until 1431 there would be many years in which the earl could skim the profits and recoup his expensive purchase. But the real business was more subtle: not only was Neville ostensibly shown favour by the sale of the wardship, but his payments were simply discharged against the gigantic debt owed to him for his service on the northern marches. He was being repaid with York's lands.[10] And to these themes is added that of marriage, for York was matched with Westmorland's youngest daughter, Cecilly, the last of twenty-three children. The marriage was eventually consummated, like most arranged aristocratic marriages, and it produced seven (or more) children, among them Edward IV and Richard III.

When Westmorland died in 1425 his widow successfully sued to retain custody of the ward, provided she also set aside 200 marks a year for his personal expenses. Eventually the minor came of age, as minors are wont to do, and in 1430 – one year early – we find York already suing to recover his holdings (without which he could never assume any sort of independent political presence). Now the administrative processes swung in his favour partly because of his high birth but mostly because he was already a petitioner for back wages due from the campaigns in France. The writs decreed that he could come into his own without furnishing formal proofs of age, a boon that may have meant the saving of several months. York's case was relatively uncomplicated, for the shares of the dowagers were neither large nor complicated and the wardship was held by his in-laws and allies. But even here he had to argue that 'by reason of his nonage the lands have been in the hands of the king and of the late king, and that during that time grievous waste has thereupon been done'.[11] Marriage was arranged between the minor and the warder's family in about 10 per cent of the cases, and it minimised friction in what could be a very sensitive area.

Not all estates went, even eventually, to the eldest surviving son or the daughter-heiress. Legal devices, uses and enfeoffments, enabled the lord to practise free dispositions to some extent, and during this period the iron hand of primogeniture was often weakened.[12] Sometimes this was done despite pressing claims by the proper heir, as when the earl of Westmorland ignored the children of his first marriage in favour of those by his second to Joan Beaufort. This was a purely personal decision, bitterly contested by the disinherited but nevertheless sustained. Other motives impelled Thomas Beauchamp, earl of Warwick, to entail his lands in 1344 so that they would stay with the earldom; the daughters were given small tokens of remembrance instead of large shares of the immense estates. The general purpose of the use was to allow the lord to treat his real property with the flexibility the common law normally allowed for personal property, and innumerable wills show how groups of friends, acting as executors, would act to prevent wardships, help younger children to disproportionately large shares, convey land to institutions without royal permission, etc. Like other developments in the history of the law of real property, these practices had no statutory base. On the other hand, they were often without any sinister or manipulative side, and the earl of Arundel certainly had kindly motives when he willed that 'oure forsaide feffees if God fortune that we decese and dye afore oure comyng ayen in to Ynglond after that oure dettes be paied that they make astate of oure forsaide brother and to his eyres maulez of his body'.[13] After 1380 the inclusion of clauses regulating the disposition of land is commonly found in the wills, and men no longer were locked in by legal custom (Doc. 33). To counter some of this new freedom, and to resolve quarrels as to whether titles and estates were separable, many fifteenth-century patents of creation for the nobles specify the manner of descent.[14]

Sometimes the devious paths of inheritance were followed for want of better alternatives. When William de Vescy died in 1297 he had already arranged for the succession of his bastard son William.[15] Though illegitimate children were frequently acknowledged in the wills, even with support they would not expect to inherit land if other claimants were around to challenge them. The earl of Salisbury sold land in the late fourteenth century to John of Gaunt and the Scropes of Bolton. John Hastings offered to make his cousin his heir if the cousin, William Beauchamp, would assume the Hastings family arms and petition the king for the earldom of Pembroke. Eccentric though this was, it shows how much scope there was, or seemed to be, for personal preference and guidance in the disposal of supposedly inviolable estates.

A different kind of qualification upon the course of simple transmission from lord to lord was the institution of the dower share, the one-third portion of the lands which went to the widow for life. Since women generally outlived their first husbands, and most died as widows regardless of how often they married, a peeress's longevity could be more than a minor inconvenience to the heir. The assessment lists for the tax of 1436 show that of the fifty-one peerages mentioned, ten were divided because of the claims of dowagers, and four more peerages were entirely in female hands for want of functioning male heirs. This sort of division could go on for years, and a peer with a living mother and grandmother might enjoy only two-thirds or one-third of his patrimony. In the case of York, which we have looked at, he had to carry the minor claims of his father's second wife, Maud Clifford, until her death in 1446, and those of Philippa Mohun, the second wife of his uncle Edward of York, until 1431. This was not too bad as such things went, but someone like Margaret Countess Marshal lived for so long, with so many jointures and dower shares bound up in her possession, that her grandson did not gain the Segrave properties until sixty years after John Segrave's death.

Some widows were well treated (Doc. 35), while others could get trampled in the rush for new wealth and new alliances.[16] The substantial grant settled on the duke of Buckingham's widow is only worthy of note because the late duke had been an ardent Lancastrian who fell at the battle of Northampton in 1460. Edward IV, Anne's cousin by virtue of the fact that their mothers were sisters, overlooked the unfortunate affiliation of the dead (but unattainted) duke and offered no objection to the widow's comfort. The grant of 39 Henry VI was confirmed, though the thirteen manors mentioned in 1461, even with all their appurtenances, came to much less than a full third of the Stafford inheritance. The extant household rolls for the Staffords from the second half of the fifteenth century show in what splendour they were wont to live, but Anne's impoverishment was relative at worst.[17]

A dower settlement from a century before listed the value of the land and property granted to Anne, widow of John Hastings, earl of Pembroke, as worth £361 19s 5d in 1375 (though it is not clear that the 'extent' of a manor was the same as its annual net worth). Because of the value of her own share of the Hastings estates the widow could afford to turn around and make an indenture with her mother whereby the old lady, our long-lived friend Margaret Marshal, received all the daughter's holdings from the wardship of the Hastings heir which the king had granted to Anne, the boy's mother (Docs. 5, 34). Anne's agreement was for her mother's life only, 'provided that if her said mother shall die within that term, the premises shall revert to the said Anne'. [18] The irony is that when the young heir, born in 1372, was killed in a tournament in 1389, while still a minor, his mother had been dead for five years while his aged grandmother had another decade before her.

Table IV

Walter Mauny = Margaret Marshal
(1310–72)   │   (d. 1399)

Anne   = John Hastings, earl of
(1355–84) │   Pembroke

John (1372–89)

But for all these permutations it is important to remember that estates usually passed from heir to heir, as defined by the common law, without undue difficulty. The laws governing the transmission of land were too basic to permit of limitless deviation. Occasionally an heir could be deprived of his share; the restraints of primogeniture were avoided or twisted sometimes, but year in and year out the bulk of the great aristocratic estates passed to the proper recipient. Since the quarrels that did arise about inheritances were protracted, colourful and sometimes bloody they receive considerable attention. They were not the normal course of events. Most of the peculiar practices only took root when a dynastic hiatus or irregular path of succession opened up. Heiresses' claims could be poached upon, and the children of a second marriage threaten those of a first, but when male followed male the law was generally firm. When Richard II began to tamper with the laws of property he was already half way to Pontefract Castle. What he could not do, few lesser men, even among the nobility, would presume to try.

If the (orderly) transmission of estates was the solid fare of landed wealth, the acquisition of new properties was the spice of the meal. To a striking degree the acquisition of land by some peers was coupled to the loss of land by others, for the gain and loss of estates was closely related to the king's efforts to reward the virtuous and to punish the opposition. These tangible rewards of political loyalty were important, for the bulk of newly acquired lands, except those coming by way of marriage and heiresses, was the result of such largess (Doc. 36 (f)). Purchase had little to do with the creation of a great patrimony. It was usually resorted to in order to round out the ragged edges of a block of holdings, and though the great bought more than they sold (and they might barter and trade as well) such transactions were rarely of much importance.[19]

The wind of royal favour could blow lands and perquisites into a chosen harbour. When Edward III raised his friends to earldoms he saw that they were properly endowed for their new honours. But the king was understandably chary about dipping into his own pocket to subsidise the new dignitaries: Salisbury got lands which were scheduled to escheat to the king when the Warennes died; Devon got lands that traditionally belonged to that earldom, etc. Edward's earls, created at a time of internal concord, did not rise at the direct expense of unfortunate rivals. Often, however, the two sides of fortune's wheel were directly paired, and what the loser lost went almost immediately, and quite nakedly, to the victor. Even the most fatuous kings realised that it was better to reward favourites with someone else's land. Many of the great reversals in political history were accompanied by equally dramatic changes in the area of land holding: after Boroughbridge, after the fall of Mortimer in 1330, after the breaking of the Lords Appellant, after the cyclical rise and fall of Yorkists and Lancastrians, after Bosworth, etc. Such local vicissitudes may have done more to bring knowledge of political reality into a locality than mere news of battles and executions did. Certainly men did not fight for their king in civil wars just for his bonny looks and his ancient lineage.

The 'carrot and stick' approach to politics is made more dignified when we speak of positive and negative reinforcement, but the essence is unchanged. When Richard II stripped Thomas Beauchamp, twelfth earl of Warwick, of his property in 1397 the lands were redistributed to various favourites and the threat which their administrative if not geographical unity posed was laid to rest. Many of them went into the hands of the king's favourite, William Scrope, earl of Wiltshire, who reinforced his unpopularity by becoming a major recipient of the spoils; his fall would be a *sine qua non* of the next reversal. However, Scrope knew the game at the top to be risky, and there is little indication that many peers chose to sit it out just because of the risk. Scrope got Beauchamp's Essex manors and their appurtenances, as listed on the *Patent Roll*, mostly for their economic return. But the grant of Paynes Castle in Wales and of Castle Barnard in Durham were as much for their political and military as for their financial value (Doc. 36 (b) and (c)). And the detailed inventory taken at Paynes Castle, down to the animals, the quarters of oats, '2 iron forks and an old chest . . . a wooden harrow, a flail', etc., indicates a depth of concern that speaks of future agricultural plans.[20] Many ends were served in one swoop by these transfers, and that the whole business of 1397 was stultified when Richard fell was hardly a unique feature of the affair.

Similar cases of turn and turn-again befell innumerable peers in the mid and late fifteenth century. After the dispersal of the Yorkists in 1459 the Coventry parliament outlawed the other side with great gusto, condemning the 'late duke of York' and the 'late erle of March' and the 'late erle of Warrewyk', etc.[21] The newly acquired royal treasure was tremendous, except that it was probably more than balanced by the newly acquired royal obligation to bestow wealth upon victors and assorted friends (and even on waverers who might be coaxed by a manor or two). Kings did not cease to display political generosity when the age of ring-givers ended and the Vikings converted. Many of the recipients of the Lancastrian largess in 1459 and 1460 were the loyal peers; some of the grants went to Lord Roos, Thomas Grey of Richemount Grey, the lofty but impoverished earl of Devon and others (Doc. 36 (d) (e) (f) (g)). The duke of Norfolk tried to keep well out of the hurricane's centre, and his circumspection needed economic as well as moral encouragement. Once again, the reversal was reversed in due course, which this time means with the accession of Edward IV in May 1461.

We have remarked on the frequency with which noble families fell only to rise again. In a similar fashion, as they lost their estates, in whole or in part, when they were toppled so they were allowed to recover them, or to try to recover them, when they were restored. Repentance was of little good if forgiveness was all it brought, and a seat in the House of Lords had to be supported. The trials which the Percys heaped upon Henry IV led to the denouement of 1408, with the earl dead at Bramham Moor and parliament passing a sentence of treason. But sure enough, by 1416 they were well along the road to recovery; two years before Henry Percy was allowed to recover lands held in tail by his father (Hotspur) and grandfather.[22] The recovery was neither smooth nor quick, and some bits and pieces remained in other hands for decades, but by 1421 Percy won back manors 'held in chief by knight service, for a fine paid in the hanaper [and] the king respited the homage of the now earl until a day now past, and commanded livery of the

said manors to be given him; and the king has taken his homage'.[23] The
Percy petition of 1414 for the recovery of land accepts the reality of the
treason, but is full of phrases of rehabilitation like 'notwithstanding' and
'if the rebellions and forfeitures . . . had not taken place'.[24] Since the
Percys were to die fighting against the Yorkists they repaid the House of
Lancaster for its renewed faith. The regranting of the lost lands was
quite common, and the belated grant to the Lumleys was a greatly
delayed, simplified version of the process the Percys had been through,
and Thomas Grey was told that 'All Actes of Atteynder and Forfaiture
made or hadde . . . [are] utterly voide, adnulled, and of noe force ne
effecte.'[25]

Land, we readily say, was money. How were acres and crops and
stock and woods and mills and other agrarian resources actually converted to the liquid assets needed to feed the great households and to
subsidise the many forms of baronial activity? The simple answer is
through a capably managed and exploitative bureaucratic structure
which turned local supervision into a segment of a widespread centralised operation. The surplus values of the manors – the profits in both
money and kind – derived from the use of people and the techniques of
absentee-landlordism were carefully collected, recorded and mar-
shalled upwards. By the late Middle Ages the administrative blocks of
scattered holdings, often gathered into blocks or 'honors', were run as
very big business. There were theories and handbooks to guide the
practitioners, and some of the administrative and fiscal techniques so
generated were borrowed in the fifteenth century by the crown itself.
Walter of Henley's thirteenth-century treatise on husbandry exists in
numerous manuscripts, and it is but the best-known product of a whole
school of instructional manuals. Lords, or rather their local agents,
were seriously concerned to maximise their profits. Nobles were not
gentlemen farmers, their approach was not that of the casual week-end
squire. The many modern examinations of baronial estates show that
most men tried to heed Walter's closing bit of wisdom: 'Look into your
affairs often, and cause them to be reviewed, for those who serve you
will thereby avoid the more to do wrong, and will take pains to do
better.'[26]

Between the thirteenth and the end of the fifteenth centuries a revolu-
tion of sorts occurred in the organisation of manors, particularly across
the south and the midlands. At the earlier date the administrative
apparatus of the landlord was still largely concerned with the extraction
of agricultural returns from the lands and direct labour services from
the serfs and labourers tied there. Though everything had a cash value
and payments in labour services were passing into desuetude by 1300,
the lord's interest was still in the details of the harvests and the fields.
By 1500 this had changed: the demesne lands were largely being

farmed, that is, leased out for set payments.[27] The ministers' accounts
which record manorial revenues now read more like financial statements
and less like granary and barn inventories. The full story behind this
transition, which is an important chapter in the whole change from a
feudal to a proto-capitalistic rural life and economy, lies beyond the
special tale of aristocratic land management. It is concerned with
agricultural booms and depressions, a rise and fall in populations, social
and political pressure towards personal freedom, horizontal as well as
vertical mobility, the growth of towns, the state's need for tax revenue,
and many other factors. But it is reflected in the documents which
illustrate manorial accounting and governance.

The nobles were absentee lords with a vengeance. This follows almost
by definition when the number of their lands and diversity of their
interests are considered. The dispersion of aristocratic land went back
to the policy of the Conqueror, and by the later Middle Ages the re-
distribution and fragmentation caused by the partition of inheritances,
by piecemeal royal grants, by barters and sales and enfeoffments and
alienation, all more than countered any rationalising efforts towards
concentration. Almost any noble family which survived and collected
wealth from its heiress-wives saw the lands come in in bits and pieces,
more diluted holdings, new problems and challenges for the administrative apparatus. William, Lord Zouche held his moderate holdings in
twenty-one different counties. As well as the thirty-nine manors the
Percys held in Cumberland and their twenty-one in Yorkshire, there
was land in Northumberland (approximately fifty-five manors, contained in three or four major baronies), Durham, Lincolnshire, Leices-
tershire, Essex, Sussex and London, plus miscellaneous bits and pieces.
York had some 135 manors in nineteen English counties, plus his vast
Welsh and Irish holdings. So obviously, the need for efficient administration was at a premium. The lord needed the money, some idea of
where he stood in relation to his debts and assets, *and* he needed freedom
from too much local responsibility, too many personal worries. It was in
each lord's interest to find a viable line between the policy of maximum
exploitation and the delegation of too much responsibility. The ascending pyramid of officials, from local reeves, stewards and bailiffs on up
through receivers and auditors to the receiver general and the household
treasurer was an absolute necessity.[28]

As a group the nobles were careful if rarely innovative or enter-
prising landlords,[29] and the financial pinch they often felt was due
more to their heavy expenditures than to a dramatic reduction of income
between the fourteenth and fifteenth centuries. Detailed examination of
some seigneurial administrations indicates trouble in collecting arrears,
in squeezing recalcitrant tenants and officials, and sometimes in finding
tenants to till the land, particularly when plague or border wars had

spread their peculiar blight. 'Defectus redditus cause pestilencie' is often encountered in the decades after 1349,[30] but there is little sign of the concomitants of real desperation: the sale of manors, the stripping of their resources, the drastic reduction of rents because of chronic depression or depopulation, etc. Fifteenth-century revenues were probably down from the pre-plague peak of the fourteenth century, but only by a factor in the neighbourhood of 10 to 20 per cent, and, in the days before inflation was eternal, the greater pressure on the barons came from a tendency to spend more rather than from an ability to collect less. Some individuals were undoubtedly desperate about their prospects but, generally, declining incomes did not drive the peers into 'political gangsterism'.[31]

A typical thirteenth- or mid-fourteenth-century ministers' account from a manor or group of manors is likely to be a long and detailed report on the sources of income, whether realised or not: which ones had been greater or less than anticipated; what expenses had been covered from the local revenues; how much of the receipts had already been discharged through disbursements; how much owed as the arrears of the following year's account. It sounds both complicated and formalised: it was. Charge-discharge accounting of this sort was far from a simple financial statement. In the ministers' account for the Percy manor at Petworth in Sussex for 1349–50 there were ten sources of revenue or charges, apart from arrears of 72s 2d.[32] The categories are rents, farms with the mills, small rents, sales of works, sales of stock, issues of the manor, sales of pasture, sales of wood, and court perquisites, and each category brackets numerous small transactions. The items lumped under sale of stock, to give one example, comprise nineteen or more separate sales, bringing an aggregate of £12 19s 3d. While forty-five pigs had been sold at 1s 1d per head (which comes to £4 5s 6d), fifty-four pelts of lambs and sheep, dead of the murrain, only fetched 12d. Against the total charges of £118 19s 9d, laid against the reeve of Petworth, he could offer eighteen types of allowed expenses or deprecia-tions, adding up to £52 12s 3d. Since the reeve had also turned over £56 13s 11d during the course of the year, mostly to the lord's receiver, he now owed £9 6s 5d, supposedly to be paid at the time of audit. A few other discharges were allowed then, and the reeve was left with the smallish obligation of £6 1s 1¼d. Then the account went on to list, in great detail, an inventory of the corn and other agricultural assets on the manor. The document was typical for the day, and it read as much like a produce report as a financial statement.

We can compare the Petworth account with a fifteenth-century ver-sion of the same kind of document. This is now short, clipped and purely financial (Doc. 37). Lord Grey of Ruthin showed a much more cursory interest in the details. Towcester was a large and prosperous

manor, which is what interested him.[33] The assets now being farmed out
brought in about 20 per cent of the revenues – a probably low figure for
the day – while the traditional payments from tenants or villeins, the
rents of assize, came to about 40 per cent and the remaining 40 per cent
came from a miscellany of sources: in the market and fair, courts, works,
pastures, etc. Once the charges upon the reeve were totalled, he, like his
fourteenth-century counterpart, had to work them off, that is either
show acceptable reasons for not having collected the money, present
evidence of discharges already made, or pay the balance in cash (now or
in the future). But fees and annuities, rather than money on enclosing
Petworth Park (£1 16s 5d) or purchasing corn (£17 8s 6¾d) or for hiring
extra hands for the harvest (£5 15s 4½d) or for salting venison (5s 8d at
17d per bushel for salt), were the channels of disbursement. Lord Grey's
obligations to his retainers and household officials were paid directly
from manorial sources, and the cash that remained went, as ready money,
to the lord's own household. We are much closer by the mid-fifteenth
century to a world of book-keeping than of agronomy.

Manorial revenues were collected by the local officials and then
funnelled upwards. At the local level the manors were supervised by
local men, traditionally of inferior or unfree social origin, though by the
end of the Middle Ages one suspects that most of them were petty
bureaucrats trying to make a bit of extra money. The agricultural pro-
ducts and money they collected went to the lord's receiver. He was an
itinerant official, working out of the central household rather than on a
local basis, though a great complex of holdings could be grouped into a
semi-contiguous block, an honor, for administrative purposes. If there
was more than one receiver there might be a chief, a receiver general,
who superintended the audit and collection. The revenues and produce
were collected or accounted for twice a year usually, with the main audit
at Michaelmas and a secondary one around Easter. It was at Michaelmas that the annual statements were prepared and audited.

The method of charge-discharge manorial book-keeping was similar
to that employed at the exchequer. Its faults were that it made it difficult to gauge the true wealth and worth of a manor, either in a given year
or as a capital asset. Since much of the trick of medieval accounting was
to ensure that someone was always responsible, the system served its
masters with some degree of efficiency for centuries. But the great
households also felt the need for immediate if cursory information,
either about 'net' or 'clear' worth, and by the fifteenth century, if not
before, summary documents were often prepared to tell something at a
mere glance (Docs. 38, 39). The valor for the Clare lands was prepared
with three vertical columns, giving gross receipts, expenses (but not
cash discharges), and clear value. Then a total for each column, for the
manors within each honor, was calculated, and from the gross total the

total expenses were subtracted, leaving a clear value (of £120 2s 4½d in this case). Then from this the miscellaneous fees involved in the book-keeping process were deducted, so the clear value (of £112 10s 8½d) remains as the annual net intake. When this was done for each honor, the value of all 'Castles, lordships, lands and tenements' was worked out and a final aggregate net (of £1,899) was stated. Thus the lord or his councillors, or perhaps the king in the instance of a minority and ward-ship, could estimate what was likely to be realised. This was valuable information. It may not have been the innovation in land management that double-entry book-keeping supposedly was to international finance and banking, but it helped to enable the great men to absent themselves from property management and to be free for the serious business of politics, bastard feudalism and rebellion.[34]

CHAPTER IV

Medieval nobles, like modern teenagers, receive disproportionate publicity for their delinquencies. Their rebellions, private violence and personal armies have all been accepted as standard characteristics of high-born laymen (and, in many cases, of ecclesiastical princes as well). The excesses of the over-mighty subjects are collectively referred to as 'bastard feudalism'. John Fortescue elaborated the view that the ungovernable behaviour of wealthy nobles lay behind the civil wars of the fifteenth century as far back as Edward IV's time, and in terms of short-term causation at least he was astute and accurate. He saw the temptation of the nobles – 'it hath come that often when a subject hath had also great livelihood as his prince he hath anon aspired to the estate of his prince' – and the way the temptation filtered down to lesser subjects— 'his subjects would rather go with a lord that is rich, and may pay their wages and expenses, than with their king that hath nought in his purse'.[1] Nor were such expressions unique, for the Pastons put the same sentiments into more practical form: 'Sundry folks have said to me that they think, verily, but if you have my Lord of Suffolk's good-lordship, while the world is as it is, you can never live in peace.' [2]

In the narrow sense bastard feudalism refers to the use of armies of paid retainers serving in lieu of vassals and sub-vassals who supposedly served under the reciprocal and personal obligations of classical feudalism. In a larger and more general context bastard feudalism simply means the private warfare and wilful anarchy of the fourteenth and fifteenth centuries, particularly as unleashed by the magnates. It was the cause and effect of dissension among the peers and of the corruption of local justice and administration as well as of royal weakness. Bastard feudalism has come to represent a whole complex of economic and military activity: the phrase is obviously a pejorative one, and few except its governors enjoyed it as a form of free enterprise.

Edward I's statute of Quia Emptores of 1290 forbade further sub-infeudation by landholders.[3] This meant that cash, rather than real property, was destined to become the basic tool used to erect the webs of private power. The statute neither began nor ended a social transition, but like the famous Capitulary of Kiersy of 877, which accepted the hereditability of Carolingian fiefs, it conveniently marks the point at which the new practices came to be seen as the norm. The traditional line of historical explanation concerning bastard feudalism runs thus: when they could no longer give out land to secure men, the barons turned to private armies, attached to their service by money and labouring under terms regulated by private contracts. As Marius supposedly tied his soldiers directly to himself with cash bonuses and promises regarding privileges upon discharge, so men now identified with the lord whose livery they were paid to wear. The private soldiers overawed the king's officials and made chronic disorder into a normal condition. Such vicious proclivities, unchecked by strong royal control or civil harmony, reached their apogee in the fifteenth century. They were the darkness of the late medieval night, coming immediately before the Tudor dawn.

Clearly this picture is overdrawn. For several generations, scholars have worked to qualify such a dramatically satisfactory explanation. The separate elements of bastard feudalism were there, but the simple explanation is lacking on several counts. One fault lies in the linear, chronological approach. Private, contractual armies were hardly novel in the later Middle Ages. They had always been found in medieval society, and Byzantine border lords as well as late-Roman dignitaries had retinues to rival those of Lancastrian times. Closer to home, the earls of Edward the Confessor's England were even more over-mighty than were Richard of York or Warwick the Kingmaker or John of Gaunt. Godwin, Mordar, Harold, Leofric and their fellows had made the realm into a private battlefield in the eleventh century more surely than did their distant imitators. When the *Anglo-Saxon Chronicle* describes the horrors of the anarchy of the 1140s there is no doubt in the author's mind as to where the blame should lie: 'Every powerful man built his castles and held them against him [Stephen] – and they filled the country full of castles.' And this was but feudalism carried to a logical extreme and receiving very bad publicity. Furthermore, the anarchy came after the rule of three successive harsh and powerful Norman kings, which indicates that no king's peace could be more than temporary. A large percentage of the military and economic resources of the polity were always in baronial hands, and the danger they posed could be controlled but never solved.

So we must realise how few of the ingredients of bastard feudalism were new. Their peculiarly volatile union in the later Middle Ages was a result of long-range factors and more immediate ones. Henry VI was a spectacular failure, and his personal shortcomings plus the decisive turn of fortune in France spelled trouble. The reasons why noble families grew richer, with interests in more counties, have been treated: the fruit of this process is relevant here. Probably neither the efficient methods of estate management nor the widening social gap between the peers and the gentry caused the civil discord, but both developments made it easier to marshal inherited resources and to justify a resort to arms for political as well as personal goals.

We can see from these comments that it does not do to explain bastard feudalism simply in terms of the indentures of military service. There is a further qualifying factor to introduce. Bastard feudalism was but the military arm of baronial private government. It should be set into the full context of the noble household and bureaucracy. If war is but the extension of national policies through the use of force, so bastard feudalism was but the extension of aristocratic ambition by means of private soldiers. The armed retainers were part of a spectrum of servants running from those who polished the boots to those who collected manorial revenues on to those who planned crusades, designed great castles like Arundel and Tattershall, and hatched dynastic rebellions.

The noble household was large and sumptuous. It was both an institution and an activity. Though the gigantic meals and courtly ceremonies are not of primary interest here, we get an idea of their scope when we see that careful rules had to be laid down: [4]

'Proclamation is made four times a year around Berkhamstead in market towns, to understand whether the purveyors, caterers, and others make true payment of my lady's money or not; and also to understand by the same whether my lady's servants make true payment for their own debts or not; and if any default be found, a remedy to be had forthwith as recompense.'

But if someone like Lady Berkeley was travelling with fifty-seven horses and supplying ninety-six meals in a day, her unwillingness to be casual about expenses and procedures is not hard to understand, and if three-quarters of Clarence's expenditure of £4,000 per year went on food and wages there must have been a small army involved in purveyance and accounting.

We are more concerned with the hard structure of officials, attorneys, receivers, treasurers, secretaries and other such trained and trusted men. Usually laymen by this period, the retinue travelled with the lord, staffed his 'headquarters', and found time to look after their own interests as well. Because the lord's interest was often best served by seeing his friends and retainers in prominent local offices and in parliament, there was a coincidence rather than a conflict in selfishness, and retainers rarely had to choose between themselves and the boss (though they might choose between different lords). Men were tied to the lord in many ways: indentures (for life or term), annual salaries, family traditions of service, local patriotism, marriage with lesser members of the house. The service might be ephemeral and opportunistic; it might be to the grave (and beyond, if one party said prayers for the other). Any individual retinue reflects both stability and transition, but 'most private civil services had a marked hereditary character'.[5] The same families served the earls of Warwick or the dukes of Buckingham for several generations. Men might stay with manors or honors, even when they changed hands. Thomas of Lancaster inherited servants from the Lacys and some of them, loyal all the way through, outlasted him. Many an official of Richard of York ultimately reached lucrative Royal office under the duke's son, as the private function now became a public one.

The bureaucrats were tied to the lord as much as were the soldiers, or even more, if we measure the years of service. The centre of the web was the baronial council, a loosely defined and often indeterminate body of men who sat with the peer or, very often, acted in his stead.[6] The great retainers made their voices heard, and because there was no dishonour attached to being retained, any more than being a vassal, important men willingly served even more important ones. A peer's circle of advisers included figures of some independent prominence: a duke would have various peers among his retainers and councillors, and so on in descending magnificence to the major gentry who handled important affairs for a baron. The earl of Lancaster numbered two lesser earls among his seventy-five or so retainers; the earl of March moved about with a dozen or so knights; Lord Hastings took a regular fee for serving the duke of York, etc. A council of perhaps eight to twenty men at a time embraced technical experts, local authorities and great men who at other times carried their own circles around with them.

A council stood in for the baron in all sorts of affairs. The earl of Northampton authorised his men 'to give, to sell and to do with the aforesaid goods and chattels what they shall see to be best'.[7] A century later Lord Lovell told Viscount Beaumont that 'y by th'avise of my counceill, shall gyf it hym in writyng undre suche fourme as shall please yow . . .'[8] This was the standard phraseology, referring to the standard practice. Dozens of entries in John of Gaunt's registers say 'porce que nous del avys de nostre conseil avons et grantez . . .' or 'par lavis et assent de nostre grant conseil avoir grantez and venduz . . .'[9] If Bishop Pecock implied that many a lord was but the cat's-paw of his own council,[10] and if contemporary verses sometimes said that retainers served themselves and told the lord whatever he wanted to hear,[11] and if Edward IV told one of Norfolk's men that he could cozen the duke but not the king, then there was certainly much dependence upon the hired lieutenants. When some of York's men were arrested he said that it 'is to his greet hurte and causeth that he can not procede with suche matiers as he hath to doo in the kinges courtes and ellus where', and he got them freed so they could 'yeve him counsail from tyme to tyme in such matiers as he hath or shal have to doo'.[12] But behind most things there stood the magnate and his wishes, and the most judicious student of the question notes 'the extent to which everything depended upon the initiative of the lord himself'.[13]

The actual indenture which stipulated the mutual bonds and obligations was straightforward (Docs. 45, 46). The indenture which York made with Sir John Fastolf neither demeaned the latter – perhaps the richest commoner of the realm – nor did it represent a repressive monopoly of his services and commitments. It was an ordinary agreement between allies of different ranks, bound at least for a while by cash and convenience. Fastolf collected annuities from York for years; he generally supported York's (or their collective) interest in East Anglia; he counselled him. On occasion the servant loaned the master a considerable sum of money with jewels as the collateral, and a separate indenture was drawn up to protect Sir John, lest 'defaulte bee made in the paiement'.[14] Nothing in these bilateral agreements gives any indication of the chaos that prevailed through the land, and this sort of non-military contract was being endorsed by dozens or scores of peers each year, with many times that number of retainers.

Two great households, those of the Black Prince and of John of Gaunt, can be examined through their extant registers. The documents reveal establishments of a size and complexity worthy of a fair-sized independent feudal principality. Gaunt's instructions to his men show a hierarchy of officials and a carefully articulated view of their duties (Docs. 41–3). The council gave advice, as the king's own council did, and at its upper level it heard members like Richard Scrope and Lord Latimer. Furthermore, this great private 'civil service' was not focused exclusively on matters of state, whether England, Aquitaine or Castile was the state in question. The duke's paid agents in the royal chancery, exchequer, common pleas, etc., had their activities (and expenses) co-ordinated. Smaller matters were carefully noted too. Feudal profits of the manors, for example wardships and escheats, villein manumissions and marriages, were tallied. The council supervised the transfer of business to Pontefract after the Savoy Palace had been burned by the rebels in 1381.

Size and complexity must have worked against the push for order and record-keeping. The latter impulses led to the creation of monthly attendance lists on which the presence or absence of retainers and servants who were paid on a *per diem* basis was noted (Doc. 44). Whether it was Katherine Swynford, Gaunt's own mistress and her illegitimate children by the duke, or simply the grooms and personal servants who were circulating from manor to manor, cash was not given away casually. No one wanted to disburse money without proper authorisation, lest the clutches of charge-discharge accounting catch him up as the responsible party. And if few other men maintained households approaching Gaunt's in size, there is little reason to think that they were any less interested in how their resources evaporated.

Gaunt's older brother had an even more quasi-royal complex at his command. Edward had 'greater and lesser' auditors, marshals, butlers, valets of the chamber, masters of the horse, keepers of arms, a hierarchy of wardrobe officials, and the vast train of minor if important menials. His chancery business was handled by the full chain of seals: a great seal, a privy seal, a signet, a secret seal. Once again, we see that it was the necessity of handling business during the lord's absence that led to many of the administrative developments, and Tout concluded that 'unity and fluidity' were the keys to success regarding the council's personnel.[15]

This kind of administrative network was the ultimate recipient of the manorial revenues and accounts, even though countless annuities and external expenses were paid directly from the moneys of the lands or honors. The main financial officials were tied to the central council, not to the local land stewards, and the appointment of Lord Scrope's receiver general shows the direct relationship. Though the Scrope patrimony in Henry V's time was hardly a major one as baronial estate complexes went, there was enough at stake to concentrate one's attention only too well. These men were often sworn to loyalty, in a style very like that of a vassal, and even if their service was for a term only, the demands and the rewards were commensurate with its import. Daily expenses were logged (Doc. 43), to be examined quarterly, and a full account, like the wardrobe account rolls of Henry Lacy from 1307–8, reflects the kinds of sums that might be involved.[16] Lacy's auditors, two old and presumably trusted servants, accounted for receipts which totalled, with arrears, in excess of £6,600. The dozens of sources of revenue included holdings like Pontefract (£699 11s 4½d) or the Receivership of Tuttebury (£719 11s 9½d) as well as minuscule but remembered bits like the Almanbury reeve's return of 14s 3d. But then they accounted for the expenditure of £5,230 18s 7½d for general household expenses, £1,079 18s 3d for bread and salt, and £1,207 7s 11½d for horses, fees, gifts and charity. Though it is possible that we have only documents from the archives of the more conscientious barons, the rolls that survive hardly support a picture of feckless or insouciant aristocrats. If a family sometimes spent itself into trouble, as the Hungerfords did to pay off some huge French ransoms, the cause at least did not lie in an inadequate accounting system which failed to note the excess of expenditure over revenue.

The private administrative apparatus has a political and economic end, rather than a military one. But when the lord's intentions ran to recruitment and the use of arms, or the threat at least of such usage, the same procedures could admirably serve his new purpose. Raising soldiers by indentures was little different, in terms of the forms involved, from the appointment of a councillor or a receiver general. The stipulated salary, the term of service, the profession of loyalty, and perhaps the designation of which revenues were to be used to pay the annual fee, are the customary ingredients of the contract, regardless of its specific purpose.

The private indenture came into use in the late thirteenth century and it was not substantially different 200 years later. Hundreds or even thousands of these bilateral agreements are extant, and scores have been printed. The agreement of 1287 was between Edmund Mortimer, a 'squadron leader', and Piers Mauley, a 'troop commander', and it is one of the earliest we have (Doc. 47). Indentures of this sort were first widely employed to recruit men to fight Edward I's Welsh wars: by the king and his barons, by his barons and their own men. The number of men needed, the length of service, the distance of the campaign from home, and so on, all compounded the problems of staffing an army with the feudal levy. The answer was the contract which called for cash in place of the loyal service which stemmed from fealty and the fief. Such troops, whether serving the king or the baron for his own ends, were but a logical extension of the process which had caused the Norman kings to prefer scutage to enfeoffment, and the Angevins to use the money fief (the 'fief-rente').[17] No one thought they were doing anything that was 'anti-feudal' in the sense that the new institution might be seen as working to replace or topple the old.

Gaunt's registers offer many examples of indentures used to recruit soldiers as well as more pacific officials (Doc. 48). Men might be attached to Lancaster for a long period, and at a higher rate of pay in war than in peace. Expeditions beyond the sea could call for money to cover transport and the expense of horses lost in service. But this costly business was a necessity, and no one could offer the expected good lordship unless he was in a position to honour promises like those Gaunt made to Raulyn Dypres, a simple esquire, in 1372. An annuity in the neighbourhood of 20 marks was usually enough to bind a man, but Gaunt went as high as £40 (plus 40 marks extra for 'special service') to bind Sir William Frank, with the money to be paid from the revenues of the seignory of Bolingbroke.[18] Payment of the annuity was often made in two equal portions, and part of the regular strain upon the administrative apparatus was caused by this need to have cash collected and available.

A century before Gaunt, the earl of Norfolk engaged Lord John of Segrave to serve him 'as well in peace as in time of war, in the lands of England, France and Scotland'.[19] A century after Gaunt, Lord Hastings was binding men along almost identical lines (Docs. 49, 50). In 1461, William Gruffity of North Wales took the lord's penny and was 'withholden and retained with and toward the said lord for term of his life, promiting and binding him by the faith of his body'. John Davers, in 1476, was 'to ride and go accompanied with as many men defensibly arrayed as he may make at such times as he shall thereto be required by the said lord, at costs and expenses of the same lord'. And the element of reciprocity was made explicit, as well as the one of obligation: 'And for this the same lord granteth unto the said Henry to be his good, loving, and favourable lord, and him aid, help, succour, and support in all his matters according to the law.' [20]

So the nobles recruited followers. The loyalty of such men was qualified, of course, by the stated conditions of the contract as well as by the unstated ones of self-interest. Money could not necessarily prevail where personal ties and the ceremonies of infeudation had failed, but there is little reason to think that it was an inferior social ligature. Kings had found vassals as unwilling to accept their dictates under unmoneyed (or pre-moneyed) feudalism as under the later kinds of ties, and if Richard III was deserted at Bosworth by indentured barons, so had John and Henry III been by men tied to them in more traditional modes. The indentured retinue was possibly a 'steadying influence in a society where old institutional loyalties were breaking down and new ones had not yet fully developed to take their place'.[21] This is a sanguine view of their utility, and one may be sceptical about what they did for non-combatants and those with ambitions but no retinues. However, they did enable barons to tie men to their interests in peace and war, to use cash as the rational basis for political organisation, and to muster their resources with some obeisance to that important new god, efficiency.

The public welfare and the ends of baronial military efficiency and flexibility were not always synonymous. The law of fortune's wheel holds that someone must come down when someone else goes up, and when the earl of Oxford told John Paston regarding a suit which concerned a tenant of the earl, 'I pray you that ye wole calle the jurry before yow . . . and opne thaym the mater at large at myn instaunce, and desire thaym to do as concyens wole, and to eschue perjury', we may wonder about the impartiality of law.[22] If the baronial wars did not ravage the countryside in a manner reminiscent of William I's harrowing of the north, or of German armies in the Thirty Years War, they hardly inspired public confidence. Major population trends and commercial life were not radically altered, but articulate voices were critical of the over-mighty who showed the arrogance and indifference of modern fox hunters while in pursuit of bigger game. Langland was a mild critic when he complained how Wrong 'maintaineth his men to murder my menials,/Fighteth in my markets and forestalleth my fairs. . . .' On the other hand the raping, stealing and looting were hardly about to be ended just because the king agreed that 'Wrong was a wicked wretch who wrought much sorrow'.[23] Protests against aristo-cratic licence were a common thread running through the fabric of public opinion, usually with full justice and considerable passion behind the complaints (Doc. 51).

The problem obviously cut deeper than the superficial if sincere wisdom of political poems and homilies. The public concern, the royal interest, and the preference of uncommitted peers often coincided in the form of statutes. Legislation, designed to tell men to be good and to eschew evil, was fairly frequent, and the laws of early years of Edward III's reign decried the same wrongs as did those of Edward IV's (Doc. 52). Restraints upon retainers were considered appropriate material for the statute book, as were efforts to limit the use of improper influence. A petition of 1347 asked that 'no councillor of the king and no other minister shall maintain pleas or disputes pending in the king's court or anywhere else in the realm',[24] while that of 4 Edward III inveighed against 'men of the realm, great ones as well as others, who have made alliance, confederacies and conspiracies to maintain parties, pleas, and quarrels . . .' [25] The statute of 1390, coming at a time when Richard II was in firm control and yet surprisingly 'congenial to baronial interests', was at best an attempt to control the private bands rather than to eliminate them.[26] Legislation like that of 1 Henry IV which spoke out against all liveries except the king's was hardly worthy of serious notice.

By Edward IV's time the use of legislation against liveried bands was a ritualistic exercise more than a serious attempt at social reform. But at least all were agreed upon the nature of the problem, and Fortescue was hardly the only critic of maintenance.[27] Retinues were supposedly con-fined to those formally within the lord's service; men were not as free to come and go in or out of service; and the baronial households were to be closed to men of exceptionally evil repute – which must have meant very evil indeed. Beyond this there was little to be done. The unmartial retinue lasted for many centuries, and the warlike one was only sup-pressed or phased out of existence when the state became strong enough to command superior coercive powers and when the nobles could no longer hope to overawe their local neighbours by the threat of arms.

As well as explicit legislation, the government in the fifteenth century resorted to the use of private oaths and bonds of good behaviour.[28] The rationale for these formal agreements was that there were higher standards of behaviour for men higher up the social pyramid (Doc. 53). There also seems to have been pressure from one's peers to enter into these ceremonial bonds, as we can see at the highest level in the pointless love-feast Henry VI got his partisans and the Yorkists to participate in in 1458. But there is an indication of the idea of the nobles as an estate, equipped to hear and judge their own, in the notice:

'that if it hap that God defend that any dissension or debate fall between Lord and Lord the remainder of the lords anon as that dissension comes to their hearing or knowledge shall leave all other things, labours and intend to the redress and appeasing of the said dissension or debate'.

In a society where it was necessary to keep the lords from acting on their own to 'take amends thereof, nor punishment of the tresspass as of their own heed or authority, but that if they find them hurt or grieved they should let the king's council have knowledge', public promises were little enough protection.[29] By the time of Edward IV and Henry VII, promises to be good were often enforced by large payments, some of which were refunded upon good behaviour, and some of which were not. Money *and* increased royal power worked small wonders at least in pacifying the countryside (Doc. 54).

Medieval legislation, we are often reminded, is a guide to the intentions of the legislator but to little else. Society was not made wholesome through acts or oaths. However, we should remember that, while general turmoil was sometimes the effect of private disorder, personal and local quarrels were often its cause. For every baronial dash aimed at a pitched battle or constitutional vicissitude, innumerable quarrels, vicious and violent in the extreme, broke out over local hegemony, office-holding, elections, law-suits and boundary disputes. Just because the nobles were not absolute brainless criminals does not mean that they were always concerned with 'large forces in history'. Local power, without which national power was likely to remain a phantom, was of immediate and pressing concern.

The quarrel between the earl of Devon and Lord William Bonville is a good example of this sort of feud (Doc. 55). Their hostilities bedevilled the West Country for some years but, nasty as they were, there was little danger of the fights spreading geographically, and neither party had the might or the opportunity to deliver a real *coup de grâce*. The ostensible cause was the stewardship of the duchy of Cornwall, though we may suspect that personal animus and a general kind of local supremacy were really behind the business. Sporadic fighting broke out in 1441 and 1442 and continued for years. In June 1452, Devon attacked Bonville, besieged him at Taunton, and then forced him to accept York's mediation. But, given the general state of the government and the many distractions elsewhere, no permanent peace could be imposed. Neither persuasion, bonds of £2,000 apiece, nor royal displeasure served to separate the antagonists. In 1455 a lawyer named Radford, a member of Bonville's council, was brutally murdered by Devon's son. This led to a pitched battle – a bit of a rarity in such baronial struggles – and Bonville was driven into Exeter. Devon proceeded to loot the cathedral and hold the canons to ransom, as though to show that he was not too partial about where he spread havoc. By now only death could end the local warfare, and Bonville's execution after the second battle of St Albans in 1461 left the earl victor by default.[30]

Though an unusually protracted episode, this quarrel was not unique or even all that unusual. Other feuds, for example between the Nevilles and the Percys, Suffolk against Cromwell and others, the duke of Exeter against the Nevilles and so on, are not hard to find. When Clifford slew the earl of Rutland he supposedly said that he was simply returning the favour that had been done to his own father. It is even possible to see the larger battles, supposedly fought between opposing dynastic factions, as being conflicts between two groups, each drawn together by common personal and familial enemies on the other side.[31] There was a politic side to the attacking, looting and killing, but there was also a strong element of the irrational in society, and the times allowed for its easy expression.

Nor was the antinomian behaviour a peculiarity of the second half of the fifteenth century. An instance of the unlicensed triumphing over the rational is provided by the Stafford-Holland episode. This quarrel, involving the royal family and an established baronial line, showed that personalities rather than geographical or economic factors could unleash violence at any time and in any place. John Holland was Richard II's uterine half-brother. In 1384 he had murdered a Carmelite friar who had been placed in his custody, and the next year this ungovernable young man killed Ralph Stafford, eldest son and heir of Henry, second earl (and third baron) Stafford. This was to avenge the death of Holland's favourite esquire, at the hands of one of the Staffords' archers.

Even the nobles of the fourteenth century thought this a bit much. Holland fled to Beverley for sanctuary, and the earl of Stafford got the king's promise that the murderer would never be pardoned. He was restored to favour, of course, a few years later, after a ceremonial appearance by Holland at court in mourning dress, begging forgiveness from the king, promising to be good, etc. The murderer rose to become duke of Exeter and to marry Gaunt's daughter Elizabeth before his own execution, after Richard II's deposition, in 1400. The Staffords founded a chantry for their fallen champion, and the sharp taste of the affair faded with time. But the concept of each deed of violence being properly provoked by a previous act, plus the formalities designed to lay the feud, are reminiscent of the *bona fide* blood feuds of Merovingian times. York composed a feud between some of his own retainers in this formalised way, and even those who directed lawless activity had some interest in keeping an element of control.[32] However, this is to see the question from above, and the poor commoners who were driven to complain of 'the said misdoers [who] be so favoured and assisted by persons of great might' were hardly cheered up by the knowledge that there were elements of conflict-resolution within the blood feud.

One form of local domination that grated harshly upon bourgeois sensitivity was the aristocratic control and use of sheriffs (Doc. 56). An article of reform from 5 Henry VI asked that 'no man being steward with any lord be neither sheriffs nor escheators in the shires that he is officer in'.[33] This speaks volumes about the contemporary trust in human nature, as well as of how bastard feudalism actually affected interests and fortunes. Over half of Hastings's indentured retainers held shrievalties in the midland counties where he was strongest; though again we must remember that to some extent he recruited men who were powerful enough to gain high local office, as well as worked to place men already bound to him into the position. There was a coincidence of interest, rather than a mechanistic push. But once again, the distinction may have been lost on men like the Pastons when they were afraid to press their claims in court because the defendant and the presiding officials openly wore the same livery.

Another obvious goal for a peer who aspired to effective local domination was via the control of parliamentary elections for the knights of the shire. There is a division of scholarly opinion regarding the extent to which such control prevailed, and some of the uncertainty springs from indecision about the early importance of the Commons. If the peers did run things, then the lower house was neither very powerful nor independent; we have to look to the future for the comforting tale of its growing power. However, if the nobles did not control the show then why did it take the Commons so long to go further on the road of self-assertion? What is the proper Whig interpretation here? Maybe the best way out is to admit that the question can be seen either way and to stress the strength of the vertical networks, embracing the peer and men of similar interest in the Commons, rather than to worry about the source of power.[34]

The idea of John of Gaunt dominating election in his territory is certainly easy to accept (Doc. 58 (a) (b)). In so far as anyone cared about what the Commons said or did, the magnates would reach out and assert themselves. Retainers, clients, and those still hoping for but not yet in the lord's eye were all pliable, and if the voters could be persuaded or overawed, the lord had men from his team in the lower house. 'The interdependence of magnates and gentry' is the key to understanding how things actually worked, and that a policy was ostensibly a lord's does not mean that it was contrary to the interests of his followers, nor that they failed to play a large role in its formulation, perhaps in his council.[35] The bold Speaker of the Good Parliament of 1376 is now widely known to have been the earl of March's steward, rather than the

Hampden or Pym of fourteenth-century England. The lions and wolves could run together with considerable harmony.

We must not sell parliamentary independence too short, particularly at the local level where the election was fought. Almost any given lord had rivals even within his own sphere of influence; so an obvious way of thwarting the wishes of one peer was to seek the help of another. *The Paston Letters* are almost as eloquent about the rivalries of the peers as they are of their power, and East Anglia was hotly contested territory between York, Oxford, Norfolk, Suffolk, Moleyns, their wives, and others (Docs. 57, 58 (c) (d) (e)). Knowing that such support might be forthcoming, the gentry could be mulish about accepting an aristocratic nominee for office. Sometimes the lord carried the day despite local opposition, sometimes he lost, and sometimes he got his way but only with considerable effort (and expenditure). The mid-fifteenth-century elections covered in some detail by *The Paston Letters* indicate how local men of substance could be far from subservient and how they could quickly scent a wind of division when larger events weakened or distracted the magnates.

CHAPTER V

The family, perhaps more than anything else, is the key to a comprehension of the incessant ambition and strife. Its prominence, extension and aggrandisement come as close to being universal motives for the wide variety of aristocratic activity as any other single force, beyond such balder explanations as power, status, or even greed. Almost everything that was done was done, at least in part, for the benefit of that collective and dynamic web of people, related by blood and then secondarily by marriage, whom we designate as the family. In a world where religion offered a formal protection against eternity and oblivion, again it was often the family which provided the efficient means to eternal remembrance. They provided a multigenerational guarantee that one would not pass beyond memory or – almost as grim a prospect – into the position of being dependent upon the prayers of subsidised strangers.

Not everything that we might wish to consider about private lives is neatly subsumed into the picture of family activity, nor was all family activity necessarily of an irenic variety. When the Nevilles complained of factions that were 'each against the other by manner of war and insurrection in late assembled great routs and companies upon the field and done furthermore great and horrible offences as well in slaughter and destruction of our people', they were referred to deeds wrought on them by their kinsmen.[1] Trevor-Roper has looked at such goings-on and cynically observed that 'in spite of all this lip-service to the family, no one really trusted anyone else, not even his sons . . .'[2] Such a nasty view of human nature: even if true, it is hardly the whole story. By the later Middle Ages the interest in collective family memory and fame has left such tangible memorials as the family cartularies, the bogus family histories of such great lines as the Beauchamps, the enumeration of vast webs of relatives in wills and private letters. For the earl of Arundel to ask for prayers for 'the souls of my father and mother, my wife and children, their successors, and all Christians', was hardly striking, but then he went on to mention specifically three sons, two daughters, one granddaughter, three grandsons, nephews and nieces, plus an uncle. His best coronet was to go to his son and heir Richard, and then 'to his heir, and so to remain from heir to heir, Lords of Arundel, in remembrance of me'. And the conclusion was that the executors should 'be good to my children'.[3] This was economic and political concern, if not necessarily love and affection: one knew and remembered one's relatives (Doc. 70).

A glimpse at the family also offers some opportunity of looking at personal concerns. Almost no one emerges from medieval records as a three-dimensional human being, but if all these beings are shadowy we do know more about the aristocrats than about almost anyone else. By the fourteenth and fifteenth centuries wills begin to complement the bleaker official records and the terse comments of most chronicles. Familiar human drives, if not familiar people, begin to take shape and leave a brief record of wishes and aspirations. The private events of many aristocratic lives catch the light for a few moments.

Marriage is a good topic on which to start. This basic social institution was second only to sex in popularity, judging from the fact that all but a tiny fraction of the nobles married. About half of them married more than once, often to women who in the course of their lives also had two or three (or even four or five) husbands. First marriages were usually made, that is contracted and consummated, between parties in their late teens or early twenties: arrangements for the marriage of much younger children would be made as business affairs, but the youngsters often lived apart for some years. At the other end of the bridge few people got more than a couple of years into their majority without a wedding.

The arranged marriages – and this probably means a large proportion of first marriages – were obviously set up with an eye to property and to political affiliations (Doc. 59). It was via marriage that estates moved to new holders, that heiresses brought in the great windfalls so regularly collected by the long-lived houses, and that the bad blood of the fathers was laid to rest through the union of the children. This is an idyllic picture and its relations to reality might be tenuous in any given case, though the story of the peerage is the story of the continuous formation of new alliances with the new sets of relatives. Of course, in a group where so many people were always related to each other there was not likely to be a single bold swathe of kinship which one unswervingly followed. Rather, kinship in some degree or other might be adduced to explain or justify almost any political decision that was made, whether the reasoning was *post hoc* or *propter hoc*. Marriage contracts were very serious, protected by indentures, hedged with conditions, deadlines, supervisors, collateral, provisions for support, and even contingency plans if one (or both) parties died before the date of final union. Nor, because of the uncertainties of life and the ceaseless quest for more allies, were younger children appreciably freer to marry according to personal inclination than their older siblings. In a medieval marriage contract the operative word really is 'contract', and as laconic an age as the fifteenth century could expend thousands of words upon one of these business ventures.[4] Huge sums were tied up through these dealings. On the other hand the nuptials of children were not wholly seen from the view of investments. Even a minor peer like Lord Burgh

left £100 of goods in Lincoln or Nottingham for the marriage of his
granddaughter Margaret, and 500 marks, plus some personal property,
for that of his younger son Thomas.[5]

Whom did the nobles marry? As a rule the peers, particularly those
who inherited their titles, married women from other noble families.
Their siblings, both male and female, also married within the peerage
on many occasions, though probably less than 50 per cent of the time in
absolute terms. There is little reason to think that being within the
peerage was, *ipso facto*, the reason for a match, that is, there are few
statements that a peer *should* marry a nobleman's daughter (Doc. 61).
But not only does like tend to marry like in most instances: this tendency is greatly reinforced by singling out the wealthiest and most
powerful, according them an hereditary position and special privileges,
and seeing them as a peerage. A propensity towards 'endogamy' is
hardly surprising here. There was also some tendency for men of higher
peerage ranks to marry women from such levels, and mere barons were
more likely to wed daughters of the great gentry than were earls or
dukes. Men were usually married till the time of their death, for, though
they might remarry, the ultimate final survivor was a widow much more
often than a widower. This leads to the headaches caused by the
dowagers, referred to above.

The Church promulgated an extensive list of forbidden unions. An
imposing collection of people were held to be related through blood,
through marriage, and through such spiritual affinities as having stood
as co-sponsors at a baptism. The practice was naturally less draconic
than the theory, and the complexities of defining and regulating what
was known as incest were more to give the Church social control over
unions than to forbid them. Regulation of people's lives, plus the collection of revenues and obeisance for dispensation from the rules was at
stake, not a dedication to the principles of eugenics and exogamy. If few
peers found themselves in the ludicrous position of the earl of March,
a great many did have to seek (and to purchase) the good offices of the
Church to effect the union they desired (Doc. 60 (a–d)). The documents
give an idea of the variety of offensive conditions which could be recti-
fied: except for the aggravated and blatantly scandalous case of Gaunt
and Katherine Swynford, the others were all very natural in a society
where an elite was closely intermarried, and men and women who survived were apt to have more than one spouse per lifetime.

For a different but related set of reasons, the king also was interested
in who, at the highest social levels, married whom. Lands, loyalties and
political networks rather than sin were his business, but through the
law, local inquisitions, and the useful incidents of feudalism he watched
the marriages of minors, royal wards, relatives of those found guilty of
treason, heiresses, and any others where he could find a toe-hold. As

with ecclesiastical interference, freedom was often available for a price. The price might take the form of money *and* allegiance, since the loss of the latter could be quite serious. We have seen how Ralph Monthermer's titles came and went with his marriages. We can also see that his constitutional inability to make a politic union got him into trouble with his second marriage, as his first to Joan of Acre had done. Eventually, like so many others of high rank who fell into royal disfavour, he begged and bought his way out (Docs. 60 (e–g), 62).

Most medieval marriages were binding until the death of one of the partners. There was no divorce in the modern sense of a civil ceremony, sufficing to terminate a civil contract. As the troubles of Henry VIII have made so familiar, the only way out of a union short of death was to discover an impediment which should have rendered the marriage invalid *ab initio*. But since there were so many possible grounds for an impediment one suspects that something could almost always be found. In fact, we may wonder if the Church purposely neglected to conduct a thorough genealogical investigation in advance so that there would be reasons, lurking around, if needed. Actually there were relatively few marital breakdowns among the aristocrats: men had enough scope for alternate activities and sex lives, women conducted their lives within the traditional framework of marriage whatever they did in private, and too much land and political fortune was involved to dissolve in a casual fashion what were often business mergers (Doc. 63). The Arundel divorce was not unique, and it does show that a strong desire for a second start had to be accommodated by the system lest people be pushed too far. Maud Clifford was able to have her marriage with John Neville, Lord Latimer, ended because of his impotence, or so she charged.

The large number of peers who succeeded to a title previously held by a brother, uncle or more distant male relative indicates how many marriages were either sterile or unable to produce children who outlived their father. We can assume in these latter cases that demographic and medical misfortune, rather than parental poverty, was the cause, just as in the former birth control was hardly a factor. If children were not always seen as precious little bundles of joy, they were at least useful pawns in higher games and their presence was desired. Against the noble couples who raised no children to legal age there were those blessed with a surplus, and many a family had five or eight or ten or even more, perhaps born by a succession of wives, to place into worthy stations in life. A great noble like Gaunt or the earl of Westmoreland with twenty-three children) or Warwick the Kingmaker could place his sons and daughters into other exalted lines, including the royal family in its more distant or even its more immediate branches. But lesser peers regularly turned some children, particularly younger sons, towards gentry marriages, where high blood could attract county acres, and such long-lived and prolific families as the Scropes were well bound into the York-shire squirearchy through the patterns of marriage. We remarked above that few families could match the Zouches' record of smooth succession, and there was no limit to the number of children needed to ensure con-tinuity. The failure of cadet lines was a regular feature of the period,[6] and the medical and gynaecological problems which plagued the royal family were reflected by many other would-be dynasties as well.

Recent studies of childhood as a social phenomenon have recalled the idea, familiar from a glance at Renaissance art, that children were generally seen as miniature adults. Though full legal age began at twenty-one, in a particular situation a boy might be called upon to assume manhood's full responsibilities some years earlier: both Edward III and the Black Prince were in arms in their mid-teens, and the earl of Rutland was killed at Wakefield in 1460 when he was yet two or three years from his majority. But children also played and learned their lessons: that same earl had complained to his father about harsh chas-tisement when he made mistakes over his books. Suffolk's parting advice to his son was full of Polonius's saws, but concern for the boy's future is probably sincerely reflected in 'drawe to you and to your company good vertuowse men, and such as ben of good conversacion, and of trouthe'.[7]

It is difficult to speak in general terms about the warmth found within the (nuclear) family circle. In some cases the wills show that children got what the law enjoined and little else. In others strong feelings of responsibility and unity, if not actually of affection, are revealed. Kin-ship terminology is pretty standardised, but many a peer spoke in strong terms of endearment when referring to relatives in his will. Gaunt referred to Dorset as 'my dear son' and to the future bishop of Winchester as 'the Reverend Father in God and my dear son'.[8] The earl of March's 'our most honoured lady and mother' may have been merely conventional wording, but it may also reflect the conventional love between mother and son.[9] Relatives in abundance were remem-bered in many of the wills. The earl of Salisbury left 500 marks for the upbringing and marriage of an illegitimate son (*filio nostro bastardo*): this was more than enough in land to put him into the comfortable if not the major gentry.[10] Children were left provided for, though occasionally there is a provision stating that they would lose the bequest if they dis-obeyed the executors. Trust might not be limitless, but it sometimes existed.

One last general point about families: they were becoming self-conscious about their past. The *Percy Cartulary* is just a notebook concerning their lands, but, like the valors and books of estate customs and of household expenses, it is a product of an age that was becoming interested in comparing past performances with preent value.[11] The more imaginative history of the Beauchamps of Warwick tied the new antiquarian and scholarly interest in the English past to contemporary status: such a literary product belonged to a century which also saw quarrels over precedent and dignity within the House of Lords (Doc. 64). And the very elaborate and protracted quarrels between the noble house of Scrope and the Grosvenor family over the right to bear certain arms and quarterings show both the strength of family pride and the unceasing level of martial activity that the mighty engaged in as a matter of course (Doc. 65). If Chaucer's knight and Henry Bolingbroke are the famous military travellers of the fourteenth century, we can see that innumerable others must have had records of equal prowess and activity. Families had private traditions which shaped the destinies of their sons just as the pressures of public business did. Wives (and mothers) helped in this, for as well as bringing family estates when they were heiresses, they brought family possessions which reinforced the idea that each new generation was an amalgamation of lines in the previous one. The countess of Arundel, a Berkeley by birth, left plate with the Berkeley and Poynings arms to her daughter, and with the Hungerford arms to her brother. Lady Morley's plate, with her paternal Bardolf crests, went to her son Thomas. There were thousands of such tangible reminders of intermarriage and dynastic merger.

Religion permeated most aspects of private life. This was true for most people in the Middle Ages, but the exact fashion in which private and family involvement was worked out is better documented for the aristocracy, so that we can follow more aspects of the interactions between Church and believers. Furthermore, the upper classes had more money to indulge in their whims towards benefaction and patronage, charity or endowment. The Church on its part was more inclined to listen to their requests, treat them seriously, and overlook or accept their human shortcomings than it was when dealing with their social inferiors. Religion was a part of daily life. Some forms of spiritual behaviour were highly personal; others followed well-worn and traditional avenues, sometimes with the family as the unit of participation. Mostly the peers were conventional: personalities and passions are usually well masked behind ritualised forms of expression and action. Though religion turned individual attention towards the transcendental, few had anything of novelty to contribute, nor was such novelty encouraged by the institutional Church. Most people found their spiritual actions to be easily integrated into a world of personal and familial aggrandisement, competition and conspicuous consumption.

From the young child's catechism to the ceremonies at the deathbed of the aged peer the conscious mind turned to spiritual matters with predictable frequency. The distinctions between clerical and lay were probably not too strong in families that regularly had members in the

Church, in high positions more often than not, and which found dispensation, licences and pardons easy to purchase. The noble household was not just the centre of a network of political administrators and caretakers. It was a self-contained domestic unit, including a full complement of chaplains, ecclesiastical vestments, ornaments and plate, prayer books and Bibles, almoners, confessors, etc. (Doc. 67 (b)). If even Henry II heard his mass regularly, albeit on horseback lest it delay his hunting, it is reasonable to suppose that lesser men were at least as scrupulous about keeping up the forms of religion. The religious side of baronial life was as ubiquitous if not as essential as the political, and we should not allow a fascination with high politics or cynicism about the depths of true piety to obscure this. Few households were as semi-monastic as that of the dowager Cecilly, in her old age, but they were probably closer to her extreme than to salons of the age of the enlightenment (Doc. 66).

Alms, dispensed by an almoner from the food and revenues of the household, were a popular form of charity. Like most other medieval forms of charity or philanthropy, the purpose was the soul of the donor rather than the happiness of the recipient. The royal court could be fairly lavish with such hand-outs, and baronial practice was probably similar though on a smaller scale. The earl of Derby gave out money regularly, if never more than a few shillings at a time.[12] Sometimes local people or institutions were helped through the mechanism of disbursements from local manorial revenues, instead of from the centralised funds. Wills, of course, often stipulated that large sums were to be handed out: to people along the course of the funeral procession; to people paid to remember the anniversary of the donor's death; to poor and infirm tenants on the manors; to deserving poor singled out by priests and college masters, etc. Society was hardly made more egalitarian through these practices, but a few poor folk lived a little better, and the sharpest edge of class conflict might be slightly dulled.

Casual alms and charity were only one alternative for those with strong inclinations towards spiritual purposes. Some peers became members of spiritual gilds or fraternities, like that in York which attracted dozens of laymen to communal activity.[13] The commitment behind such steps was not necessarily a great one, but it was some sort of half-way step between the passive and the partially active. Membership of knightly or chivalric orders, like the Order of the Garter – which always had a strongly aristocratic membership – carried quasi-religious connotations: purity, dedication and renewal were its moral ends. In a larger sense knighthood had an element of dedicated service, though by this period it was more a sign of social status than of elite devotion. All these activities were small steps from the ranks of the holy towards those of the sacred. Many nobles, with money and sometimes time to spare, went on pilgrimages: Spain for a short foreign journey; Rome for a more extensive holy voyage; and Jerusalem for those like the earl of Warwick who could really pick and choose their voluntary behaviour (Doc. 67 (d–f)).

Except for younger children who were steered into the Church as a career, or dumped into a nunnery to get them out of the running as heiresses, the peers mostly knew regular life from a distance. But the idea of the spiritual retreat, particularly when not accompanied by over-rigorous asceticism, was attractive, and many a nobleman and/or his wife petitioned to spend a few days each year within the walls of some congenial house (Doc. 67 (a)). A few people went further and sought, in old age, actually to leave the world and enter the cloister. Lord de Lisle was one of a small handful of men who forsook the world of pomp and splendour in order the assume 'the habit of religion' (Doc. 68). Among widows, the cloister, or at least a vow of chastity, was both a refuge from the pressures for remarriage and a kind of retirement tranquillity. Most of those who took such vows had a smoother course than the countess of Lincoln (Doc. 69), and the pressures of public life were avoided by a withdrawal that Christian society honoured and understood.

The preamble to the last will and testament was a standard place or opportunity for the expression of religious concern. Whether the imminence of death made people less reticent about their deeper convictions or more eager to get some platitudes down on paper (or parchment) is a matter of interpretation, but few other sources show us people speaking with such an appearance of sincerity. There was nothing unusual in Lord Roos's invocation of the 'Holy and undivided Trinity, the Father, Son and Holy Spirit and most blessed and most glorious Virgin Mary, the mother of our Lord Jesus Christ and of all the saints of heaven'.[14] After this introduction the least he could do was to commend his soul to 'God omnipotent and the Blessed Virgin Mary, and St Thomas the Martyr and all Saints', before simply asking for burial at Christ Church, Canterbury. This was the common style, and Duke Henry of Lancaster ended his *Book of Holy Medicine* by asking 'May God pardon his misdeeds'.[15] Even the most pious – or perhaps we should say especially the most pious – approached their worldly end with trepidation, if not with doubt. An astounding flood of prayers might be unleashed and subsidised. We have seen that the funeral procession could become a sort of political parade, the alms that accompanied it a major form of public charity. The precise directions concerning the tomb, the services, the funeral cortège, etc., are another of those combinations of the religious, the political and the grandiose which mark so many aspects of aristocratic life.

The most splendid of all forms of activity which combined ecclesiastical benefaction and individual advertisement was the *de novo* foundation. Though the great age of monastic foundation was over by 1300 the aristocrats were prominent among the founders of monasteries, colleges, hospitals, and the innumerable chantries that continued to spring up. The size and value of the foundations varied, as did the depth of the commitment, whether measured by the amount given or by the duration of individual or family concern with the project. As befits the greatest lay subjects of the realm, the nobles as a group made some contribution to almost every sort of foundation. But in this regard they were acting in accord with all other Englishmen: a heavy leaning towards the more private and smaller kinds of foundations, some affection for the mendicants (largely as reflected in the choice of burial sites), and not too much interest in the old regular orders.

There were some new regular establishments which stemmed directly from aristocratic largess. The history of such houses is usually a tale of generosity on the part of one family over the course of several generations, a theme well illustrated by the Montagues and the house of Augustianian (or Austin) canons at Bisham (or Brustlesham) in Berkshire (Doc. 71). In 1336 William Montague was permitted to alienate land on the grounds of a former preceptory of the Temple. Within a year or two he sought and gained the right to alienate land, rent and advowsons 'whether held in chief or otherwise, to the value of £300'.[16] Through the century gifts continued to come from the Montagues, in life and in death, and in the fifteenth century, when the Nevilles succeeded to the Montague lands and positions, they picked up the continuity of obligation: various members of the Neville clan were buried there, endowed prayers there, gave personal possessions, vestments, etc. With little help from anyone else – there was a sort of tradition of keeping hands off another family's pet foundation (Doc. 67 (g)) – the house was built up so that its declared worth in the 1535 Valor was £185 per annum.

This record of sustained endowment is far beyond the average in terms of the number of generations and the amounts, but on a lesser scale it was matched by many noble families. Few peers, and fewer of their families, failed to make some kind of gift, bequest or endowment to some branch of the Church. The shortest aristocratic wills may only have something for the burial church, as did the will of Edward Courtenay, earl of Devon, to be buried in 1419 in Forde Abbey, a 'foundation of our ancestors'.[17] Some of the briefer ones remembered a local house or two, and little more: Lord Roos, with strong Yorkshire ties, left money for Beverley and Rievaulx but nowhere else (except the burial church at Canterbury). At the other end of the spectrum a huge number of establishments were remembered and enriched, as the pressures of local status, old favours, and the remorseless need for prayers all loosened the purse strings. The countess of Suffolk made bequests to religious establishments at Campsey, as well as to Redlingfield priory, the four orders of friars in Suffolk and Norfolk, the priory at Snape, the priory at Mendham, the nunnery at Bruisyard, the monastery at Thetford, the house at Flixton, the famous Norwich recluse Juliana Lampett and others.[18] Though each person felt free to pursue his individual preferences, there were both traditions and obligations which helped to guide the seemingly free hand of benefaction.

After the Statute of Mortmain in 1279 the king licensed all alienation in mortmain, and the *Calendars of the Patent Rolls* record hundreds of benefactions made by the nobles through this device. To alienate land to the Church was relatively inexpensive, in terms of what the licence might cost, and it was a vehicle equally well suited for the transfer of a small plot or tenement or the profits of several large and valuable manors. This kind of endowment was more popular in the fourteenth century than in the fifteenth, but it was pursued into Tudor times. Alienation in mortmain was one of the ways in which the major foundations were enriched: the Montagues received a number of licences regarding Montagues. Alienation could also be a completely isolated affair, almost a random activity, and when Gilbert Talbot granted three messuages of land, sixty-four acres of various kinds of land, and a rental of 23s 10d [19] he was definitely not beginning a family tradition. Through alienations a steady if not huge stream of property continued to pass from aristocratic to ecclesiastical hands, and we can only suppose that the prayers and good-will which they gained in exchange repaid the peers for what to us might seem like a one-way transaction.

The nobles did not just give tangible goods to the Church. A great many of them placed sons and daughters, nephews and nieces, etc., in the clerical or cloistered ranks. About one-sixth of the bishops came from noble families, including a fair number of the archbishops, and numerous other high positions in the Church and in the two universities were held by men of aristocratic origin. In a negative sense these figures indicate how much room there was for others, by the upward path of 'social mobility', but if aristocratic control was less than a stranglehold, there was little chance of a capable and well-supported noble youth failing to rise high. The career of George Neville is a little extreme, with all the dispensations in his favour and the backing of the Warwick faction (Docs. 67 (c), 72), but not many peers' sons or brothers had to cool their heels awaiting advancement. Some of the most active archbishops, like Arundel and Courtenay, were from great families. Archbishop Bourchier used his Yorkish connections and his trimmer's personality to keep his hand on Canterbury from his appointment in 1457 until his death in 1486. The royal family steered none of its sons or daughters into the Church in this period, for they were badly needed for diplomatic purposes and they were generally in short supply. But had Prince Arthur lived, Henry VIII might have been archbishop of York, which fact should appeal to our sense of irony. Because aristocratic men entered the Church early, their careers tended to be a bit longer; a longer career meant both more years of milking personal riches from the Church and more years of shaping her policies and politics.

The story of aristocratic children in the Church is also one of family policies. Daughters were still steered to or placed within the cloister for the traditional reasons: personal preference, a parental wish to 'dedicate' a child to God, the too-complex situation on the marriage or dowry market, the desire to get an heiress out of the way. Nuns who ultimately became heiresses were apt to be passed over in the division of estates; some of the Beauchamp women got cash and personal remembrances when the law really should have given them dozens of manors, thousands of acres and tenants. Some houses, like that of the Minoresses in London, were very popular in high circles, and daughters, endowments and burial plots were all directed towards it. An occasional noblewoman became the abbess of her house, but one suspects that most of the women pushed into the cloister were rather lacklustre, despite their economic and family advantages. We can see from the numerous bequests of personal possessions, made to daughters within regular houses, that such women were allowed to have personal property and that they often took heavy advantage of this privilege.

It may flatter the nobles unduly to end this essay with some comments about their intellectual life. England was relatively untouched by the mainstream of the Italian Renaissance and all that it connoted, and aristocratic intellectual activity was very much that of medieval patronage, derivative literary exercises, and benefaction and endowment with an eye on education. In assessing the aristocratic contribution there is a question of emphasis: should we give the peers credit for the level of activity and culture they did attain, or should we condemn them for not reaching a general level which compares with their compatriots of Italy or perhaps Burgundy? At least it is no longer fashionable simply to dismiss them as a collection of muscle-bound bullies, gulled by their reeves if not by their wives. The testimony of their administrative and diplomatic ability and their supervision of the intricacies of estate management should indicate that they could use their heads. The evidence on education, book collecting, patronage and educational supervision, and occasional authorship shows that in some instances they could use those same heads for gentler arts than siegecraft.

By the fifteenth century, if not by the fourteenth, the majority of noblemen (and their wives and their children) were probably literate.[20] This cannot be proven, of course, but it follows from the separate bits of evidence concerning books (Doc. 74), tutors, prayer services and the indications of supervision of accounts and household expense lists. The 'hierarchic bilingualism' of the day was changing so that English was taking first place and French second,[21] and the *Lay Folks' Mass Book* and other such vernacular prayer guides were quite popular. About one aristocratic will in six or seven contains a mention of books among the bequests. They were mostly religious in nature, prayer books and hymnals and primers, plus a sprinkling of Bibles, saints' lives, works of meditation and contemplation, and a little bit of theology. Histories, romances (where French probably held its own against English unusually well), instructional literature and a few travel books rounded out the variety, and most of the books listed in the wills went to lay recipients rather than to ecclesiastical ones. Family feeling ran through this activity, as when Lord de la Warre left his French books to his wife, and then to his eldest son John, and then on from heir to heir, with the stipulation that they were not to be alienated or sold.[22] Memory of the maternal line was often preserved through the transmission of books with arms on the covers, and pride in status shows in a bequest like that of 'a faire prymar which I had by the yifture of Queen Elizabeth'.[23]

These were books for personal use or private pleasure. The peers sometimes put their weight into the world of formal education. Two Cambridge colleges were founded by fourteenth-century aristocratic dowagers, Pembroke by the widow of Aymar de Valence and Clare by Elizabeth de Burgh, heiress of the great Clare earls of Gloucester of the thirteenth century. Otherwise, higher education was more entrusted, both for its support and its manpower, to the gentry. But an aristocratic foundation such as the de la Pole alms house at Ewelme was expected to contribute something, at least at an honest if pedestrian level, to the educational structure. One of the priests was to be 'a wele disposed man, apte and able to techyng of grammer, to whose office it shall longe and perteyne diligently to teche and informe childer in the faculte of grammer'.[24] Such institutions helped with the local situation, and simple grammar, music and liturgy were about as high as they could aim. Within the noble households there were tutors or clerks with specific educational tasks, no doubt, but there is little reason to think that any of the households became beacons of any larger renown.

A few of the peers were bibliophiles and patrons on a larger scale. The earls and then dukes of Lancaster had both an interest in literature and a special concern that their children be well educated in books as well as arms. The Bohuns were serious collectors of manuscripts for several generations, and their family arms on book covers were fairly common. Humphrey of Gloucester, Henry V's youngest son, enjoyed a fame that has lasted because of his benefactions to Oxford (Doc. 73), while the important library of his own brother, Duke John of Bedford, was scattered. Literary patronage in fifteenth-century England is a serious topic on its own, but a good share of the tale must be devoted to

Humphrey, John Tiptoft, earl of Worcester, and Antony Woodville, Earl Rivers.[25] The books which these men collected, inspired, and even helped to write indicate that some of the Tudor Renaissance sprang from ground that they at least softened. The duke of Suffolk was no earl of Surrey when it came to creative verse, but his efforts, like those of the duke of York concerning the hunt,[26] remind us that men we are quick to write off as political failures had versatile, curious minds (Docs. 75, 76). They were the realm's leaders, and they had more to offer than undisciplined retainers.

DOCUMENTS

1. Summons to Parliament (1313)

FROM: *RDP*, III, 221–3 (6 Edward II)

The King, to the venerable father in Christ, Richard, by the same grace, archbishop of Canterbury, primate of all England, greetings.

Because on the third Sunday of Lent next to come, We decree to hold a parliament at Westminster. God willing, we will talk with you and other prelates and peers of our realm, and treat of divers affairs and the state of our realm. We order you, in the faith and love you bear us, and we firmly command you to be present in person on the day and place aforesaid, with us and our prelates and peers as aforesaid, in order to deal with the business which will be discussed, and to supply us with your advice . . .

And in no wise should you neglect to do this.

Witnessed, by the King, at Windsor on the 8th day of January.

[Similar writs went to 19 other bishops, 45 abbots, 3 priors, and the Master of the Order of Sempringham]

The king, to his beloved and faithful Thomas of Brotherton, earl of Norfolk, greetings.

Because on the 3rd Sunday of Lent, etc., to which we order you, because of the faith and homage which you bear to us, as we firmly order all others to whom this pertains, that you will be with us in person on the day and place aforesaid, with us and our prelates and peers aforesaid, for the aforesaid discussion of our business.

And in no wise should this be neglected.

Witnessed as above, etc.

In the same manner, written to those below:

Thomas, earl of Lancaster
Gilbert of Clare, earl of Gloucester and Hertford
Aymar de Valence, earl of Pembroke
Edmund, earl of Arundel
John of Warenne, earl of Surrey
John of Brittany, earl of Richmond
Robert de Veer, earl of Oxford
Guy de Beauchamp, earl of Warwick
Humphrey de Bohun, earl of Hereford and Essex
Robert de Clifford   John de la Warre

Henry de Percy
Hugh le Despenser
Henry de Lancaster
Roger Mortimer of Chirk
John Hastings
Hugh de Veer
John St John
William Martin
Thomas Bardolf
Thomas Berkeley
John Somery
Ralph de Gorges
Edmund Deincourt
John Sudley
Henry Beaumont
John Botetourt
John Moubray
John Segrave
Robert of Monte Alto
Bartholomew Badlesmere
Payn Tibbetoft
Robert FitzPayn
Hugh Courtenay
John Grey
Richard Grey
Thomas Furnival
John Gifford of Brimpsfield
John Clavering
William Roos of Hamelak
Marmaduke Thweng
Robert Felton
Ralph Neville
Ralph Monte Hermerii
Nicholas Meinill
Miles Stapleton
Aucher FitzHenry
Alan Zouche
Adam Everingham
Thomas Multon of Egremont
Edward Burnel
Robert Fitz-Walter
Thomas FitzBernard
John de la Mare

William Paignel
Peter Corbet
John Beauchamp of Somerset
Ralph Basset of Drayton
Philip Kyme
William de Grandisson
William Botiller of Wemme
John D'Engayne
John Thorpe
William Marshal
Fulk Le Strange
John Northwood
William Latimer
William Vavassour
Hugh Neville
Nicholas Audley
Maurice Berkeley
Henry Tyeys
Roger Bavent
William de Echingham
Maurice Brun
Fulc FitzWaurin
John Lovel of Titchmarsh
William Brewes
John de Rivers
John de Mohun
Peter Mauley
Walter Fauconberge
John St John of Lageham
William Ferrers
William Zouche
Henry Husee
Robert Scales
Roger Mortimer of Wigmore
John of St Amand
John Le Straunge
Simon Montague
Edmund Hastings
Nicholas Segrave
Theobald Verdun
Robert Bayard
William Vescy
Henry de Cobham
Ingelram de Guisnes

2. Creation of an Earl (1337)

FROM: *RDP*, V, 32

The king, to the archbishops, etc., Greetings.

Know that, because much of the grace of the state lies in the wisdom and eminence of those mentioned hereinafter, and in particular the throne of the realm is elevated and the rule of the kingdom is strengthened when there are many men of noble status and lofty excellence.

Therefore, we, at the request of the prelates and peers and the commons of our realm in the present parliament assembled at Westminster, in our wish to enhance the order of the kingdom and to bestow new honours as much as to restore old ones, and to secure the safety of the state and to add to the number of nobles by whose counsels we are directed, and for support in times of adversity;

Have presented our most dear first born Edward, by our prerogative and for his special merits, to the Duchy of Cornwall, which Duchy we have given because it is vacant due to the deaths of its former holders, and we have invested him and girded him with the sword, as is customary.

Furthermore, considering the others whom we might promote to an earldom, we choose for his probity, vigour and wisdom as well as for the renown of his ancester our beloved and faithful William de Monte Acuto. We do this because of the promptitude with which he has submitted himself to danger on our behalf, and that this honour will add to his wealth as to the love he bears us, and in grateful commemoration of the service and use which he has devotedly provided for us.

We gird him with a sword and invest him with the county of Salisbury, to him and his heirs of his name, and we freely concede the authority of the said county to the same earl and his heirs, and in support of this grant the decision of parliament is pleasing to us and in accord with our own council.

And to support the burden we give and concede and confirm in this charter to the same earl and his heirs £20, returned from the profits of the county of Wiltshire each year at the Feasts of Easter and St Michael in equal portions, to be received from the hand of the sheriff who will be there, in perpetuity.

Wherefore we will and specially affirm by us and our heirs that the aforesaid earl and his heirs shall receive the aforesaid £20 returned from the profits of the said county, each year at the aforesaid feasts, in equal portions, receiving from the hands of the sheriff of that county who will be in that time, in perpetuity, as is stated above.

In witness of this: our venerable father, John, Archbishop of Canterbury, primate of all England, our chancellor . . .

Given by our hand at Westminster, 16 day March.

By the king himself and all the commons in parliament.

3. Ennoblement by Letters Patent (1387)

FROM: *RDP*, V, 81

The King, to all to whom, etc. Greetings.

Be it known that for the good and willing service rendered to us by our beloved and faithful knight, John Beauchamp of Holt, steward of our household, and for service given in the place and time of our crown-wearing, and which he will offer to us in our future councils and parliaments, and for the noble and faithful race from which he is descended, and because of the wisdom and good counsel of the said John, we make him a peer and baron of our realm of England, and we will that the same John and male heirs begotten of his body shall hold the status and title of lord of Beauchamp and baron of Kidderminster.

In which thing, etc. Witnessed by the King at Woodstock, the 10th day of October.

By writ of privy seal.

4. Creation of a Viscount (1440)

FROM: *RDP*, V, 235

The king to the archbishops, bishops, abbots, priors, dukes, earls, barons, justices, sheriffs, reeves, bailiffs and his other faithful to whom this comes, etc. Greetings.

Know that we observe from our majesty that those who exhibit continuous faithful service to us, especially in those matters which touch on our prerogative we proceed to elevate to special honours with great liberality. And this is especially the case with those whose progenitors were of noble memory and whose virtues were demonstrated by clear evidence in the past, as well as with their intrinsic merit. We now act in order that virtue be strengthened and many people be led to upright acts.

Therefore, considering the noble progenitors of our most dear cousin John, lord of Beaumont, and the service which his parents faithfully rendered to our ancestors, and the way in which he has laudably and faithfully devoted himself to our service in these times, and that he should continue to act thus in the future, we act so that our lofty prerogative shines to honour him.

By our grace in our present parliament the aforesaid John, lord of Beaumont, our kinsman, and his male heirs begotten of his body, shall be assigned the name of Viscount Beaumont, and he shall be invested with the rank of Viscount Beaumont, and he shall have a place in our parliament and councils and other gatherings over all barons of the realm. And we assign this in as much as it will especially adorn him when he stands in the aforesaid status of viscount, according to our accustomed liberality.

We give and concede by us and our heirs, as is in our power, to the aforesaid John and his heirs with his name, rank, and position: 20 marks, to be received annually by him and his heirs male begotten of his body, from the profits of the farm of the county of Lincoln, paid by the hand of the sheriff of that county, whoever he shall be, by equal portions at the terms of Easter and St Michael. He is to have and to hold, for him and his heirs in perpetuity, the aforesaid name, insignia, position and 20 marks, notwithstanding other gifts or concessions made to the same John by us in a previous time, according to the form of this edict, made and enrolled in this present form and all others notwithstanding.

In which thing, etc.

Witnessed by the king at Reading, 12th day of February.

By writ of privy seal.

5. Duchess in Her Own Right (1398)

FROM: *Rot. Parl.*, III, 355   (21 Richard II)

Item: our lord the king wishes to honour, enhance, and increase the name and estate of his honourable cousin, Margaret Marshall, Countess of Norfolk.

On this same day, in full parliament, in the absence of the countess, the countess is made and created a duchess, and she is given the style, title, honour and name of Duchess of Norfolk, to have for the term of her life.

The charter of creation will be sent on this aforesaid matter.

6. The Perquisites of Elevation (24 April 1337)

(*a*) FROM: Rymer, II, iii, 166

The King, to the collectors or keepers of the stampage of tin in the county of Cornwall, greetings:

Wishing to honour our beloved and faithful William de Monte Acuto, we have recently in person given him the name and honour of the earl of Salisbury and we award him in the county of Salisbury and we gird him with the sword, as was shown.

And among other things in which county, by which this honour shall be sustained and in every way supported, we concede from us and our heirs, in the aforesaid county, 1,000 marks. Each year, at the feasts of Easter and of St Michael, in equal portions, from the profits of the tin aforesaid, by your hands and those of other collectors and keepers of the same stampage, now and in the future, it will be paid.

He shall have and hold in the same county, and his legitimate male heirs begotten of his body, 800 marks thus, until the Castle and Manor of Trowbridge and certain other manors which our beloved and faithful John of Warenne, earl of Surrey, and Joan his wife hold for the term of their lives; the reversion of which is to go to the said earl of Salisbury after the decease of the said earl of Warenne and Joan, under the form we have conceded, and it shall come to the hands of the aforesaid earl of Salisbury, or his heirs male.

And the remaining 200 marks, which is also for the said earl of Salisbury or to his said heirs, it shall be of 200 marks of land and annual rent, in a fitting place within our realm, as will be provided by us or by our heirs, in perpetuity, in the form as is contained in full in our letters patent.

Therefore we order to you that the aforesaid earl of Salisbury receive 500 marks at the Easter term next, from the profits of the aforesaid stampage, to be paid according to the tenor of our aforesaid letters.

The aforesaid earl of Salisbury shall receive his letters patent testifying to the aforesaid 500 marks, and we shall allow the payment in your account in our Exchequer.

Witnessed by the king at Windsor, 24 day of April.

(*b*) FROM: *CCR*, 1337-9, 18.

26 March, 1337. To the treasurer and barons of the exchequer. Order to cause the sheriff of Wiltshire to have due allowance, from time to time, in his account for what he shall be found to have paid henceforth to William de Monte Acuto, earl of Salisbury, by virtue of the king's order as the king granted it to the earl by the name of earl of Salisbury, £20 of revenue of the issues of Wiltshire to be received yearly by the hands of the sheriff.

7. Impeachment of Suffolk (1450)

FROM: *RDP*, V, 277-8)

To the king, our sovereign lord.

The commons pray that whereas in your last parliament held at Westminster the commonalty of this your realm in the same parliament assembled, accused and impeached William de la Pole, then duke of Suffolk, as well of divers great, heinous, and detestable treasons as of many other falsities, deceits and other untrue misprisions done and committed by him. Unto which accusations and impeachments he, being put to answer thereto, gave no answer sufficient after the laws of this your land as in the acts and process had upon the said accusation and impeachment, the tenor whereof is annexed more plainly. By cause whereof judgement of attainder of the said treasons ought to have been given against him and he convicted of the said misprisions after the course of your said laws. And forasmuch as such judgement against him then was not had, as justice after his merits required: please it your highness to grant, ordain and establish by the advice and assent of the lords spiritual and temporal in this present parliament assembled that by authority of this same parliament the said William de la Pole be adjudged, deemed, declared, published and reputed as traitor to you against your royal dignity and your crowns of your realms of England and of France; that he is culpable and defective of all the said treasons, falsities, untrue coloured deceits and misprisions, and that his blood be corrupt and his issue and other persons be unable and fore-judged to be heirs to him of blood to inherit any lands, tenements, rents, services or any other manner inheritances or possessions of fee simple as heirs to him, and that no issue of him lineally coming shall have, enjoy, obtain or inherit the name or estate of duke, marquis or earl, nor any place or pre-eminence to any such estate. And that all the manors, lands, tenements, and all other inheritances and possessions . . . of the same William or of his heirs . . . be forfeit unto you for ever . . .

Your great wisdom, right wiseness, and high discretion considering that the said William de la Pole hath not only done and committed the said treasons and mischievous deeds, but was the cause and labourer of the arrest, imprisoning and final destruction of the most noble, valiant true prince, your right obeisant uncle the duke of Gloucester, whom God pardon, and of the abridging of the days of other princes of your blood, and estranged from your good grace, favour and conceit full great lords who are right nigh to you. And he was moreover the most dangerous councillor and unprofitable person to your high estate and your said realms that can be remembered of in days past.

Le Roi s'advisera.

8. A Dispute over Position (1445)

FROM: *RDP*, V, 269

Memorandum, that in the parliament held at Westminster, the 23rd year of the reign of our sovereign lord king Harry VI, after the conquest, there was a controversy moved between William, earl of Arundel, on the one party and Thomas, earl of Devonshire, on the other party, in the presence of our said Sovereign, for the seats, places and pre-eminence of the same earls in the king's high presence as well as in his high court of parliament as in his councils and elsewhere, as by divers writings made, shown and declared between the said parties in the same parliament. Which matters and declarations with all their incidents the king of his highness, by the advice of his lords spiritual and temporal then being in the same parliament, committed to certain lords of the same parliament for them to examine and decide . . .

Which judges, hearing and seeing these claims and all the writings presented to the king's highness by the said earls thereof with an act exemplified, made in the parliament held at Westminster the 11th year of the reign of our said sovereign lord. For John, late earl of Arundel, the judges say and declare after their conceits that it is a matter of parliament belonging to the king's highness and to his lords spiritual and temporal in parliament, by them to be decided and determined. Howbeit that the said act [of parliament] made mention but only that the said John, late earl of Arundel, brother of the said William, whose heir he is, should have his set place and permanence in the king's presence as well in his parliament and councils as elsewhere as earl of Arundel, as in the same act more openly appears. In which act is not expressed in writing [that] the heirs of the same late earl, notwithstanding that he was seised and inherited of the castle, honour, and lordship of Arundel whereto the said name, estate and dignity of earl of Arundel is, and from time that has no mind has been, united and annexed, and by that reason he bore and had that name; and not by way of creation, as the same judges understand by the same act. And that it belongs to be discussed and determined by the king and his lords, and in no other wise. Whereupon the king our sovereign lord, by the advice and assent of the lords spiritual and temporal being in the same present parliament and considering the title and right of the said earl of Arundel in these claims, as opened, shown and declared by the great consideration of time as well in writing as otherwise between the said earls in diverse parliaments, declared, determined and decreed that William, now earl of Arundel, is to have, keep and enjoy his seat, place and permanence in the high court of parliament and in the king's councils and elsewhere in the king's high presence, as earl of Arundel by reason of the castle, lordship, and honour of Arundel as worshipfully as ever any of his ancestors, the earls of Arundel, did before this time, and him and his heirs for evermore, above the said earl of Devonshire and his heirs, without letting, challenge or interruption of the said earl of Devonshire or of his heirs or any other person to any title shown, declared or pretended by the said earl of Devonshire in the premises notwithstanding. Saving always to the same earl of Devonshire his lawful suit to the king our sovereign lord, and to his heirs and successors in his high court of parliament for his right touching his [own] seat, place and permanence before mentioned, against the said earl of Arundel and his heirs, as right law and reason require.

9. The Degradation of George Neville from the Name of Duke (1478)

FROM *RDP*, V, 409   (printed from the Rolls of Parliament, 17 Edward IV, m. 16)

Where before this time the king our sovereign lord, for the great zeal and love he bore to John Neville, late named Marquis Montague, and other consideration, moved him to erect and make George Neville, eldest son of the said marquis to be duke of Bedford. And at that time for the great love his said highness bore to the said John Neville, proposed and intended to give to the said George, for sustaining the same dignity, sufficient livelihood. And for the great offences, unkindnesses and misbehaviours that the said John Neville has done and committed to his said highness and is openly known [to have done], he has no cause to depart any livelihood to the said George. And for so much as it is openly known that the same George has not nor by inheritance may have any livelihood to support the said name, estate and dignity, nor any name of estate, and oft-times it is seen that when any lord is called to high estate and has not livelihood conveniently to support the same dignity, it induces great poverty, indigence, and causes oft-times great extortion, embracery and maintenance to be had, to the great trouble of all such countries where such estate shall happen to be inhabited. Wherefore the king, by the advice and assent of his lords spiritual and temporal and the commons of this present parliament assembled, and by the authority of the same, ordained, established and enacted that from henceforth the same creation and making of duke and all the names of dignity given to the said George or to the said John Neville, his father, be from thenceforth void and of no effect. And that the same George and his heirs from henceforth not be duke or marquis, earl or baron, for any erection or creation afore made; but that that name of duke and marquis, earl and baron, in him and his heirs, cease and be void and of no effect, the said erection or creation notwithstanding.

10. A Return to Grace: Lord Lumley's Restoration (1461)

FROM: *Rot. Parl.*, V, 486–7

To the king, our sovereign lord:

Meakly we show and in the most humble wise beseech your highness and good grace, [from] your true and faithful liegeman, Thomas Lumley, knight, cousin and heir to Ralf Lumley, knight, i.e., son to John, son to the said Ralf. [Know that] the said Ralf and others [who] were cruelly murdered and slain by Henry the fourth, late in deed and not in right king of England, for the true faith, duty and allegiance that they bore to the right noble prince, King Richard the second in his days, and after his decease unto Edmund Mortimer, late earl of March, next heir to the said King Richard, and after his decease the very true heir to the crown of England. And that in a parliament held at Westminster, the second year of the usurped reign of the said Henry, after the death of the said Ralf and the others, a declaration, act and judgement of treason was given against the said Ralf and others, in manner and form as in an act thereof made in the said parliament as it appears.

Wherefore [may it] please your Highness, of your most noble and abundant grace, to ordain, establish and enact by the advice of your lords spiritual and temporal and of your commons, in this your present parliament assembled, and by the authority of the same, that the said declaration, judgement and act [of treason] be deemed and taken for nought, annulled, damned, void, and of no force or effect. And for as much as the said Thomas is next cousin and heir to the said Ralf, as aforesaid, the which Thomas has been always faithful and true unto your Highness and has done true service to the uttermost of his power unto your Highness and to the most noble prince your father, whom God aid, and [to] other true lords of your noble blood, and yet at this day continues and abides in the North parts in your service, for the defence and surety of the parties there, to his great costs and charge.

It be ordained, established, and enacted by the advice and assent of your lords spiritual and temporal and of your commons, in this your present parliament assembled, and by authority of the same, that the said Thomas, as cousin and heir to the said Ralf [may come] upon and into all the castles, honours, manors, lands, tenements, knights fees, fee farms, advowsons, services, annuities, franchises, courts, privileges, liberties and all other inheritances and possessions, with their appurtenances, which were seized by the said Henry, late called king, or which came to his hands by reason or colour of the said declaration, act or judgement, whereof the said Ralf, or any person or persons acting on his behalf, were in demesne or held in reversion or possessed at the time of his death, of estate of inheritance lawfully entered, as well upon your possessions as the possession of any other person or persons, and them seize, have, hold, enjoy and inherit, to the same Thomas and his heirs, in as ample and large form and estate as the said Ralf or any other had them on his behalf at the time of his death . . .

Which petition, read, heard, and fully agreed to in the aforesaid parliament, by the advice and assent of the aforesaid, received this response:

Let it be done as desired.

11. The Loss of Fortune: Thomas Holand, Earl of Kent

(a) FROM: *CCR*, 1399–1402, 67

13 March, 1400   To the sheriffs of London. Order upon sight, etc., to cease every excuse and to take down the head of Thomas, late earl of Kent, which is upon London Bridge, and deliver it to Joan, who was the earl's wife or to her deputies or attorneys, to be taken for burial whither she shall please.

(b) FROM: *CPR*, 1408–13, 416

11 July, 1412   Licence, at the supplication of the king's kinswoman Lucy, countess of Kent, for Joan, late the wife of Thomas, late earl of Kent, to take up the bones of the said earl, who was captured for certain treasons against the king at Surcestre and killed there and buried within the abbey of that town, and bury them within the priory of Mountgrace, of which he was founder.

12. Death of the Duke of Suffolk (1450)

(*a*) FROM: *PL*, I, 124–5

To my right worshipful John Paston, at Norwich [from William Lomner].

Right worshipful sir, I recommend me to you, and am right sorry of what I shall say, and have so washed this little bill with sorrowful tears that you can scarcely read it.

As on Monday next after Mayday there came tidings to London that on Thursday before the duke of Suffolk came unto the coasts of Kent full near Dover with his two ships and a little spinner; the which spinner he sent with certain letters to certain of his trusted men unto Calais to know how he should be received. And a ship called Nicholas of the Tower met with him, with other ships waiting on him and by him that was in the spinner the master of the Nicholas had knowledge of the duke's coming. And when he spied the duke's ships he sent forth his boast to know what they were, and the duke himself spoke to him and said he was sent to Calais by the king's commandment, etc.

And they said he must speak with her master. And so he, with two or three of his men went forth with him in her boat to the Nicholas; and when he came the master bade him, 'Welcome, Traitor', as men say, and further the master desired to know if the shipmen would hold with the duke, and they sent word they would not, in no wise; and so he was in the Nicholas till Saturday next following.

Some say he wrote many things to be delivered to the king, but that is not verily known. He had his confessor with him, etc.

And some say he was arraigned in the ship on the matter of the impeachment, and found guilty, etc.

Also he asked the name of the ship, and when he knew it he remembered Stacy who had said that if he might escape the danger of the Tower he should be safe. And then his heart failed him, and he thought he was deceived, and in the sight of all his men he was drawn out of the great ship into the boat, and there was an ax and a block. One of the lewdest men of the ship bade him lay down his head, and he should be fair fared with and die on a sword, and he took a rusty sword and smote off his head with half a dozen strokes, and took away his gown of russet and his doublet of velvet mail, and laid his body on the sand of Dover. And some say his head was set on a pole, and his men were set on land with great care and deference. And the sheriff of Kent watched the body, and sent his under-sheriff to the judges to learn what to do, and also to the king to learn what shall be done.

Further I know not, . . .

(b) FROM: F. W. D. Brie (ed.), *The Brut* (Early English Text Society, O.S. 136, 1908), II, 516

And for to appease the commons, the duke of Suffolk was exiled out of England for five years, and so, during the parliament, he went into Norfolk and from there took shipping to go out of the realm of England, unto France. And this year as he sailed on the sea a ship of war called Nicholas of the Tower met with his ship and found him therein. They took him out and brought him into their ship before the master and captains, and there he was examined and at last judged to the death. And so they put him in a cabin and his chaplain shrove him, and that done they brought him into Dover Roads, and there set him into the boat and there smote off his head and brought the body to land, upon the sands, and set the head thereby. And this was done on the fifth day of May.

Lo! what availed him now, all his deliverance of Normandy, etc. And here you may learn how he was rewarded for the death of the duke of Gloucester. This began sorrow upon sorrow, and death for death.

13. An Earl's Burial (1463)

FROM: *A Collection of Ordinances and Regulations for the Government of the Royal Household* (London, 1790), 131–3

The interment of the Earl of Salisbury at Breshall, in the shire of Buckingham [was made] the fifteenth day of February in the second year of King Edward the Fourth, and of Sir Thomas his son, in two coffins, in one chariot with six horses in trappings, the first in St George's arms, the other covered in black, a banner of St George before him, and two behind. First, before the conveying of the body and bones of the said earl and his son, the earl of Warwick, son and heir of the said earl, rode after the chariot, Lord Montague on the right side afoot, Lord Latimer, his son, on the left hand with many knights and squires afoot on every side to the number of sixteen; the earl's banner and standard came next and immediately after the chariot; and before the earl of

Warwick, meeting with the corpses a mile without the town, came two heralds and two kings of arms, bearing the coats of arms of the said earl at every corner of the chariot . . . At which place [of interment] they received the bodies and the bones so coffered. The bishop of Exeter, chancellor of England, the bishop of Salisbury, the bishop of St Asaph, and two other abbots mitred, in solemn procession accompanied by the Lord Hastings, the king's chamberlain, the Lord Fitz-Hugh, and many other knights and squires in great number, conveyed the corpses, the son before the father, into the choir, where the hearse of the said earl . . . was prepared and ordained in solemn and honourable wise, as appertained to the estate of an earl . . . The earls within the parclose and pall covered with black, where the coffer with the bones of the earl's son Sir Thomas was laid under the coffer of the earl his father, were the lords that followeth: the duke of Clarence, the king's brother, the duke of Suffolk, the earl of Warwick, the earl of Worcester, the Lord Montague, the Lord Hastings, the Lord Fitz-Hugh, with many other knights and nobles without. At the corners of the head of the said hearse, on the right side of the banner, stood Garter king-of-arms in the coat of the said earl's arms; on the left side [of] the standard there stood Clarencieux king-of-arms; and at the corners of the feet of the said hearse were two other heralds, Windsor and Chester, in coats of the said earl's arms, with many other heralds and pursuivants, during the observance of the dirge till the void was done . . .

Item, the earl of Warwick, coming again, for himself offered twenty pence. Item, the residue of ladies and gentlewomen with other knights and esquires and gentlemen offered, the lords and ladies returning into the hearses before said. Item, the lords, returned into the pall and parclose of the hearse, made their presentation and offering of cloths of gold of baudekin unto the corpses then present; that is to say, one a length [i.e., along] the corpses and the other over, like a cross; the youngest baron first, the two barons after, and so the third. Every baron offered one cloth, every earl two, the duke of Suffolk three, the duke of Clarence four; the earls after the barons, the dukes after the earls, at every time till they had offered their cloths; the youngest of estate first beginning, the most noble the richest cloths . . .

14. Veneration for a Political 'Martyr': The Office of St Thomas of Lancaster

---

FROM: Thomas Wright, *The Political Songs of England* (Camden Society [1839] VI, 68–72), printed from British Library, Royal Manuscripts, 12. c. xii, fo. 1^r

Anthem – Rejoice, Thomas, the glory of chieftains, the light of Lancaster, who by thy death imitates Thomas of Canterbury; whose head was broken on account of the peace of the Church, and thine is cut off for the cause of the peace of England; be to us an affectionate guardian in every difficulty.

Prayer – O God, who, for the peace and tranquillity of the inhabitants of England, willed that the blessed Thomas, thy martyr and earl, should fall by the sword of the persecutor, grant propitious, that all who devoutly reverence his memory on earth, may merit to obtain worthy reward along with him in heaven, through Our Lord.

Prosa – The pouring out of prayers to Thomas restores the sick to health; the pious earl comes immediately to the aid of those who are feeble; they are relieved from their infirmities by the suffrage of one who was infirm. So that it is shown by the evidence of the miracles of St Thomas, that the royal vessel is beheaded for the cure of the Kingdom. O how the cure of diseases declares the sainted leader! Therefore with rejoicing let us sing the praises of St Thomas; for he who asks him devoutly, immediately without doubt he will return healed.

Sequence – Let us honour the highest King, for the memory of the sweet martyr, whom we join in praising with utmost reverence. He is called Earl Thomas, of an illustrious race; he is condemned without cause, who was born of a royal bed. Who when he perceived that the whole commons were falling into wreck, did not shrink from dying for the right, in the fatal commerce. O royal flower of knights, preserve ever from evils this thy family, bring them to glory. Amen.

Declare, my tongue, the martyrdom of the glorious earl, and of the precious blood of Thomas, the flower of knights, and of the praise of the noble sprout, the light of earls – Thomas sprung from a royal race by both his parents, whose father was the son of a king, and whose mother Navarre raised to be a queen – The faithful leader when he saw his flock was dispersed, and he called to mind that his king was moved with jealousy towards him, soon according to the law of the flesh he trembled wonderfully – The blessed man is taken on the vigil of St Benet, on the third day he is suddenly made an unconquered champion, he is delivered to dire death, on account of which England mourns – Alas! he is beheaded for the aid of the commons, he is deserted by the company of his knights, while he is treacherously deserted by de Hoyland – At whose tomb are frequently performed miracles; the blind, the lame, the deaf, the dumb, paralytics, by his prayer obtain the help they desire – Praise and honour, virtue and power be to the Trinity, Father, Son, and Holy Ghost, for ever, which preserve us from sin through the intercession of Thomas! Amen.

O now the piety of Christ, and the charity of Thomas, shine openly! Alas! equity now pines away, and impiety flourishes, truth is made vile; yet the goodness of Thomas, and his sanctity, daily increase; at whose tomb health is given to the sick, that the truth may now be clear to all.

O Thomas, strenuous champion of plentiful charity, who didst combat for the law of England's liberty, intercede for our sins with the Father of Glory, that he may give us a place with the blessed in the heavenly court. Amen.

15. Military Summons (1276)

FROM: *RDP*, II, 36–8

Edward, by the grace of God, king of England, lord of Ireland and duke of Aquitaine, to his beloved and faithful brother, Edmund earl of Lancaster, greetings.

Because Llewellyn, son of Griffin, prince of Wales, and his fellow rebels attack us and our lands and our faithful servants in the parts of the [Welsh] Marches, and from day to day perpetrate invasions, murders, and other enormous damages in that place, and the same Llewellyn should owe us obedience but he is contemptuous of us and he acts to our harm and contempt, and also to you and to our other faithful men does grave damage and manifestly works to disinherit us.

We have ordered a muster of our army to be made at Worcester in the Octave of St John the Baptist next, to put down the rebellion of the said Llewellyn and his accomplices. We order you to be present on the said day and place, with horses and arms to do the service you owe us, and to go on the expedition with us against the said Llewellyn and his associates in rebellion.

Witnessed by the king himself at Windsor, the 12th day of December, the 5th year of our reign.

16. Charges against the King's 'Wicked Advisers'

(a) FROM: N. Denholm-Young (ed.), *Vita Edwardi II* (London, 1957), 8–9

When the Christmas respite was over the barons met at London by royal edict [on 8 February 1310], but they were unwilling to come to the normal meeting place of our parliament, and when the king enquired the reason for the unusual delay, they answered the royal messengers thus, that it was their bounden duty to come at the command of their king and natural lord, but as long as their chief enemy, who had set the baronage and the realm in an uproar, was lurking in the king's chamber, their approach was unsafe, and this they protested with one accord, that in this the king's mandate would not be obeyed; adding that if it was absolutely necessary to present themselves before the king, they vowed that they would make their appearance not unarmed as they are wont to do, but armed. His royal majesty should not on this account feel offended or injured, since everyone is bound by natural feeling to choose the safer way.

(b) FROM: Ordinances of 1311, in *SR*, I, 157

13. And whereas the king, as aforesaid, has been badly advised and guided by evil councillors, we ordain that all the evil councillors shall be put out and utterly removed, so that neither they nor other such persons shall be near him or shall be retained in any office under the king; and that other persons who are fit shall be put in their places. And the same shall be done in the case of domestics, officials, and other men in the king's household who are not fit.

14. And whereas many evils have been incurred through such councillors and such ministers, we ordain that the king shall appoint the chancellor, the chief justices of both benches, the treasurer, the chancellor and the chief baron of the exchequer, the steward of the household, the keeper of the wardrobe, the comptroller and a fit clerk to keep the privy seal, a chief keeper of the forests on this side of Trent and one on the other side of Trent, also an escheator on this side of Trent and one on the other side, as well as the king's chief clerk of the common bench, by the counsel and assent of the baronage, and that in parliament. And if by some chance it may happen that there is need to appoint any of the

said ministers before parliament meets, then the king shall make such appointments by the good counsel [of those] whom he shall have near him up to the time of the parliament. And so let it be done henceforth with regard to such ministers, whenever there is need.

(c) FROM Roger Twysden, *Historiae Anglicanae Scriptores, Decem* (London, 1652) col. 2765

Articles of accusation against Edward II.

It has been decided that Prince Edward, the eldest son of the king, shall have the government of the realm and shall be crowned king, for the following reasons:

First, because the king is incompetent to govern in person. Throughout his reign he has been controlled and governed by others who have given him evil counsel, to his own dishonour and to the destruction of Holy Church and of all his people, without his being willing to see or understand what is good or evil or to make amendment, or his being willing to do as was required by the great and wise men of his realm, or to allow amendment to be made.

Also, throughout his reign he has not been willing to listen to good counsel, or to adopt it, or to give himself to the good government of his realm; but he has always given himself up to unseemly works and occupations, neglecting to satisfy the needs of his realm ...

17. On Holding a Parliament

FROM: *Modus Tenendi Parliamentum*, printed in Maude Clarke, *Medieval Representation and Consent* (London, 1936), 374–5

Here is described the manner in which the parliament of the king of England and of the English was held in the times of king Edward, son of king Ethelred; in which manner it was recited by discreet men of the realm before William, duke of Normandy, conqueror and king of England. The Conqueror himself commanded this to be done, and this usage is through his approval, and in his time and in that of his successors, kings of England ...

Concerning the laity: Item, each and every earl, baron and their peers should be summoned and should come, i.e., those who have lands and revenues to the value of a whole earldom, i.e., namely 20 knights' fees, with each fee computed at £20, which makes £400 in all, or to the value of a whole barony, that is, thirteen and a third knights' fees, with each fee computed at £20, which makes in all 400 marks, and no minor laity should be summoned or should come to the parliament, by reason of tenure, unless their presence for other causes will be useful or necessary for the parliament, and then about the others it should be done as is said for the minor clerics, who by reason of tenure are too unimportant to come to the parliament.

18. Bishop Russell's Sermons on the Role of the Lords

FROM: S. B. Chrimes, *English Constitutional Ideas in the Fifteenth Century* (Cambridge, 1936), 169–73

... And therefore the noble persons of the world which – some for the merits of their ancestors, some for their own virtues – be endowed with great honours, possessions and riches may more conveniently be compared unto the firm ground that men see in islands than the lower people which, for lack of such endowments (not possible to be distributed among so many) and therefore living by their casual labours, be not without cause likened unto the unstable and wavering running water. *Many people from many waters.* It was said to St John in the Apocalypse, *The waters which you have seen are peoples and multitudes.* To lay the ground of nobility upon virtue joined to possessions and riches, though it be a matter disputable and disputed at large by diverse authors and perhaps some other opinion there taken therein than the common use of every region requires, yet for reputation of nobility there is recited the custom of this land and many others adjoining ... It is not of any school denied but that riches are a proper instrument for the execution of virtue, adding thereunto the definition that Aristotle makes in the fourth chapter of his *Politics*, that 'nobility is virtue and ancient riches'. It seems that conveniently such firmness of ground as may be best found in this world ought to be assigned to the lords and noblemen, and so they to be signified and understood by what is found most stable, that is to say by the islands and not by the water nor floods ...

The cause why lords and noblemen ought more to be persuaded to agree and each amiably to hearken to another than the whole generality of all the people is plain and evident enough, considering how the politic rule of every region well ordered stands in the nobles. For after

Rome was peopled, the first institution of the thing public there made by Romulus was a Senate of one hundred. Likewise Moses, the leader of the children of Israel, by the advice and counsel of Jethro, his cousin, chose out of the whole multitude a certain number of wise and noble men to have power under him in all causes reserved to the greatest – like as in these days in every region where is a monarchy and one prince the same policy is observed. To you then, my lords, pertains principally the office of hearing of the state of every case falling among yourselves or the people under you, yourselves to be reduced [to peace] by loving treaty, the people by true justice. You be like to Moses and Aaron who ascend unto the mount where the law is given. The people must stand afar and not pass the limits; you speak with the prince, who is *as our God on earth*, as they did with God, mouth to mouth; but it suffices the people to receive with due obedience the prince's commandments by the direction of his wise ministers and officers, saying to each of you, as they of Israel did to Moses, *Speak to us and we will hear, but let not God speak to us* . . .

19. Peers in the King's Council

FROM: J. Fortescue, *Governance of England*, C. Plummer (ed.) (Oxford, 1885), 145–9

The king's council was wont to be chosen of great princes, and of the greatest lords of the land, both spiritual and temporal, and also of other men who were in great authority and offices. Which lords and officers had near hand also many matters of their own to be treated in the council, as had the king. Wherethrough, when they came together, they were so occupied with their own matters and with the matters of their kin, servants and tenants, that they attended but little, and at other times nothing to the king's matters . . .

And what lower man was there sitting in that council who dared say against the opinion of any of the great lords? And why might not then men make by means of corruption some of the servants and councillors of some of the lords to move the lords to partiality, and to make them also favourable and partial [to one side] as were the same servants, or the parties that so moved them? . . .

How may the king be counselled by such great lords to restrain giving away of his land, the giving of offices, corrodies, or pensions of abbeys to other men's servants, since they most desire such gifts for themselves and their servants . . .

Which things considered, and also many others which shall be shown hereafter, it is thought good that the king had a council chosen and established in the form that follows or in some other form like thereto:

First, that there were chosen twelve spiritual men and twelve temporal men, of the wisest and best disposed men that can be found in all the parts of this land . . . And that these twenty-four be always councillors, but if there be any default found in them, or it list [please] the king, by the advice of the more part of them [to] change any of them.

And that every year be chosen by the king four lords spiritual and four lords temporal to be for that year of the same council, in like form as the said twenty-four shall be . . .

The said eight lords also, which by reason of their baronies and estates, be councillors of the king by birth, and therefore ought to counsel him at all times when he wills, need not have great wages for their attendance to his council, which shall last but for a year . . .

20. The Trial of Peers in Parliament (1341)

FROM: *Rot. Parl.*, II, 127

Honourable lord, to your reverence, it seems to the prelates, earls and barons, with one assent, that the peers of the land ought not to be arrested, nor brought to judgement, except in parliament, and by their peers. And on this there have recently been some discussions whether any of the peers, who is or had been chancellor, treasurer or any other office whatsoever, ought to lose this exemption, as well by reason of his office as in any other manner. The peers of the land are advised that all the peers of the land, officers or otherwise, either by reason of their office or of the things relating to their office, or for any other cause, ought not to be brought into judgement, nor lose their temporalities, lands, tenements, goods or chattels: nor be arrested, imprisoned, outlawed or condemned, and ought not to respond or be judged, except in full parliament, and before the peers where the king takes part. Saving to our lord the king the laws rightly used by due process, and saving the suit of the party . . .

21. Privileges of Peers (1388)

FROM: *Rot. Parl.*, III, 244 (11 Richard II)

In this parliament all the lords then present, spiritual as well as temporal, claimed, as their liberty and privilege, that the great matters which were moved in this parliament and will be moved in other parliaments in the future, touching the peers of the land, will be treated, adjudged and discussed by the court of parliament and not by the civil law nor the common law of the land [which is] used in other, lower courts of the realm. Which claim, liberty and privilege the king graciously allowed and heard in full parliament.

22. Privileged Position of Peeresses (1442)

FROM: *Rot. Parl.*, V, 56

The Commons pray:

That it please you, by the advice and assent of the lords spiritual and temporal, assembled in this present parliament, to declare that such peeresses as are indicted, or, after having been indicted of any treason or felony committed by them, be treated as barons are. And that they be put to answer, and that judgement be rendered and judged upon them, before such judges and peers of the realm as are peers of the realm. And that if they be indicted or impeached of such treasons or felonies it be in such a manner and form, and in no other.

Response: Le Roi le voet.

23. Lords Intercede and Advise (1404)

FROM: *Rot. Parl.*, III, 350 (5 Henry IV)

Item, as several supplications and requests of the commons made in Parliament to our lord the king for Benet Wilman, who is prevented by certain malevolent persons, and is detained in prison and is ordered to respond before the constable and marshal, contrary to the statutes and the common laws of England: Nor our lord the king, by the advice and assent of the lords in parliament grants and orders that the said Benet shall be governed and ruled according to the statutes and the common laws of England, notwithstanding any commission made to the contrary, or hindrance placed on him before the constable and marshall as above is mentioned. And this brief will be followed in the form which follows . . .

24. Act to Enforce Parliamentary Attendance (1453)

FROM: *Rot. Parl.*, V, 248 (32 Henry VI)

Memorandum, that on the last day of February, the year of our said lord the 32nd, a certain petition was shown to the same lord king in the present parliament, which contains these words:

Please it the king our sovereign lord that for as much as divers and many lords of this land, as well spiritual as temporal, the which have been summoned and commanded by your writs directed to each of them separately to have come and [to] be at this your present parliament, who in no wise do come, nor have been at your said parliament at your palace of Westminster since the 14th day of February last until today, that is to say, the Lady Day of February the year of your reign the 32nd, but have absented them since the said 14th day of February of coming to the said parliament, whereto they have been called, summoned or warned; to ordain and establish by authority of this present parliament that every of the said lords who comes not but, being absent, be charged to give and pay unto you and to your use such sums of money and in such manner as follows: that is to say, every archbishop and every duke, £100; every bishop and every earl, 100 marks; every abbot and every baron, £40; to be levied upon their lands and goods wheresoever they be within this your realm. And that by all means and processes to be made out of your exchequer, such as has been accustomed to be had for the levying of other grants made unto you in your parliament.

Provided always that the bishops of Bangor, St Asaph, and Llandaff that have not come to this said parliament as above be not charged but only each of them £20.

Provided also that such lords that for feebleness and sickness are not able to come, nor may come to the said parliament at this time, be informed of this act; so that such feebleness or sickness be sufficiently and duly proved by just and indifferent examination, before the lords of the king's council, and by no other trial to be had thereof; and that it be ordained and established by the said authority that every lord as for such feebleness or sickness [may] not come as above, make such fine to you as shall be thought reasonable by the discretion of the said lords of your council, so always that the said fine exceed not the sum in the act charged upon the said lord for his absence, as it is declared above.

Provided also that this act extend not to the duke of Somerset, nor to the Lord Cobham, being in prison; nor to the Lord Rivers, the Lord Welles, nor the Lord Moleyns, being beyond the sea by the king's commandment.

Provided also that this act extend not nor be prejudicial to the Lords Beauchamp and St Amand, being about the king's person in the time of his infirmity.

Provided also that this act attain not to any hurt, prejudice, burden or charge of the said lords so absent, or any of them, saving only of payment of the said sums or fines; and the said sums to be applied to the safe-guarding of your town of Calais, your Castle of Guisnes, and your marches there, and to no other use; this present act to extend to such lords only as be not come as above for this time and no longer.

Which petition, read in the aforesaid parliament, heard and fully understood, the same petition, by the advice and assent of the aforesaid, was assented to in these words:

Le roi le voet.

25. Attendance at Parliament (11 Feb 1452)

FROM: *PPC*, VI, 116

By the King,

Right trusty and well beloved. How be it that we thought that you, according to your duty, had been and would have been waiting upon us as other lords that but lately was called to come to our council do, and attended upon us and to our service as our true liegeman ought to do, namely, considering the great untruths and disobedience that is meant and proposed against us and against our estate and against our universal policy and welfare of this our land, the which, with the grace of Our Lord shall not take such effect as the authors and labourers thereof propose and intend, but shall be so rebuked and chastised as it shall be to the pleasure of God and to the worship of us and to the weal of this our realm. Nevertheless you wilfully absent yourself from us and withdraw yourself otherwise than you ought in any wise to do. We therefore write unto you, charging you straightly upon the faith and allegiance that you owe unto us, that as soon as you see these our letters, you, without delay or tarrying, come to our presence, there to wait upon us and do service such as it fits our true liegeman [to do], and especially [one] of your estate and degree to do, and fail not so to do as you would eschew our indignation and the peril that may ensue therefrom.

Given, etc., at Westminster, the 17th day of February, the year, etc., xxx.

To our right trusty and well beloved the Lord Cobham.

By order of the king, by advice of his council.

26. Exemption from Parliament

(*a*) FROM: *CPR*, 1381-5, 185

5 November, 1382: Exemption, for life, on account of the weakness of his eyes, of John de la Warre, Lord of Wakerless, from attendance in parliament, notwithstanding his tenure from the crown by barony.

(b) FROM: PRO, C 66/188, membrane 13 (22 December 1336)

The King to all to whom, etc., greetings.

Know that we order, to our beloved and faithful Robert de Insula, who is enfeebled and whose body has been injured by dangerous labours, that we are moved by compassion and that of our grace we specially concede, for us and our heirs, to the same Robert that he be excused throughout the time of his life from coming to us or our heirs in our wars, or in parliament, or to our councils or those of our heirs. And furthermore we will that he be not compelled to do service to us or our heirs, nor that he be compelled to be a minister or official of us or our heirs, according to his wishes as aforesaid.

And therefore we order you that the same Robert be allowed what we have conceded and that he be not molested in this matter.

In which it is written, etc., by the king at Doncaster, 22nd day of December,

By writ of privy seal

27. Debate in the Lords (1449)

FROM: A. R. Myers, *English Historical Documents* (London, 1969), IV, 468–9

Present – The cardinal of York, the archbishop of Canterbury, the bishops of Winchester, Carlisle, Llandaff, Bath, Worcester, Chichester, Norwich, [Chester], Coventry, Bangor, the abbots of Westminster, and Gloucester, the duke of Suffolk, the earls of Warwick, Devon, Wiltshire, Worcester, Viscounts Beaumont and Bourchier, the prior of St John of Jerusalem, Lord Roos, Grey of Ruthin, Groby, Moleyns, Dudley, Lisle, Cromwell, Sudley, Stourton, Southwick.

The question is how supplies may be found for the setting forth of the armies in Normandy and Guienne.

Lord Stourton thinks there should be certain commissioners of oyer and terminer to enquire of murders and riots against the peace. Also of liveries and that every sheriff should certify to the commissioners all the names of knights, squires, and all other men of might within his shire, that they may know whom they may empanel, such as be sufficient.

Lords Sudley and Cromwell think that due justice might be had and a good agreement amongst the lords first.

The bishop of Chichester thinks there are two ways to have goods.

One is that all those who have incomes should bind themselves to give the value of that income to defend the land. Also that those who have grants and annuities of the king's grant give a year's value of the grant and annuity beforehand to help the arms for the defence of that country.

The bishops of Norwich and Chester hold that justice may be had without difference, and that half the shire knights should be sent forth with the grants that are granted for the defence of those parts.

The bishops of Bath and Worcester hold the same.

The bishops of Salisbury and Ely hold that the precedents that have been in such matters should be seen.

The lord treasurer thinks that the diligence that the lords do for this matter, both for ordnance and for men to be sent forth and to see the ways how goods may be procured for them to be sent forth, should be laid before the commons. And they to be entreated to consider this great diligence and to put their hands to their good benevolence to see how supplies may be had to perform the purpose of sending forth the said armies.

The lord of Winchester holds that due justice may be had and then to ordain of others of the shire archers.

The lord cardinal and the lord of Suffolk hold to the same opinion.

The conclusion of this communication is to take the usual grant of goods for the defence of the land.

Also this day the letter that Sir Francis le Arragonois sent to the duke of Suffolk was read before the lords in the parliament, the which was thought right notably written.

28. Passage of a Parliamentary Bill

FROM: R. Tottell (ed.), *The Year Books*, 33 Henry VI, fo. xvii (London, 1924), pp. 150–1)

If any bill, private or otherwise, is first presented to the commons and is passed by them, it is customary for the bill to be endorsed in this form: 'Be it delivered to the lords.' And if the king and the lords agree to the bill and do not wish to alter or change it in any way, it is not the custom for them to endorse the bill, but it is given to the clerk of parliament, to be enrolled. If it is a common bill it is enrolled and enacted, but if it is a private bill it is not enrolled but is filed on the file, and that is sufficient.

If the party wishes to have it entered, in order to be more secure, it may be enrolled.

If the lords wish to make any change in the bill, it is not returned to the commons if the change is such that the commons have already agreed to it. Thus, if the commons grant Tunnage and Poundage for four years, and the lords consent to this grant, but only for two years, then the bill is not returned to the commons because their consent may be assumed. But if, on the other hand, the commons make a grant of Tunnage and Poundage, or of something similar, for two years, and the lords prolong the grant to four years, the bill must be returned to the commons, and the lords must draw up a note expressing their intention or else they must endorse the common bill to this effect: the assent of the lords is given for a period of four years.

When the bill has been returned to the commons, it may not be enacted if they do not wish to agree to it. But if the commons wish to agree with the lords, then they endorse their answer on the margin at the bottom of the bill in this form: 'The commons have agreed to the note of the lords which is attached to this bill.' Then the bill is delivered to the clerk of the parliament.

If a bill is first of all presented to the lords and is passed, then it is not the custom for them to endorse it in any way, but it is sent to the commons. In such case, if the bill passes the commons, it is endorsed by them in this form: 'The commons have assented.' This proves that the bill has first passed the lords.

29. York's Claim to the Throne

FROM: *Rot. Parl.*, V, 376

. . . [They] said that they were the king's justices, and have to determine such matters as come before them in the law, between party and party, and in such matters between party and party they may not be of counsel, and so this matter was between the king and the said duke of York as two parties, and also it is not the custom to call the justices to counsel in such matters, especially since the matter was so high and touched the king's high estate and crown, which is above the law and passed their learning, wherefore they dare not enter into any communication thereof, for it pertained to the lords of the king's blood, and the condition of this land, to have communication and to meddle in such matters; and therefore they humbly besought all the lords to have them completely excused of having to give any advice or counsel in this matter.

And then the said lords, considering the answer of the said judges, and intending to have the advice and good counsel of all the king's councillors, sent for all the king's serjeants and attorneys, and gave them direct orders in the king's name that they gravely and wisely should search and seek into all things that might be best and strongest alleged for the king's avail, in objection and the defeat of the said title and claim of the said duke.

Whereupon the said serjeants and attorney, the next Wednesday, answered and said that the said matter was put to the king's justices, and how the Monday before the same justices said and declared to the said lords that the said matter was too high and of such great weight that it passed their learning, and also they dare not enter any communication in the matter, to give any advice or counsel therein; and so the said matter was so high that it passed the learning of the justices, it must needs exceed their learning, and also they dare not enter any communication in that matter; and they prayed and besought all the lords to have [them] excused of giving any advice or counsel therein.

To whom it was answered, by the advice of all the lords, by the said chancellor, that they might not be so excused, for they were the king's particular councillors, and therefore they had their fees and wages. And he said to the said serjeants and attorney that they were the king's councillors in the law, in such things as were under his authority or by commission, but this matter was above his authority, wherein they might not meddle, and humbly besought to the said lords to have them be excused of having to give any counsel in the matter. And it was answered again that the lords would not have them excused, but let the king's highness have knowledge of what they said. And thereupon the said chancellor reminded the lords spiritual and temporal of the words and excuses of the justices, and the words and excuses of the serjeants and attorney, and also the great command of the king's highness that they had to find all such objections as might be most mighty to defend the king's right and title, and to defeat the title and claim of the said duke of York. And also that the king might understand that the said lords did their true and faithful labour and acquittal in the said matter, desired all the lords, that every one of them should say what he could say in fortifying the king's title, and in defeating the claim of the said duke. And it was agreed by all the lords that each lord should have his freedom to say what he would say, without any reporting or account to be had for his words. And thereupon, after the saying of all the lords, each after the other, it was concluded that the matters and articles written below should be alleged and objected against the said claim and title of the said duke . . .

30. An Inquisition Post-Mortem

(a) FROM: *Calendar of Inquisitions Post-Mortem*, XV, 1–7 Richard II

William la Zouche, or Souche, of Haryngworth, knight

Writ: 26 April, 5 Richard II [1382]

(No. 630): Devon: Inquisition taken at Bruggeton Pomeray, Tuesday before Ascension Day, 5 Richard II. He was seised in his demesne as of fee of the undermentioned castle and manors:

Totteneyse. The castle and manor, with the members of the castle, to wit, Lo—— and Hywyssh.

Corneworthy. The manor.

All held of the king in chief by knight's service.

He held no other lands, etc., in the escheator's bailiwick.

He died on Wednesday the feast of St George last. William la Zouche of Bramfeld, knight, aged 40 years and more, is his son and heir.

Writ: 26 April, 5 Richard II

(No. 631): Worcester. Inquisition taken at Upton on Severn, Thursday after Corpus Christi, 5 Richard II. He held the undermentioned messuage, etc.

Le Mersshe by Interberewe. A messuage so called, and 40 acres land and 20 acres meadow held of the earl of Pembroke by knight's service.

Date of death and heir as above . . .

Writ: 26 April, 5 Richard II

(No. 635): Hertford. Inquisition taken at Retbourne, Monday after Ascension Day, 5 Richard II. He held the undermentioned messuages, etc., jointly with Elizabeth his wife, deceased, for the term of their life, with remainder for life to Thomas, their son, who is still living, by grant of John, bishop of London, Simon Warde of Carleton, deceased, Jean Holt and John Tame, deceased.

Whethamstede. A waste messuage, called 'Youngesplace', with 140 acres arable, 20 acres wood, 5 customary tenants owing $39\frac{1}{4}$ summer works, and 24s 6d rent of assise, out of which 20s has to be paid away to the abbot of Westminster, held of the said abbot by knight's service.

Retbourne. A waste messuage called 'Cuttysplace', 53 acres arable, 6 acres pasture, 2 acres meadow, 4 acres wood, and 9s rent of assise, out of which 13s 4d has to be paid away to the abbot of St Albans, held of the said abbot by knight's service.

Date of death and heir as above . . .

(b) FROM: PRO, E 149/47, no. 2

Inquisition held at Dockyng in the county of Norfolk before John Rose, escheator of the lord king in that county, the 11th day of May, the year of the reign of King Richard II after the conquest, 5; by virtue of writs of the said king, to the said escheator, directing the same escheator that this inquisition is to be taken by oath of John de Mordere and the jury, called on oath. They say that William la Souche of Haryngworth, knight, deceased, held in that county in demesne as of fee on the day he died the manor of Dockyng, called 'Zouchesmaner' in part in Dockyng in the County of Norfolk from the lord king in chief, by service of a sixth part of a knight's fee, in which manor there is one capital messuage which is worth nothing, per annum, beyond reprises. Item: there are in that place 100 acres of arable land which are worth per annum, 33s 4d, per acre 4d: and also in that place 10 acres of pasture which are worth per annum 11s 8d, per acre, 14d. And also in that place from rents of assize, 40s per annum, paying at the feast of All Saints, Easter and the Advent of St Peter in equal portions. They say that the aforesaid William died the 23rd day of April, and that William la Souche of Bramfeld, knight, son of the aforesaid William la Souche of Harryngworth, is heir of the aforesaid, and his age is 40 years and more.

Sum of the extent, £4 5s 0d.

(c) FROM: PRO, E 152/207, no. 18

Inquisition taken at Oxford, Monday next after the Feast of Corpus Christi in the year of the reign of King Richard, after the Conquest II, 5, before Edmund Giffard, escheator of the lord king in the county of Oxford, by virtue of writs of the said king to the same escheator, directing that this inquisition be taken by oath of William Avener and his companions in the county who say on their oath that William de la Zouche of Haryngworth, knight, deceased, did not hold any lands or tenements in the said county that were in fee on the day he died, from the lord king in chief, in the aforesaid county; but that he held on the day he died in his demesne as of fee 20s rent with part in Hempton, from the earl of Buckingham as of his manor of Dadyngton, by which service they do not know. And they say that the said William de la Zouche died Wednesday on the feast of St George last, and that William la Zouche, knight, son of the aforesaid William is his nearest heir, and he is age 30 years and more.

(d) FROM: PRO, C 136/23, no. 24

. . . They say on their oath that William la Zouche of Haryngworth,

knight, deceased, held neither land nor tenements in his demesne as of
fee on the day he died of the lord king in chief in the aforesaid county.
But they say that he held in the same county on the day he died the
manor of Alvenlegh, with part that he holds from the countess of
Norfolk as of the Castle of Framlingham, by service they are ignorant
of; and part of Sir Richard Waldegrave, knight, by service of 4s 6d rent
of the manor of Buris, and another parcel he holds of John Good by
service of 12s rent per annum, and 1d of 'wardesilver' as of the manor of
Codynham. And they say that he held the aforesaid manor of Alvenlegh
and parts for the term of his life, and Elizabeth his wife, deceased,
similarly, by gift and concession of John, bishop of Lincoln, Simon
Warde of Carleton, deceased, John Hoolt and John Tame, deceased. So
that after the death of the aforesaid William and Elizabeth the said
manor with its parts, to his son Thomas, the aforesaid William and
Elizabeth to this heir, and it remains to Thomas for the term of his life.
In which manor is one capital messuage which is worth nothing, in
value per annum, beyond reprises. Item: in that place, 120 acres arable
land which are worth per annum 40s, price per acre, 4d. Item: there are
there 10 acres meadow, value per annum 20s, price per acre, 2s. Item:
there are there 6 acres pasture which are worth per annum, 7s, price per
acre, 14d. Item: there is in that place one acre of wood which is worth,
per annum, 6d, and there is there, from rents of assize, 16s 3d, paying at
the feast of Easter and St Michael in equal portions . . .

31. Land Inherited through the Wife

(a) FROM: *CCR*, 1381–5, 313

22 June, 1383   To James de Pykeryng, escheator in Yorkshire. Order
to give Thomas de Nevylle and Joan, his wife, daughter and heiress of
William de Furnyvall, knight, seisin of the said William's lands; as Joan
has proved her age before the escheator, and the king's commissioner
John de Neville of Raby to take her husband's fealty.

(b) FROM: Ibid., 1405–9, 201

3 May 1407   To William Colclogh, escheator in Salop and the Marches
of Wales adjacent. Order in presence of the heirs and parceners or of
their attorneys to make a partition into two equal parts of three mes-

suages and 1 virgate of land in Pueton and Dudilbury in Corsdale, and to give John Talbot and Maud, his wife, seisin of her purparty, but to remove the king's hand and meddle no further with the other purparty, delivering to Joan daughter of Thomas Nyvylle, knight, any issues thereof taken; as it is found by inquisition, taken before the escheator, that at his death the said Thomas held the premises of others than the king, and that the said Maud his daughter by Joan, sometime his wife, and the said Joan by Ankaret late his wife, are his next heirs, both being within age; and the king has taken the fealty of John Talbot for lands which the deceased held in chief by the court of England in right of Joan his wife.

(c) FROM: *CFR*, 1405–13, 74

3 May, 1407   Order to Thomas Egmanton, escheator in the county of York, to cause John Talbot and Maud, his wife, daughter of Thomas Nevyll, 'chivaler', deceased, to have full seisin of all the lands which the said Thomas on the day of his death held by the court of England as of the right of Joan his late wife, a tenant of Richard II in chief and the mother of Maud, her heir; as the king has taken John's fealty.
The like to the following:
    John Bagot, escheator in the county of Stafford.
    Richard Whityngton, mayor of London and echeator therein.
    Edmund Brundell, escheator in the county of Buckingham.
    William Colclogh, escheator in the county of Salop and the adjacent Marches of Wales.
    John Brugge, escheator in the county of Hereford and the adjacent Marches of Wales.

32. A Wardship Granted

(a) FROM: *CFR*, 1422–30, 64

13 December, 1423   Commitment to Ralph earl of Westmorland – by mainprise of John earl marshal and earl of Nottingham and Richard Nevill, 'chivaler', and by and with the advice and assent of the king's council – of the wardship of Richard son and heir of Richard late earl of Cambridge, and kinsman and heir of Edward late duke of York, together with the marriage of the said heir (which marriage pertains to the king

by the death of the said late earl and duke, who held of Henry V in chief on the days of their death, and by reason of the minority of the said heir), and so from heir to heir until one of them shall have attained full age and Ralph shall have duly effected the marriage, rendering 3,000 marks for the said wardship and marriage, to wit, 1,000 marks in hand, 500 marks at Midsummer next, 500 marks at Christmas following, and finding fit maintenance for the heir; and for this maintenance the king wills that the said Ralph have 200 marks a year from the issues and profits of the lands late of the said duke (which are in the king's hand by reason of the minority of the said heir) by the hands of the keepers, farmers, bailiffs, reeves, occupiers or other ministers of the same, or by the hands of the treasurer.

(b) FROM: *CPR*, 1422–30, 343

26 May, 1426   Grant to Joan, countess of Westmorland, by advice of the council, and on her petition, she having the custody of Richard, duke of York, as executrix of Ralph, earl of Westmorland, her late husband, of 100 marks a year during the minority of the said duke, out of the lordships, lands and tenements of Edmund, late earl of March, in Dorset and Suffolk, which are in the king's hands, in addition to 200 marks a year, which she already has, for the sustenance of the said duke, who is being made a knight.

33. Enfeoffment of Lands by William, Seventh Lord Lovel

FROM: Andrew Clark (ed.), *Lincoln Diocese Documents* (Early English Text Society, O.S. 149 [1914], 83–8) from John Chedworth's Register in the Lincoln Diocesan Archives, fos. 22–6

I, the said William, Lord Lovel, declare my will and intent to the said feoffment in the following manner and form:

That is to say, that my said feoffees soon after my decease make estate in and of the said manors of Brideshurth, Ubbedon, Knoke, Erdescote, Estwamburgh, Berley, Estwykham, Rotherhigh, Wydefore, fee farm, and in all the said other lands or tenements in the same towns, in all the said lands and tenements in Bampton, litell minster, and elsewhere in Oxfordshire that were sometime belonging to Eleanor Hill, with all the appurtenances, to William my second son and to the heirs male of his body, lawfully begotten, under the following form and condition; that if the same William my son or any of the heirs male begotten of his body do or suffer anything to be done by which the said tail should be discontinued, in part or totally, longer than for the term of the life of the same William my son or of the life of any of his male heirs begotten of his body, or during the life of any of the wives of my said son or of any of the wives of the male heirs of his body, that then all the said manors . . . specified in the tale remain unto the right heirs; and the said entailed estate to be utterly void.

And I pray and require my said feoffees to help and assist my right heirs in this matter:

And in case the said William my son die without male issue of his body, or else that he or any of his said male heirs (for lack of any other issue of mine) inherit from me and become Lord Lovel, and no such discontinuance made by him or any of his said male heirs otherwise than is mentioned above, then half of the same manors, lands, tenements and fee farm, with the appurtenances, remain unto Robert Lovel, my third son, and to the male heirs begotten of his body, under proper form and conditions to be observed and kept by the same Robert and his male heirs as is mentioned above to be observed and kept by the said William and the male heirs of his body. And in case the said Robert dies without male issue begotten of his body, or else that he or any of his said male issue becomes my heir and become Lord Lovel, and no discontinuance is made by the same Robert or any of the male heirs begotten of his body of the same moiety or any parcel thereof otherwise than is mentioned before, then the said moiety remains to Henry Lovel, my fourth son, and to the male heirs begotten of his body, under proper form and conditions to be observed and kept by the same Henry and his male heirs (as is mentioned before) to be observed and kept by the said William and the male heirs begotten of his body. And for lack of such male issue of the said Henry the remainder thereof [goes] to my right heirs. And that the other half of the said manors, lands and tenements, with the appurtenances, remains unto the same Henry and to the male heirs gotten of his body, under proper form and conditions to be observed and kept by him and his said male heirs (as is mentioned above), to be observed and kept by the said William and the male heirs begotten of his body; and in case the said Henry dies without male issue begotten of his body, the remainder thereof unto the same Robert and the male heirs begotten of his body under proper form and conditions, as is mentioned above. And for lack of such male issue of the said Robert, the remain thereof goes to my right heirs . . .

34. Widows and Dower Shares

(a) FROM: *CCR*, 1374–7, 187–8

11 November 1375   To John Rokwode escheator in Norfolk and Suffolk. Order to deliver in dower to Anne who was wife of John de Hastynges earl of Pembroke, tenant in chief, such as are in his bailiwick of the following manors and lands of her said husband which the king has assigned to her, having taken of her an oath that she will not marry without his licence; namely the manor of Sutton, extended at £21 2s 8d a year, the manor of Wynferthyng at £13 18s 4d, the manor of Asshele at £6 6s 8d in Norfolk, the manor of Lydgate at £9 4s 0d, the manor of Badmondesfeld at £4 5s 0d, the manor of Otteleye at 10 marks, the manor of Wridlyngton with three burgages in the town of St Edmunds at 60s in Suffolk; the manor of Thoryton at £4 7s 0d, the manor of Esthanyngfeld with divers other lands in Westanyngfeld thereto pertaining at £16 12s 0d, the manor of Southanyngfeld with other lands in Franges thereto belonging at £4 4s 4d in Essex; the manor of Totenham at £20 in Middlesex; the manors of Padyngden and Westcote and a tenement in Suthwerk at £24 in Surrey; and the manor of Benham at £10 in Berkshire; divers lands in Fitelton at 13s 4d in Wiltshire, the manor of Brampton at £78 18s 4d and the manor of Lymyng at 66s 8d in Huntingdonshire, the manor of Blounham at £20 and the manor of Kempston at £24 in Bedfordshire; certain lands in the town of Repyngdon at £4 in Derbyshire; the manor of Allesleye at £22 13s 6d, the manor of Filongleye at £13 12s 0d, the manor of Aston Cauntelowe at £39 0s 21d, and the manor of Pillardyngton at £4 13s 4d, in Warwickshire; and the manor of Nayleston extended at £11 12s a year in Leycestershire.

(b) FROM: Ibid., 333

7 March 1376   Indenture made between Margaret Mareschall countess of Norfolk and dame de Segrave and Anne countess of Pembroke, dame de Bergeveny and de Mauny, being a lease for eight years by the said Anne to the said Margaret her mother of all her castles, lordships, lands whatsoever, fees and advowsons in England and Wales, making no waste or destruction, rendering every year one rose at Midsummer, and performing the services due to the chief lords, power being reserved to the

said Ann in case the said Margaret shall die within that term again to enter and hold the premises without gainsaying of her executors, assigns or any other.

Dated London, Candlemas eve, 50 Edward III [1 Feb. 1376].

(c) FROM: Ibid., 448

1376 Indenture made between Margaret Mareschall countess of Norfolk and dame de Segrave of the one part, and Anne, her daughter, countess of Pembroke and dame de Mauny of the other part, witnessing a grant made by the said Anne to her said mother of all the manors, parks, fisheries and the profits thereof arising, the wardship whereof the king by letters patent has granted and to farm let to the said Anne until the full age of John, son and heir of Sir John de Hastynges, earl of Pembroke her husband, the same having come to the king's hand by reason of the nonage of the said heir, paying to the king the farm to him reserved by the said letters patent and all other charges whatsoever, provided that if her said mother shall die within that term, the premises shall revert to the said Anne during the same term, this grant notwithstanding; and covenant by the said Margaret that if her said daughter shall survive her during that term she shall hold the premises as aforesaid, and the said Margaret's executors shall be bound to discharge the same toward the king and every other of all manner of farms and charges for the time that the said Margaret shall have the occupation thereof.

Dated London, St Matthew's day, 50 Edward III [24 Feb. 1376].

(d) FROM: CPR, 1385–9, 423

25 March 1388 Grant – reciting letters patent (dated 25 October, 6 Richard II [1383]), granting to Robert de Veer, earl of Oxford, and Philippa, his wife, daughter of Ingelram and Isabella de Coucy, the king's aunt, the lands of Joan, late the wife of John de Coupeland, for the support of the said Philippa, and upon her petition in the present parliament for provision, as all the lands of the said Robert de Veer, duke of Ireland, are seised into the king's hands by judgement of parliament – with the assent of the prelates and nobles of parliament, and in consideration of her being of royal stock, to William, archbishop of Canterbury, Robert, bishop of Lincoln, Thomas, bishop of Ely, chancellor, the king's uncle Thomas, duke of Gloucester and John de Waltham, keeper of the privy seal, of all the lands aforesaid from the date of the said duke's forfeiture to the use of the said Philippa, for life, to whom or to her attorneys all the profits are to be from time to time delivered and paid, to be expended upon her maintenance without account to the king, and further at her nomination the grantees are to

present proper persons to benefices falling vacant to be instituted as vicars, rectors, or wardens therein.

By the King in Parliament.

(e) FROM: Ibid., 1461–7, 6

9 April 1461   Confirmation without any fine or fee to Anne duchess of Buckingham, late wife of Humphrey duke of Buckingham, of letters patent dated 4 February, 39 Henry VI [1461], being a grant to her for life in dower, in amplification of a grant by letters patent dated 19 September, of the manor and lordship of Kynges Hatfeld, free chace and hunting in the hay of Hatfeld, the manor and lordship of Fobbyng, the hundreds of Ongre and Harlowe with courts and perquisites, co. Essex, the manor and lordship of Desenyng, the manor of Haverhull with the hamlet of Hersham, cos Suffolk and Essex, the manors of Wotton and Tissho, co. Warwick, the castle, manor, and lordship of Okeham, co. Rutland, the manor and hundred of Rothewell with the fee farm of the town and the borough there, the manor of Slapthorn, alias Clapthorn, co. Northampton, the manor and lordship of Okham, co. Surrey, the manor of Pakynton, co. Stafford, the manor and lordship of Agmondesham and the manor of Little Birkehill, co. Bucks, with their appurtenances and knight's fees, advowsons, and other franchises, parcel of the possessions of the late duke in England, Wales, the Marches of Wales and Calais.

35. Support for a Widow

FROM: *CPR*, 1388–92, 117

18 October, 1389   Grant, with the assent of the council and considering that she lately had by grant of her husband Robert de Veer, late duke of Ireland, 100 marks a year for life from the manors and lands in England which were his before forfeiture, to the king's kinswoman Philippa, duchess of Ireland, of 1000 marks a year from the farm of the said lands, payable by the countess of Oxford so long as she is farmer thereof, and, if she be amoved, then by the farmers or tenants for the time being, so long as the same continue in the king's hand by reason of the forfeiture aforesaid.

By privy seal.

36. Political Gains and Losses

(a) FROM: *C.Ch.R.* (1300–26), III, 448, 9 July 1322

Gift, for good service rendered and to be rendered, to Hugh le Despenser, earl of Winchester, of the castle, town, manor and honour of Denbigh and the cantreds of Ros and Royewynok and the commote of Dynmael in Wales, late of Henry de Lascy, sometime earl of Lincoln, which by the death of Thomas, late earl of Lancaster, tenant of the foregoing, a rebel and enemy to the king, have come into the king's hands, and which while in the king's hands Alice de Lascy, daughter and heir of the said Henry, late the wife of the said Thomas, quitclaimed to the king; to be held by the said earl and his heirs, with all appurtenances, as the said Henry held them by the services rendered to him.

(b) FROM: PRO, C 66/347, membrane 10 (29 September 1397)

The King, to all to whom, etc.

Know that through our special grace we concede to our beloved and faithful William Lescrope, earl of Wiltshire, the manor of Welkhampstowe and Loweholle, with their appurtenances in Essex, with all manner of hamlets, lands, tenements, rents and services of free and unfree tenants whatsoever, of this manor above said, with all meadows and pastures and wood lands, fishponds, mills, chases, wardships, marriages, reliefs of age, franchises, liberties and other profits, emoluments possessed there of members and appurtenances whatsoever, with knights' fees and advowsons of churches, vicarages, chapels, chantries and other benefices of the Church whatsoever belonging to the abovesaid manor, in any manner, which belonged to Thomas, late earl of Warwick and which are to us by virtue of the indictment against the same late earl of Warwick in our full parliament, and now the same manor is forfeit and is, with all its appurtenances, of the earl of Wiltshire and his heirs male, held from us and our heirs by the service which was freely and wholly done by the earl of Warwick in times past, to us and our heirs.

Witnessed by the king at Westminster, the 29th day of September.

By writ of privy seal.

(c) FROM: *CPR*, 1396–9, 267 (29 September 1397)

Grant, in tail male, to William Lescrope, earl of Wiltshire, of the castle, town, and lordship of Castle Bernard alias 'Bernardescastell' in the bishopric of Durham, the manors of Middleton and Gaynesford, and a messuage in Queryngton, together with all lands, tenements, rents and services within the same, late of Thomas, earl of Warwick and forfeit by virtue of the judgement against him in the parliament at Westminster on Monday after the feast of the Exaltation of the Cross in the 21st year, together with the towns, hamlets, members, and fee farms, knights' fees, advowsons, etc., pertaining to the premises, except advowsons of abbeys and priories, if any, as fully as the said earl held the same.

(d) FROM: *CCR*, 1454–61, 407 (10 March 1460)

To the receivers, bailiffs, reeves, farmers, tenants or occupiers for the time being of the manors of Yaresthorp, Appulton, Scorby and Hund-burton, co. York. Order to pay to Thomas Roos, knight, Lord Roos, or to his assigns during his life, a yearly rent or annuity of £40 which the king has granted him for life of and in the said manors, which are in the king's hands by forfeiture of Richard late earl of Salisbury, a rebel, and by virtue of an act against the earl and others published in the parliament lately held at Coventry.

(e) FROM: Ibid., 408 (19 December 1459)

To the bailiffs, farmers, receivers or other the occupiers for the time being of the lordships or manors of Wendover and Whaddon, co. Buckingham. Order to pay to Thomas Grey of Regemond Grey, knight, £40 a year for life; as in consideration of his great assistance, loyalty and grievous charges and travail while the king in person was resisting the rebels and traitors, Richard late duke of York, Richard late earl of Warrewyk, Richard late earl of Salisbury and other their accomplices, and frustrating their designs, the king has given him for life £40 a year of the issues, profits, revenues, etc., of the said lordships, in the king's hands by reason of the duke's rebellion and by force of an act against him and others in the parliament holden at Coventre, 20 November last.

(f) FROM: Ibid., 410 (1 January 1460)

To the bailiffs, farmers, receivers or other the occupiers for the time being of the manor and borough of Milverton with the tithings there, and of the manor of Mersshwode. Order to pay to Thomas earl of Devon 100 marks a year for life and the arrears; as in consideration of his assistance and true loyalty, and of his grievous charge and travail when the king in person was travailing to resist the rebels and traitors Richard late duke of York, Richard late earl of Warrewyk, Richard late earl of Salisbury and their accomplices and to frustrate their accursed designs, by letters patent of 19 December last, the king gave him for life 100 marks a year of the issues, profits, revenues, etc. of the said manors and borough, which are in his hands by the said duke's rebellion and by virtue of an act against the duke and others in the parliament holden at Coventre, 20 November last.

(g) FROM: Ibid., 418 (11 December 1459)

To the abbot and convent of Ramesey for the time being. Order to pay to John duke of Norfolk £50 a year for life, which the king has granted him of the yearly farm which the abbot and convent used or ought to render to Richard late earl of Salisbury and Alice his wife, in her right, for the fair or residue of the fair in the town of St Ives co. Huntingdon, the same having come to the king's hands by reason of divers treasons by them committed, for which they were attainted and convicted in the parliament holden at Coventre on the feast of St Edmund king and martyr, 38 Henry VI.

37. A Minister's Account (1467–68)

FROM: R. I. Jack, *The Grey of Ruthin Valor* (Sydney, 1965), 66–9

County of Northampton
Towcester: account of John Burwood, bailiff there, for the seventh year of the reign of King Edward IV.

Rent of assise and at the lord's will in Towcester	– sum is £20 12 0
Farm of the city off the manor	– sum is £1 5 4
Farm of the demesne lands	– sum is 4 0 9½
Farm of the common oven	– sum is 3 6 8
Farm of the mills	– sum is £8
Farm of Buckby	– sum is 10s
The fair and the market	– sum is, this year 40s
The perquisites of the courts	– sum is 6 0 6
Rent in Caldecote	– sum is 59s 6½d
The works in Caldecote	– sum is 9s 3d

Rent in Burcote	– sum is 50s 1d
Works in Burcote	– sum is 3s 8d
Pastures in Towcester	– sum is 66s 8d
Medesyluere (meadow?)	– sum is 114s
Rent of assise with farms in Apthorpe, Foxcote, and Wapton	– sum is 12 10 4½
Rent of capons and hens	– sum is 17s
Works in Apthorpe and Foxcote	– sum is 13s 8d
	Sum total is – £76 19s 6½d

Decayed rents:

First is the allowance of the rent of a tenement, late John Blondell, the which my lord gave to John Holt and Elizabeth, his wife, for the term of their lives, by the year, 40s. Also the allowance of the works of a tenement late [of] John Deyfte, in Towcester, for they are not levy-able, by year, 14d. Also, for one, a goose and a half and one hen and a half with the rent of them in Apthorpe, 11¼d. Also in the allowance of the rent of a cottage, late held by Maud Hawkin, which is granted her for the term of her life, 4s. Also in the decay of the rent of a shop in Troust', late held by William Waxchandler, for it lies in my lord's hand, 14s. Also in the allowance of the rent of a shop, late in the tenour of William Scote, cause abovesaid, 3s 4d. Also another tenement, late in tenour of Bole, for the same cause, by the year, 8s. Also another shop, lately held by Robert Broune, by the same cause, 5s. Also in the distress of the rent of a shop, lately held by Alice Hony, which yielded 6s 8d per year, and now pays but 2s by the year, 4s 8d allowed. Also in the decay of 4 acres of land in Apthorpe, lately held by John Ward, lying in my lord's hands, 2s. Also in the decay of the motehyll in Towcester, by the same cause, 16d. Also a parcel of London called Writhehaches, by the same cause, 16d. Also 6 acres of land laying in Wiggenhall, by the cause above said, 16s. Also in the allowance of the rent, late Thomas Vane(s), for the house is not well repaired this year, 16d. Also in the allowance of the rent of 9 shops, for they are not at the full rent this year, 17s 4d.

Sum, 106s 4¾d (recd)

Expenses of the Steward and his clerk	– sum is at certain 34s 8d
Repairs of houses	– sum is 6s 9d
Repair of the mills	– sum is 20s

Fees and annuities:

First in the fee of John Dyve, is	– 8d
Item, in the annuity of John Harpour	– 48s
Item in the fee of John Byrwode, bailiff	– 60s 8d
Item in the fee of William Assheby, attorney	– 40s

Item in the fee of William Newenham   – £4 13s 4d
Item in the fee of William Coberford   – 40s
Item in the fee of John Humfrey of the stable   – 8s
Item in the fee of Thomas Colyns, woodkeeper   – 22s
Item, for his own rent, for the term of his life   – 8s
                                          Sum   – £19 6s 8d

Expenses of my lord's council and of this account.   Sum is 13s 8d
Money paid to my lord and my lady.   Sum is £40
Item paid to my lord for expenses of My Lady Grey,
    coming from London.   6s 8d
Money delivered to Richard Carlile, steward of the
    household   – Sum is £6 0s 12d

Sum of all the allowances and £74 15s 9¼d, and so there is owing,
40s 8¾d, of which is allowed to the bailiff for his costs in . . . Henys,
Slapton, and Foxcote, 2s 0¼d. And so there is owing by William
Assheby, 38s 8½d.
And so the valor of this manor is this year, over £40 paid to my Lady,
£8.

38. A Manorial Valor

FROM: Westminster Abbey Muniment 12158 (temp. Richard II)

. . . Buckingham and Oxfordshire

Whaddon

Summary of value of rents and farms, beyond deductions – £25 16s 6d
Profits of the courts there in that year – £1 2s 9d
    = £26 19s 3d

Stipend to reeve there per annum, 10s
Expenses to steward for holding the court there, in this year, 7s 4d
For repairs in enclosing the park there this year, 11s
Balance due to the reeve in that year, 1s 1d
    = £1 9s 5d   and clear value
                        = £25 9s 10d

Claydon

Summary of the value of all the rents and farms there, beyond deductions – £22 6s 2d

From there, in fees to the parker – 10s and clear value there = £21 16s 2d

Finmere

Summary of value there of the rents and farms beyond deduction = £10 7s 9d

Profits of the courts there in that year = 4s 2d = £10 11s 11d

From there, in fees to the reeve, per annum, 5s

Expenses to the steward for holding the court there in that year – 3s 4d = 8s 4d

and clear value there = £10 3s 7d

Bierton

Sum of the value per annum in rents and farms, beyond deductions = £10 0s 6½d

Profits from the court there, value this year £1 0s 1d

From there, expenses to steward for holding court this year – 4s 8d

Fees paid to the bailiff there this year – 6s 8d

Balance due to John Borwick, 12s 5½d
    = £1 3s 9½d
        Clear value there
        that year = £9 17s 10d

Wendover Borough

Value there, per annum, of rents and farms, beyond deductions, £9 3s 9½d

Profits from courts there, value this year, £1 1s 0d
    = £10 4s 9½d

From there, expenses to steward for holding courts this year, £1 18s 8½d

Fees to bailiff there that year. 1s 6d
    = £2 0s 2½d
        Clear value there
        = £8 4s 7d

Wendover Foreign

Sum of all values, per annum, in rents and farms, beyond deductions, £48 6s 1d

Profits of the court there this year, £1 14s 1d

From there, expenses to steward for holding court there that year £2 9s 2d

Fees to bailiff there that year, £3 0s 8d
    = £5 9s 10d
        And clear value there
        £44 10s 4d

Sum of the total value of all the lands in the aforesaid manors in the aforesaid counties – £131 3 11½d

From which:

Fees to the bailiffs in those places paid that year	– £3 8s 10d
Fees to the parker, as aforesaid, in that year	– 10s
Fees to the reeve there that year as abovesaid	– 15s
Expenses to the stewards there that year, as mentioned above	– £5 3s 2½d
Repairs for the enclosing of a park that year	– 11s
Surplus balance returned that year	– 13s 6½d
	= £11 1s 9d
And so there remains	– 120 2s 2½d

Expenses of the account: paper, parchment, ink and travel around the county	– 5s
Fees to Robert Pygot, Receiver there that year	– £3 6s 8d
Fees to Nicholas Talbot, the lord's steward in the county, per annum	£4
	= £7 11s 8d

And so there remains clear £112 10s 6½d

39. Survey of an Estate

FROM: Marie Clough (ed.), *Two Estate Surveys of the Fitzalan Earls of Arundel* (Sussex Record Society, 1969), LXVII, 2–3

Manor of Arundel:
There are 4½ acres in demesne, worth 12s 4½d at 2s 9d an acre, and 153½ acres worth £10 4s 8d at 1s 4d an acre. The town of Arundel owes rent as follows:

On St Thomas' day (21 December) . .	1s 10d
On Whitsunday	£6 12s 2d
Geld, due on the above dates, total . . .	5s 0d
From the Broke, at Midsummer . . .	13s 4d
Rent of weirs and fish traps, due at Christmas, Lady Day, Midsummer, and Michaelmas, total	£1 12s 0d

The mills on the Swanebourne pay their dues to the prior of Arundel's leper-house and to the chaplain of Arundel Castle, and so are worth nothing to the lord. There is a windmill, worth £1 a year in the usual instalments. The grazing in the small park is worth 5s 0d, and 2 bucks and 2 does may be taken every year. The garden fruit is worth 5s 0d. There is also a large park with grazing worth £1 and 5s 0d in pannage; 5 bucks and 7 does may be taken there every year. There is a great forest; it contains the pasture called Madehurst, whose appurtenances bring in 6s 8d. Pannage is worth £1, the dead and fallen wood can be sold for £2, and £30 worth of green wood may be sold annually without making waste. The pleas of the forest are only worth 10s 0d because they have been badly kept, and the Weypanies bring in 1s 0d. The court at Arundel is worth £3.

There are eight hundreds in the lord's hand (owing rent in equal instalments at Easter and Michaelmas):

Palinges – at farm for £1 10s 0d	Value of its court:	£5 0s 0d
Avesford – at farm for £1 10s 0d	,,	5 0s 0d
Boxe – at farm for 15s 0d	,,	2 10s 0d
Stokebrug' – at farm for 15s 0d	,,	3 0s 0d
Bury – nothing from its farm	,,	13s 4d
Eswride – at farm for £1 0s 0d	,,	4 0s 0d
Ruserebrugh – at farm for 13s 4d	,,	2 10s 0d
Midhurst, now called Esbourne, at farm for £1 10s 0d		
	Value of its court:	£5 0s 0d

Pleas of the court at Chichester are worth 3s 0d with 'La Foune'. Wreck of the sea brings in 10s 0d.

Total due from Arundel –   –   –   £99 11s 6d
Rents and farms from the Hundreds, apart from the lady's share – £17 7s 8d

Rents due: at St Thomas and Christmas –		14s 10d
Lady Day		13s 0d
Easter	£3	11s 8d
Whitsunday	£6	17s 2d
Midsummer	£1	6s 4d
Michaelmas	£4	4s 8d

40. Receiver General Appointed (22 June 1415)

FROM: PRO, Ancient Deeds, E 40/A 6094

To whomsoever this writing comes, Henry, lord LeScrope, greetings in Our Lord eternally:

Know that we have confirmed our beloved John Foxhole, clerk, to be our receiver general for all debts with arrears, farms, and other receipts and profits from all our lordships and lands within the kingdom of England.

The said John, for receiving and acquitting these revenues, shall make as often and wheresoever it is necessary full consultation, hear and be aided by all and singular of our officials and ministers, and the aforesaid John shall be aided and obeyed as is appropriate. In our name he does the aforesaid business in all matters.

Witnessed by this seal which we affix. Given at our manor of Faxflete, the 22nd day of June, year of the reign of King Henry V after the Conquest, 3.

41. Appointment of Household Official (26 June 1380)

FROM: E. C. Lodge and R. Somerville, *John of Gaunt's Register*, 1379–83, no. 1072 (Camden Society, third series), Vols 56 and 57

John, etc., to all, etc.

Know that we, by the advice of our great council and by the great assurance which we have in our very dear and well beloved esquire William Overbury, and being entirely confident of his loyalty, ordain, constitute and assign him to be our chief pantler and our chief butler of our household, giving to the said William full power and mandate to well and loyally do the purchasing and purveying which pertains to the dsai office, and to carry out and execute all which duly pertains to the offices of chief pantler and butler, as the governors of our household will properly inform him and furnish him with what is reasonable on our part.

And the said William shall take annually for his fee £10 for all the time that he shall hold this office, receiving the fee from the hands of our receiver general in equal portions at the terms of St Michael and Easter.

By which we order to all our ours, etc.

In witness, etc.

Given, etc., at our castle of Hertford, the 26th day of June, the year, etc., 4.

42. Household Government: The Transfer of Office (3 December 1382)

FROM: *John of Gaunt's Register*, 1379–83, no. 787

John, etc., to our very dear and well beloved clerk Sir William de Norneby, chancellor of our exchequer in the county of Lancaster and our receiver there, greetings.

Because we have given instructions to our most dear and well beloved monsieur Robert de Plesington, formerly our steward within the said county and chief baron of our exchequer, to deliver to you, either by himself or by his attorneys or deputies, all the rolls, records, accounts and other materials which have remained with the said Robert or his deputies touching both the office of chief baron of our exchequer of the county of Lancaster and the offices of our steward and justice in the same county, we order you for the maintenance of our instructions, to receive from the said monsieur Robert or from his attorneys or deputies the rolls, records, accounts and remembrances aforesaid.

And also we order you to occupy the office of chief baron of our said exchequer and to continue to hear the pleas regarding the exchequer until some one else is ordered to do so or until you receive another order, notwithstanding our letters previously sent to you regarding the receipt of the rolls, muniments and remembrances aforesaid of the monsieur Robert, his attorney, or deputy, by indenture between you. And these our letters will be your power of attorney.

Given, etc., at Westminster, the 8th day of December, the years, etc, six.

43. Household Expenses (6 May 1383)

FROM: *John of Gaunt's Register*, 1379–83, no. 803

John, etc., to our very dear and well beloved clerk Sir William Oke, clerk of our great wardrobe, greetings.

We order you to pay, from the issues received in our chamber, to the following persons, the sums named below:

To Herman Goldsmith, for a pair of silver basins with gold plate and engraved on the borders with swans, and embossed with escutcheons of arms of our brother of Buckingham, given by us to the daughter of our said brother on the day of her baptism at Plessy, £46 18s 2d . . .

And to Geoffrey our barber, for the private expenses of our chamber, by indenture made between us, the 16th day of May, £20.

And to distribute to poor men to the value of the 2 nobles bestowed upon us and our charger at the jousts at Chelmsford, 13s 4d.

And to various heralds who were at the same jousts, from our gift, 10 marks.

And to various minstrels who were there, from our gift, 10 marks.

And to pay for a pair of paternosters, containing 16 great chorals and 150 aves, bought from William at Mille and handed over to us in person, 13s 4d.

And for a primer containing the matins of Our Lady, seven Psalms, and Dirige with other devotions, delivered to our own hands, 46s 8d.

And to Geoffrey, the aforesaid barber, for the expenses of our chamber at Tuttebury the 13th day of September, by indenture made between us, £20.

And to John of Brampton, tailor of London, for an order bought from him for the use of our daughter of Pembroke, £8.

And to William Palmer, for another order bought for the use of the same daughter, £6 7s 2d.

And to pay £11 1s 11d for the expenses of our said daughter Pembroke, going from Hereford to Henley with the king for 9 days, and show on your accounts the parts which include this sum.

By these things and by the indentures mentioned above or by acquittances we wish that the sums you have paid shall be duly allowed in your account.

Given, etc., at our Castle of —— [blank in the manuscript], the 6th day of May, the year, etc., six [of Richard II].

FROM: East Sussex Record Office (Lewes), Glynde Manuscript 3469, sheet 6 of Wednesday, 1 – (29 or after, of either March or November, 1391), Rolls B6.

N.B. The 'y' indicates that only 1½d was paid on those days.

Name	Attendance
Monsieur de Derby – 4d per day	x
Monsieur John Beaufort – 6d per day	x x x x x x x x x x x x x x x x x x x x x x x
Monsieur Robert Jeffers – 4d	x
Monsieur John Deincourt – 3d	x
Dame Katherine Swynford – 12d per day	
Henry Beaufort – 6d per day	
Jane Beaufort – 6d	x x x x x x x x x x x x
Thomas Beaufort – 6d	x x
Man Servant – 4d	x x
Robersham – 3d	x x
Lancaster Herald – 2d per day	x x x x x x x x x x x x x x x
Leicester Herald – 2d per day	x x x x x x x x x x x x x x x
Arnold Fancouer – 2d	x x x x x x x x x x x x x x x
Robert Bladwell – 2d	x x x x x x x x x x x x x x x
Edward Ferrers – 1d per day	x x x x x x x x x
Dugelm messag – 1d	
Thomas Greene, messenger – 1d	
Philip Gallechith – 2d	
Lewes Jumpet – 1d	x x x x x x
William Whinewell – 1d per day	x x x x x x x x x x x x x x x x x x x
John Gor – 1d.	x
John Restell – 1d	
Dame – Blount – 2d per day	x x x x x x x
Dame E. Parr – 1d	x x x x x x x x x
Dame E. Sherley – 1d	x x x x x x x x x
Rubbyn Shalminster – 3d	x y y y y y y y
Jolebyn Cranminster – 3d	y y y y y y y y y
— Brombard – 3d	x x x y y
Eleanor Walerer – 3d	y y
Nicholas Norwold, 1 charger at 7½d per day	x x x x x x x x
William Wrawe, 1 charger at 7½d per day	x x x x x y x x
Thomas Fehwell, 1 charger at 7½d per day	x x x x x x x x x x
David Carere, 1 charger at 7½d per day	x x x x x x x x x x x x x
William Sedewell, 1 charger at 7½d per day	x x x x x x x x

45. An Indenture (12 May 1441)

FROM: British Library, Additional Charter, 14,598

Richard, duke of York, earl of March and Ulster, lord of Wigmore and of Clare, lieutenant general and governor of the kingdom of France and of the duchy of Normandy,

To all to whom the present letter comes, greetings.

Know that we, for the noteworthy and laudable service and good council which our beloved councillor John Fastolf, knight, has rendered and will render to us in the future, we give and concede to the said John an annual revenue of £20, to have and to receive annually for the duration of his life, from the tax moneys which we receive annually by hereditary right from the customs and subsidy on wool and wool pells in the port of London from the hands of the collectors of those revenues, being paid at the terms of St Michael the Archangel and Easter, in equal portions.

In witness whereof we will cause letters patent to be made.

Given, under our seal at London, 12th day of May in the 19th year of the reign of King Henry VI after the conquest.

46. An Indenture for Service (1442)

FROM: British Library, Additional Charter, 17,234

John, duke of Norfolk, earl Marshal and Nottingham, marshal of England, lord of Mowbray, of Segrave and of Gower; to all to whom the present letters come, greetings.

Know that we, from our special grace, for the good and laudable service rendered and to be rendered to us by our well beloved servant, William Berdewelle, esquire,

Give and concede and by the present confirm to the same William an annual revenue of 10 marks to be received by him annually from the profits and issues of our manor and lordship of Stoneham in the county of Suffolk. He is to have, hold and receive the aforesaid annual revenue of 10 marks in lawful English money in equal portions at the feast of St Michael the Archangel and at Easter, for the term of his life, and he is to be paid through the hands of the receiver, bailiff, farmer or other occupier of the said manor and lordship of ours of Stoneham, aforesaid through the stipulated time.

Wherefore we will and order our auditors that when the aforesaid receiver, bailiff, farmer or other occupier of our said manor pays the aforesaid annual revenue of 10 marks from year to year and from term to term, they shall make allocation, for all the life of the aforesaid William, that the aforesaid payment should be made to him for that term.

In witness of this our letters patent shall be made.

Given under our seal in our Castle at Framlingham, 20th day of Ascension, in the year of the reign of King Henry VI after the Conquest, 20.

47. An Early Indenture

FROM: N. B. Lewis, 'An Early Indenture of Military Service, 27 July 1287', *Bulletin of the Institute of Historical Research* (1935–6), XIII, 89

This is the contract made at Wigmore on the Sunday next after the Feast of St James the Apostle, in the year of the reign of King Edward, 15, between that noble man Lord Edmund de Mortuo Mari on the one part and Lord Peter de Malo Lacu on the other:

That the aforesaid Lord Peter will abide with the aforesaid Lord Edmund in a military expedition to Wales against Reese the son of Meredith and his accomplices, malevolent rebels against our said lord king.

With 10 horses, covered by this appraisal: one with black feet and having one white foot, price 60 marks: and one other black horse, price of 40 marks: and one other black horse with 2 white feet, price of 30 marks: and one other horse, price of 20 marks: and one other bay horse, price of 18 marks: and one other 'farranto' horse, price of 40 marks: and one sorrell horse, price of 18 marks: and one other bay horse, price of 18 marks: and one 'Lyard' horse, price of 18 marks: and one piebald horse, price of 14 marks: and one rouncey horse, price of 100 shillings.

And if it happens that any of the horses are lost when the said Lord

Peter is in the service of the said Lord Edmund, in any manner, then the said Lord Edmund and his heirs who hold from him shall pay in property to the said Lord Peter whatsoever shall be the assessed value of the horses, in this fashion:

Half the payment for however many or one of the horses as shall be lost, to be paid at the feast of the Purification of the Blessed Mary next to come, and the other half at the feast of the Blessed John the Baptist which follows:

And for the greater security of this agreement, it should be done thus. The aforesaid Lord Edmund and the aforesaid Lord Peter make their cyrographs or affix their seals to this, to the effect that the aforesaid Edmund makes the agreed payment in the chancery of the Lord King in the fashion he has recognised, and this agreement shall be enrolled in the chancery. And Edmund agrees that if the aforesaid payment is not made then his lands, goods, and cattle in the county of Hereford and elsewhere shall be taken by bailiffs of the Lord King and paid to the aforesaid Peter as by this agreement. Given at Wigmore, in the year and day aforesaid.

And it is recorded that the aforesaid Edmund came to the chancery of the Lord King and recognised that the aforesaid writing contained the manner of the aforesaid agreement.

48. Indenture for Peace and War

FROM: *John of Gaunt's Register, 1379–83*, no. 27

This indenture is made between John, king of Castile and of Leon, duke of Lancaster on the one part and John Skargull, esquire, on the other part:

Witnessing that the said John is retained and resides with the said John, king and duke, for the term of his life, in time of peace as in time of war, in the manner which follows.

That is to say, the said John shall be held to serve the said king and duke in time of peace as in war, for the term of his life, and to work with him in such matter as shall please the said king and duke, and to be well and properly arrayed for war.

And the said John shall receive in time of peace wages and food at court at divers places whither he shall be sent and ordered by letters of the said king and duke. And the said John shall take 20 marks each year in time of war, as his fee of war, plus food at court, from the hands of whoever shall be the treasurer for war of the said king and duke.

And if it happens that in the future the said John changes his estate and takes the order of chivalry then he shall take, in time of war, for himself, his esquire, and his men at arms, well and properly arrayed for war, 40 marks per year as their fee for war, from the hands of the aforesaid treasurer for war, plus food at court for himself and his said esquire.

And in regard to the horses of war taken and lost in the service of the said king and duke, if there are any from the moment of the beginning of the year at war, and regarding prisoners or other profits of war taken by him or won by his men, and for the freight and harnesses of horses used for the said king and duke, it shall be done for him as it is for other esquires of his estate and condition.

In witness, etc. Given at London, the 23rd day of June, the year, etc., four.

49. Indenture for Service

FROM: W. H. Dunham, *Lord Hastings' Indentured Retainers, 1461–1483* (New Haven, 1955), 124–5

This indenture, made the 22nd day of November, the 9th year of the reign of King Edward IV, between William, Lord Hastings, on the one part, and his entirely beloved cousin, Sir Simon Montfort, knight, on the other part, witnesses that the said Sir Simon of his mere motion and free will grants and by these presents faithfully promises for term of his life to be retained and bound with the said lord as his servant; and his full part and quarrel to take against all others during the said term, the allegiance of the said Sir Simon only excepted and reserved; and over that the said Sir Simon grants and promises to be ready at all times and places within this realm of England to attend upon the said lord, or where[ever] as he shall by the said lord be appointed by his writing or commandment, as well in time of peace as war, upon reasonable warning accompanied with such people as thereto shall be required and as accords to the worship that the said Sir Simon is of, or shall be called unto.

And in consideration of the premises the said lord accepts and takes the said Sir Simon according to his desire and promises him to be his good and faithful lord and to aid, assist, comfort and fortify him in all lawful and reasonable causes as a lord ought to do. And moreover the said lord grants by these presents to pay and satisfy the reasonable expenses of the said Sir Simon and company so labouring with him in time of war or otherwise, coming to the said lord by his commandment or writing. And the same Sir Simon promises again to the said lord upon his faith and honour of knighthood to perform the premises and every part of them, never in his life to attempt the contrary. In witness whereof to the one part of these indentures remaining with the said lord the said Sir Simon has set his seal and sign manual, and the said lord to the other part of these indentures remaining with the said Sir Simon has set his seal and sign manual thereto,

the 22nd day of November, the said 9th year of the reign of our said sovereign lord, King Edward IV [1469].

50. An Indenture (12 December 1474)

FROM: W. H. Dunham, *Lord Hastings' Indentured Retainers, 1461 1483* (New Haven, 1955), 126–7

The indenture made the 12th day of December the 14th year of the reign of King Edward the fourth between William Hastings, knight, Lord Hastings, on the one part and James Blount, esquire, on the other part, witnesses that the said James granted to the said lord, as well by the faith of his body as by this present indenture, of his own free will and motion, is retained [sic] with the said lord to be his true and faithful servant and to do him true service during his life, and his part take against all earthly creatures, his allegiance and the lord Mountjoy, his nephew, when he comes of full age, excepted.

And the said James shall at all times be ready to go and ride with the said lord whensoever he shall be required, within the land, with all such men as he may make at the costs and charge of the said lord. And for this thus doing the said lord promises and grants to the said James that where the town of Derby has granted and ordained the said lord to have the rule and governance of the said town, that the said James shall occupy and have the rule in his absence of the said town in manner and form as the said lord and the said James between them agree. And over that to be his good and favourable lord and to aid him, to help and succour in all such things as shall belong to him according to right under the king's laws.

In witness whereof the said parties have set their seals and subscribed their names, the day and year abovesaid.

51. Complaint against Violence

FROM: First Version of John Hardyng's Chronicle, *c.* 1457; printed in *English Historical Review* (1912), XXVII, 749–50

(From a section entitled 'How the kynge shulde reule moste specialy the comon profyte of his Reme with pese and lawe . . .')

In every shire, with jackets and salades clean,
Misrule doth rise and maketh neighbours war:
The weaker goes beneath, as oft is seen:
The mightiest his quarrel will prefer
So poor men's cause is ever pushed back far;
Which, were the peace and law now well conserved,
Might have amended been, and thank to God deserved.

They kill your men always by one and one,
And who says aught he shall be doubtless beaten;
For in your Realm Justice and Peace be none,
That dares now the belligerents oppress.
Such sickness now hath taken them and access,
They will know nothing but of riot and debate,
So common is it now in each estate.

But this I dread full sore without gabbe,
From such riots shall arise more mischief
And from the sore unheeded will come a scab
So great that it may not be restrained;
Wherefore, good lord, if you will give me leave
I would say this unto your excellence,
Withstand the first misrule and violence.

Withstand, good lord, the beginnings of debate
And well chastise also the rioters
That in each shire are now associate
Against your peace, and all their maintainers.
Truly, if not, will fall the fairest flowers
Of both your crown and noble monarchy,
Which God defend and keep through his mercy.

Who prays to you for any contekoure,
Whether he be duke, earl, or other estate,
Blame him as for the very maintainer
Of such misrule, quarrel, and each debate;
Which else your law would chastise and abate,
If maintainors would suffer it have the course
That plaintiffs might, to law have their recourse.

The law is like unto a Welshman's hose,
To each mans leg that shapen is and mete;
So maintainors subvert it and transpose,
Through might it is laid full low under feet,
And maintenance, up instead of law complete;
All, if law would, things were by right reversed,
For maintainors it may not be rehearsed.

52. Statutes against Livery and Maintenance

(a) FROM: *SR*, I, 256 (1327)

14. Also, because the king desires that common right be administered
to all, to rich as well as to poor, he commands and forbids that any of his
councillors or of his household or any of his other ministers or any great
man of the realm, by himself or through another, or any others in this
land, great or small, by orders sent through letters or in any other way,
shall take upon them to maintain quarrels or parties in the country, to
the disturbance of the common law.

(b) FROM: Ibid., II, 74–5 (1390)

The king to the sheriff of Kent, greeting.
    Whereas by the laws and customs of our realm, which we are bound,
by the oath made at our coronation, to preserve, all our lieges within the
same realm, as well poor as rich, ought freely to sue, defend, receive and
have Justice and Right, and the accomplishment and execution thereof,
in any our courts whatsoever and elsewhere, without being disturbed or
oppressed by maintenance, menace, or in any other manner; and now so
it is, that in many of our parliaments heretofore holden, and namely, in
the parliaments last holden at Cambridge and Westminster, grievous

complaint and great clamour hath been made unto us, as well by the lords spiritual and temporal as by the commons of our said realm, of great and outrageous oppressions and maintenances made to the damage of us and of our people, in divers parts of the same realm, by divers maintainers, instigators, barrators, procurers, and embracers of quarrels and inquests [juries] in the country, whereof many are the more encouraged and bold in their maintenance and evil deeds aforesaid, because that they be of the retinue of lords and others of our said realm, with fees, robes and other liveries called liveries of company.

We have ordained and strictly forbidden by the advice of our great council that no prelate nor other man of Holy Church nor bachelor nor esquire nor other of less estate give any manner of such livery, called livery of company, and that no duke, earl, baron or banneret give such livery of company to knight or esquire if he is not retained with him for the term of his life, for peace and for war, by indenture, without fraud or evil device, or unless he be a domestic and familiar, abiding in his household. Nor to any vale called 'yeoman archer' nor to other of less estate than an esquire, if he be not, in like manner, a familiar abiding in his household.

And that all the lords spiritual and temporal, and all others of whatever condition or estate, shall utterly oust all such maintainers, instigators, barrators, procurers and embracers of quarrels and inquests from their fees, robes and all manner of liveries and remove them from their service, company, and retainer without receiving any such on their retainer, in any manner, in any time to come; and that no lord spiritual or temporal, nor any other, that hath or shall have people of his retinue, shall suffer any that belong to him to be a maintainer, instigator, barrator, procurer or embracer of quarrels and inquests in the country, in any manner; but shall put them away from his service and retinue, as afore is said, as soon as it can be discovered; and that if any lord do oust any such maintainer, instigator, barrator, procurer or embracer from his company for this cause, that then no other lord do retain or receive him of his retinue nor of his company in any manner.

And that none of our lieges, great nor small, of what condition or estate he be, whether he be of the retinue of any lord or other person whatever who belongeth not to any retinue shall not undertake any quarrel other than his own, nor shall maintain it, by himself nor by other, privily nor apertly. And that all who use and wear such livery called livery of company, contrary to this our ordinance, shall take them off altogether within ten days after the proclamation of this same ordinance without using or wearing them any more afterwards; and that this our Ordinance be held and firmly kept, and duly executed, in all points, as well by those who have or shall have people of their retinue as by all other persons, in that which to them belongeth touching the same ordinance, upon pain of imprisonment, fine and ransom, or of being punished in other manner, according as shall be advised by us and our council . . .

Given under our Great Seal at Westminster, the twelfth day of May,
By the King himself and the Council.

(c) FROM: Ibid., II, 426–8 (1461)

Forasmuch as by the giving of liveries and cognisances, contrary to the statutes and ordinances thereof made concerning these things in the past, the maintenance of quarrels, extortions, robberies and murders has been multiplied and continued within this realm to its great disturbance and lack of peace.

The king is willing to have remedy for such inconveniences and that his laws shall have their course. Therefore he charges and commands that no lord, spiritual or temporal, shall from henceforth give any livery or cognisance, mark or token of company, except at such times when he has a special command from the king to raise people for the king's aid, to resist his enemies, or to repress riots within his land . . . upon the penalty contained in the statutes made in this connection, and upon pain of incurring the great displeasure of the king.

Also, he wills that no lord, or other person of lower estate or degree, spiritual or temporal, shall give any livery of clothing to any person except in his household and to his serving men, his officers, and his learned counsellors, spiritual and temporal, and he also wills that no man . . . shall take it upon him to wear the livery of clothing of any lord . . .

Also, that no lord . . . shall knowingly receive, keep in his household or maintain thieves, robbers, oppressors of the people, those guilty of manslaughter, ravishers of women, and other open and notorious perpetrators of misdeeds, against the law . . . upon penalty of the king's great displeasure and the perils that may ensue therefrom.

53. Promise to Behave (16 April 1430)

FROM: *PPC*, IV, 36–7, 8 Henry VI

Also it was accorded and assured there that for no manner quarrel that is or may be between lord and lord or party and party no bonds to be taken nor riot nor gather of people made, but that if it hap that God defend that any dissension or debate fall between lord and lord the remainder of the lords anon as that dissension comes to their hearing or knowledge shall leave all other things, labours, and attend to the redress and appeasing as the said dissension or debate and that without holding of partiality or more favours showing to one party than the other, to stand whole, united and knit together and the said lords between whom peradventure such division shall fall, to be assured to stand in high and low to the redress and rule of the remainder of the lords.

Whereupon at Canterbury even forthwith, my lord the duke of Norfolk and the earls of Huntingdon and Warwick among other there being present, at the instance of my said lord the Cardinal made assurance in the hands of my lord of Gloucester that for every manner of dissension or quarrel which fell or will fall, which God forbid, hereafter between them or between their friends, kin, or servants, either here or in France, or between them, their servants and the servants of the duke of Bedford or of Burgundy or of any other of the king's allies or subjects, they shall not make amends thereof, nor punishment of the trespass as of their own heed or authority but that if they find them hurt or grieved they should let the king's council have knowledge of their grief and that if such reasonable redress as the said council should ordain or purvey for them in the case they shall hold them content.

54. Bonds to Keep the Peace

(a) FROM: *CCR*, 1468–76, 25–6

10 June 1468   John, earl of Shrewsbury, John, Lord Duddeley, and Walter, Lord Mountjoy, knights, to the king.

Recognisance for £1,000 to be levied in Salop.

Condition that from now on to All Hallows next the earl shall be of good behaviour towards John Shirley, Nicholas Knyveton, William Basset, Ralph Pole, esquires, and all other the jurors in certain inquisitions taken at Derby on Wednesday after the close of Easter last, before George, duke of Clarence, Richard, Earl Ryvers, William, Lord Hastings, and others concerning the treason, trespasses, and other evil doings in Derbyshire, shall until then do or procure no hurt or harm to Henry, earl Grey or any servant of his in breach of the peace, and on November 6 next shall appear in person in chancery.

(*b*) FROM: Ibid., 244

14 April 1472   James Haryngton, knight of Lancashire, to the king.

Bond in 3,000 marks payable at the Feast of St Peter *ad vincula* next or levied, etc., in the above named county.

Conditions, that if the said James stand and obey the award of arbitrators indifferently chosen by the King in the suit between him and Thomas, Lord Stanley, concerning the custody of the manor of Horneby, county Lancaster, and all the manors, lands, rents, revenues and advowsons of abbeys, priories, churches or chapels formerly of Sir John Haryngton and John, son and heir of Thomas Haryngton; and shall obey the king's award touching all trespasses, offences and demands between the said James and the said lord and his servants, and carry out the same, this recognisance shall be voided, etc.

Thomas, lord Stanley, to the king. Bond in 3,000 marks, etc. Like conditions, *mutatis mutandis*, under the same date.

55. The Devon-Bonville Quarrel

(*a*) FROM: *PPC*, V, 173–4

28 November 1441   It was rehearsed by my lord chancellor by the king's commandment to the earl of Devon that time being there present, that the king considereth well the great riots, disorders, dissensions and debates the which now late[ly] have grown and been between the said earl of Devon and his servants and friends, and Sir William Bonville, knight, and his servants and friends, the which have caused manslaughter, the king's peace [to be] greatly troubled and broken, to the great unquietness of his shires of Cornwall and of Devon and also of other places, to the unease not only of them and theirs but also of his subjects dwelling therein. And as it is done him to understand for the said discords, divers companies of men have been so arrayed in guise of war as with jacks and other arrays and weapons for the war the which was of more likelihood to trouble the king's peace than otherwise. And the king, willing his peace to be well and duly kept without any interruption or breach of it by any of his subjects of any estate, degree or condition that he be of, for it fitteth to none [being] his liege man to take it into his own hands to avenge his own quarrel, neither by way of feat nor otherwise, for he is their sovereign lord which will do right,

hath therefore charged the said earl of Devon upon the faith and allegiance that he owes unto him, and as he would show his grievous indignation, that neither by way of feat abetting, procuring nor otherwise, he neither do nor procure in all that he can or may suffer to be done or procured, in that he can and may let it, any bodily harm, hurt or damage bodily [come] to the said Sir William, nor to any of his servants, friends, well wishers or allies . . . The said earl shall in all goodly haste . . . notify it unto the said Sir William to the intent that he and his may eschew such bodily hurts as above.

And forthwith at the same time it was demanded by my lord chancellor by the king's commandment if that the said earl would do and perform the king's will and commandment as above. And he said and promised yea. And that to do he took my lord chancellor by the hand and promised by his faith so to do. . . . [To the same question] the said William said and promised yea. And that to do he took my said lord chancellor by the hand and promised by his faith so to do.

And furthermore it was rehearsed then by my lord chancellor to either of them, apart [separately] in the king's presence, that there as they have promised for all manner of dissensions, discords and debates that have been and are hanging between them, and also for the office of the stewardship of Cornwall, etc., to stand to the award and arbitration of certain lords and judges so that the said award be made by the first day of March next.

The king will and chargeth both the said earl and Bonville so to do.

And considering that the said office hath as it is supposed to be great cause of the said debate, wherefore the king wills that neither of them shall occupy it as yet, but that an indifferent man shall occupy it.

(b) FROM: Ibid., 408

November 1441

By the King [to the earl of Devon]

Right trusty and well beloved cousin, it must needs be in your fresh remembrance that at your last being with us and our council ye were willed, desired, and also commended upon pain of £1,000 that neither you nor none of yours should trouble our peace nor bear no hurt to our liege people and especially to our right trusty and well beloved the Lord Bonville, his servants, nor tenants, the which notwithstanding, as we are informed, whereof we marvel, there have divers of the said servants and tenants since that time grievously been let and hurt by such as belong unto you whose names we send to you enclosed herein. For so much we write unto you, willing and charging you straightly upon pain of £[blank] that you, demeaning as it appears to, your estate, attempt nothing by you nor none of yours, nor suffer to be attempted [anything] whereby

our peace may be hurt or troubled, calling to mind what jeopardy you
stand in as towards the said pain if it so be as it is surmised. And over
this we will and charge you that you come and be with us and our said
council at our palace of Westminster, the 25th day of this present
month, there to answer to the premises and such other things as shall be
opened and declared unto you at your coming, having with you there at
that time the said persons whose names we send unto you herein as
above. Given [etc.].

Thomas Phillip Walshman
John Hoye late of Bokevell
Thomas Davy late of Honyton
William Appulton
Thomas Inglond
John Knoweston

(c) FROM: *Rot. Parl.*, V. 285–6

Item, the Monday the 17th day of the said month of November, it was
shown to the said lieutenant and all the lords, by the mouth of Burley,
accompanied in notable number of the commons, in the name of all their
fellows, that how the said commons had divers times made requests to
their good lordships, that they should be good means to the king's
highness, that there might be chosen and made a protector and defensor
of this land, of the which requests as yet they have no answer. And
where as it is yet thought by them that be come to this high court of
parliament for the commons of this land; for as much as this day they
have knowledge and understanding by such persons which the said
lords send to them, that there be great and grievous riots done in the
West Country at the city of Exeter, by the earl of Devonshire, accompanied with many riotous persons, as it is said with 800 horsemen and
4,000 footmen, and there have robbed the church of Exeter and taken
the canons of the same church and put them to 'fynaunce' and also took
the gentlemen in that country, and done and committed many other
great and heinous inconveniences; that in abridging of such riots and
inconveniences, such a protector and defensor must be had, and that
they might have knowledge of him, his power, and authority; and that
he, in abridging of such riots and offences, should ride and labour into
that country, for but if the said riots and inconveniences were resisted,
it should be the cause of the loss of that land, and if that land were lost,
it might be cause of the subversion of all this land, wherefore they that
be come for the commons of this land, desired the said lieutenant and
lords, for as much as the Holy Feast of Christmas approaches, so nigh,
that rather than the land shall be lost, it might like the said lieutenant
and all the lords, this present parliament to prorogue, adjourn, or dis-

solve, to the intent that these said riots and inconveniences might be resisted.

(*d*) FROM: Ibid., 332 (1455: 33 Henry VI)

To the King our sovereign Lord, Prayen the Commons:

That where divers, many and great riots, commotions of your people, robberies and murder have been done in the shires of Cornwall, Devonshire and Somerset between Thomas, earl of Devonshire, his servants and adherents on the one party, and William Bonville, knight, Lord Bonville, his servants and adherents on the other party, to the over great hurt of these parties, and likely to be perpetual destruction thereof, without due remedy be had in that behalf. Wherefore please it your highness, for part of remedy thereof, to ordain and establish by the advice and assent of the lords spiritual and temporal in this present parliament assembled, and by authority of the same, that as well the said earl, as the said William Bonville, knight, shall be and abide in prison without bail or mainprise, till your commissioners of oyer and terminer be directed by indifferent commissions, to inquire, hear and determine all the premises; and into that time that all the premises, by virtue of that commission, be fully determined and executed. And that by the said authority, Andrew Hillersdon, now sheriff of the said county of Devonshire which is supposed verily to be unlawfully favourable to the party of the said William Bonville, intermeddle not as sheriff of any process dependent upon the said commissioners, but that by the same authority another person, indifferent, be ordained to execute all the processes dependent upon the said commission that belong to the office of sheriff to execute and serve.

The king will be advised.

56. A Local Quarrel

FROM: *PPC*, V, 305–6

12 July 1443 (21 Henry VI)   Be there made a letter to the Lord Grey of Ruthin reciting how that the king is informed that there is division, dissension, discord and debate between him on the one party and the town of Northampton on the other party wherethrough inconvenience might fall, that God defend. And therefore the king wills and charges

him straightly as he will eschew his grievous indignation that to the said town neither to no one of him coming to the town nor going out of the town to market or elsewhere nor being in any place in the said town or without it, he in his person, neither by him nor by his abetment nor procuring to do no harm to any of the said town. But that he do and see that the peace be kept against him in all manner wise.

57. Local Disorder and Elections (27 May 1454)

FROM: *PPC*, VI, 183–4

To the right honourable and most discreet council of the king, our sovereign lord.

Sheweth unto your right honourable and wise discretion that John, duke of Norfolk, at the shire meeting held at Ipswich in the shire of Suffolk, the Monday next after the feast of St Valentine last, came with divers servants and tenants to the election of the knights of the shire for the last parliament, there to have given their voice to the knights of the shire according to the law of this land.

Thomas Sharnburn, at that time sheriff of the said shire, imagining and purposing to make knights of the shire after his own intent and for his singular purpose, and to hurt the servants and tenants of the said duke, returned in the Common Pleas a writ against many and divers servants and tenants of the said duke whose names be annexed to this bill, submitting by his return that his officers dared not hold the aforesaid shire meeting because of the affronts and threats made to his officers, as he returned in the Common Pleas aforesaid. Whereas the said servants and tenants of the said duke never made any such manner of force, threats nor affronts as the said sheriff has returned, but they peacable came to the shire house for the election of the knights of the shire after the law of this land. Wherefore please it your right wise and noble discreet lords to send our sovereign lord's letters to the justices of the Common Pleas commanding them to admit all the servants and tenants of the said duke contained in the said bill to appear by attorney and to answer the attorney, considering that full many of the said servants and tenants which are innocent persons be returned in the said complaint against all manner of reason and conscience, of the which servants divers and many were not there at that time, as shall sufficiently be proved at the reverence of God and in way of charity. . . .

In the Palace of Westminster, 27th May, etc., the 32nd year of King Henry VI, by advice of his council in the presence of the above named lords, the king ordered the keeper of the privy seal to make his seal to the letters . . .

58. Parliamentary Elections

(a) FROM: H. G. Richardson, 'John of Gaunt and the Parliamentary Representation of Lancashire', *Bulletin of the John Rylands Library* (1938), XXII, 47. (PRO, DL d/1/123)

On Behalf of the king of Castile and of Leon, duke of Lancaster. [to the chancellor of the Duchy of Lancaster].

Very dear and well beloved. Because we have been commanded and charged by our very redoubtable lord the king to ordain two able and sufficient knights from within our duchy of Lancaster, and from each city two citizens and of each borough two burgesses within our same duchy, who are to be at Westminster the quinzaine of Easter next to come, in the parliament which will be held in that day and place, we order and charge you, by writ under our great seal, that Monsieur Adam de Hoghtone and Monsieur Roger de Pylkyngtone or Monsieur William de Athyrtone should be at that parliament on the said day, and with regard to the two citizens and burgesses, we order that you ordain and carry out this writ as it seems best to you, that they be at the said parliament, at the place and day aforesaid. And do not omit to do this. And may Our Lord protect you.

Given, under our signet, at Doncaster, the 5th day of March.

(b) FROM: Ibid., 47–8 (DL 42/14, fo. 18b)

To cause Monsieur John Butiller and Monsieur William de Athertone to be warned to be at the next parliament.

John, etc., to our dear and well beloved friend, Monsieur Nicholas de Haryngton, our sheriff of Lancaster, greetings.

Because we have elected our very dear and well beloved bachelors, Monsieur John Buttiller and Monsieur William de Athertone as good and sufficient men to be at the next parliament, among others of our duchy, they are to treat there and to do what pertains in accordance with the writ under our lord the king's great seal which was directed to us.

We order you to accept and to receive for this business the aforesaid Monsieur John and Monsieur William, elected by us, as has been stated, and cause them to be duly warned to be among the others at the parliament at Westminster on the Monday next after the Feast of St Hilary next to come, and to do what pertains to them in this matter. And also we order you to make good and due execution of the writ which we sent you under our great seal touching the aforesaid business, according to the purport of it, so that neither default nor slackness be found in you in anything touching your office. And do not neglect this.

Given, etc. at Newark, the 17th day of November, the year, etc., the third [of Richard II: 1380].

(c) FROM: *PL*, no. 119 (16 October 1450?)

[The duke of Norfolk to John Paston]

Right trusty and well beloved, we greet you well.

And forasmuch as our uncle of York and we have fully appointed and agreed upon two persons to be knights of the shire of Norfolk as our said uncle and we think convenient and necessary for the welfare of the said shire, we therefore pray you, in our said uncle's name and ours as well, as you hope to stand in the favour of our good lordship, that you do not labour contrary to our desire. And God have you in his keeping.

Written at Bury St Edmunds, the 16th day of October.

(d) FROM: Ibid., no. 120 (18 October 1450?)

[The earl of Oxford to John Paston]

Right well beloved, I greet you well.

And as touching upon tidings, I have naught to say, saving that my lord of Norfolk met with my lord of York at Bury on Thursday, and there they were together until Friday, 9 of the clock, and then they departed. And there a gentleman of my lord of York gave to a yeoman of mine, John Deye, a token and a sign of my lord's intent, i.e. whom he would have as knights of the shire, and I send you a note enclosed in this letter with their names, wherefore I think we do well to perform my lord's intent.

Written the 18th day of October, at Wynche.

County of Norfolk: Sir William Chambirlayn
Henry Grey

(e) FROM: Ibid., no. 244 (8 June 1455)

[The duchess of Norfolk to John Paston]

Right trusty and well beloved, we greet you heartily well.

And for as much as it is thought right necessary for divers causes that my lord have at this time in parliament such persons as belong to him, and be of his menial servants, wherein we conceive your good will and diligence to be advantageous, we heartily desire and pray you that at the contemplation of these letters of ours, as our special trust is in you, you will give and apply your voice on behalf of our right well beloved cousin and servants, John Howard and Sir Roger Chambirlayn, to be knights of the Shire, exhorting all others whom your wisdom shall help lead, to the good execution and conclusion of this business.

And in your faithful attendance and true labour in this matter you shall do a thing of great pleasure to my lord and to us, and cause us hereafter to thank you, as you shall be agreeable and contented with the grace of God, who shall ever have you in his keeping.

Written at Framlingham Castle, the 8th day of June.

59. Marriage Agreement (1445: 23 Henry VI)

FROM: PRO, DL 41/2/8

This be the appointment, accord, and conclusions made the 10th day of August, the 23rd year of the reign of King Henry the Sixth, by the high and mighty prince John, duke of Exeter upon the one party and Thomas, Lord Scales, Sir John Fastolf, and Sir Andrew Ogard, commissioners [together] with Ralf, Lord Cromwell, having full power and authority of Richard, duke of York under his seal of his arms to entreat, appoint and conclude with the said duke of Exeter for marriage to be had by the grace of God between Sir Henry, son and heir apparent of the said duke of Exeter and Anne, daughter of the said duke of York, the tenor of which power binds with these words Richard, duke of York, etc., in manner and form that follows:

First, it is appointed, awarded and agreed that the said Henry shall by the grace of God wed and take to wife the said Anne, daughter of the said duke of York within half a year next after the date hereof, lawful dispensation within the same half year therefore had. And moreover it is appointed, awarded and agreed between the said duke of Exeter and the said commissioners that the said duke of Exeter within six months after the marriage had between the said Henry and Anne, the said duke of Exeter shall make or do to be made a fair and sufficient estate to certain persons as well named by the said duke of York as by the said duke of Exeter of certain lordships, manors, lands and tenements in England, to the yearly value of 400 marks, over the reprises and charges. To have and to hold the said lordships, manors, lands, and tenements to the said persons so to be named to their heirs and assignes to the intent that the same feoffees shall make or do to be made a sure and sufficient estate unto the said Henry when he shall be of the age of 16 years and to the said Anne that time being his wife. To have and to hold certain lordships, manors, lands and tenements parcel of the same to the yearly value of £100 over the charges and reprises to the said Henry and Anne and to their heirs of their body lawfully coming. And for default of such issue which God defend, the remainder thereof to the said duke of Exeter and to his heirs and of the remains of the said lordships, manors, lands and tenements, the said feoffees shall make a sure and sufficient estate at the said 16th year to the said Sir Henry and Anne, to have and to hold the said lordships, manors, lands and tenements to them both and to their heirs male of the body of the said Henry lawfully coming, and for default of such issue which God defend, the remainder thereof to the said duke of Exeter and to his heirs, provided always that the said estate shall be made by the said feoffees unto the said Henry and Anne, and delivery made upon such conditions that if the said Anne disagree to such marriage before her age of 13 years so that by such disagreement the said marriage is void, that then the estate of the said lordships, manors, lands and tenements so made to the said Henry and Anne be void, cease and endure no longer. And so immediately after such disagreement and voidance of marriage the said lordships, lands and tenements remain to the said duke of Exeter and his heirs. And so happen that after marriage had between the said Henry and Anne the said Henry die before the age of 16 years, which God defend, the said Anne so married being alive, then the said feoffees shall do and make a sure and sufficient estate or parcel of the said lordships, lands, manors and tenements to the yearly value of 300 marks over all charges and reprises to the said Anne for term of her life. The remainder thereof to the said duke of Exeter and to his heirs and for the said marriage in the form above, as appointed awarded and agreed by the said commissioners. That the said duke of York shall pay or do to be paid to the said duke of Exeter the sum of 4,000 marks and 500 marks in manner and form following. That is, to pay the day of the said marriage to the said Henry and Anne £1,000, and 1,000 marks the same day 12 months then next following, and a 1,000 marks the next following. And also it is accorded, appointed and agreed by the said commissioners that the said duke of York shall in the day of marriage find sufficient surety to the said duke of Exeter to pay or do to be paid to the said duke the remainder of the said sum of 4,000 marks and 500 marks at the day and hour rehearsed; and if the said Anne die, which God defend, afore any estate made to her in the said manors, lands and tenements after marriage had as it is before rehearsed, that then the said duke of Exeter or his executors shall pay to the said duke of York or to his executors half the sum of money of that that the said duke of Exeter or his executors then shall have received for the said marriage within two years next after the death of the said Anne. And the said duke of Exeter or his executors shall release and quitclaim, by his deed enancealed sufficient in the law, all accounts that they may have for the residue of the said sum of 4,500 marks. And if the said Henry disagree him to the said marriage so that the said marriage be void in the law by such disagreement, then the said duke of Exeter or his executors shall repay to the said duke of York or his executors all that the said duke of Exeter or his executors then shall have received for the said marriage within two years . . .

Also, it is appointed, accorded and concluded between the said prince the duke of Exeter, the said Thomas, Lord Scales, Sir John Fastolf, and Sir Andrew Ogard, knights, commissioners aforesaid, that their said appointments, accords and conclusions shall be made in form of indenture and enancealed with the seals of the said two princes and signed with their sign manual in as goodly haste as it may be done. In witness whereof to this schedule remaining toward the said mighty prince the duke of Exeter, the said Lord Scales, Sir John Fastolf, and Sir Andrew Ogard, knights, have put to their seals and signs manual, the day and year aforesaid.

60. Aspects of Aristocratic Marriage

(a) FROM: *CPL* (1404–15), VI, 456

16 Kalends February, 1415   To Edmund, earl of March and Ulster. Dispensation to him – who desires to have children, but being related to divers magnates cannot find a wife suitable to his rank whom he can marry without papal dispensation – to marry a fit woman related to him in the third degree of kindred or affinity.

(b) FROM: Ibid. (1362–1404), V, 375

12 Kalends November, 1390   To the bishop of Ely. Mandate to separate for a time and then to absolve from the sentence of excommunication incurred by marrying, knowing that they were related in the fourth degree of affinity, Thomas de Morley, knight and Anne de Despenser, damsel, of the diocese of Norwich; to grant dispensation to

them to contract marriage anew and remain therein, and to declare past
and future offspring legitimate. Thomas and Anne told Henry, bishop
of Norwich, who ought to have been written to in this case, for a certain
reason suspect. Whichever of the two survive the other shall remain
perpetually unwed.

(c) FROM: Ibid., p. 67

Kalends of July, 1369   To the archbishop of Canterbury. Mandate, on
petition of King Edward, to dispense, if the facts be as stated, John de
Hastings, earl of Pembroke, and Ann, daughter of Walter de Many,
knight, damsel, of the dioceses of Canterbury and Cambray, to intermarry, notwithstanding that Ann was related, in the third and fourth
degrees of kindred, to the late Margaret, daughter of King Edward,
damsel, whom the said earl had married. The said earl and Ann are
exhorted, if the dispensation be granted, to give 1,000 gold florins
towards the repair of the church of the monastery of St Paul, Rome.

(d) FROM: Ibid., 545

Kalends of September, 1396   Ratification and confirmation of the
marriage contracted by John, duke of Lancaster, and Catherine de
Swynforde, damsel, of the diocese of Lincoln, with dispensation to
remain therein, offspring past and future being declared legitimate.
Their petition contained that formerly, after the death of his wife
Constance, duke John and Catherine contracted and consummated
marriage (not being ignorant that John had been godfather to a daughter
of Catherine by another husband, and that, afterwards, while Constance
was still alive, he had committed adultery with the said Catherine, an
unmarried woman, and had offspring by her); and that they considered
such marriage to be lawful, inasmuch as, the said impediment of com-
paternity not being notorious but private, their orator to the apostolic
see had taken back to them from the pope a letter of credence marked
by the pope's hand, and related to them that, as was also contained in the
letter itself, the pope had given his *viva voce* consent. They now doubt
lest, the said impediment having been afterwards divulged and apostolic
letters on the subject of such consent not being forthcoming, their
marriage may not be impugned, divorce follow, and grave scandals arise.

(e) FROM: CFR, 1307–19, 380

20 November 1318   Order to the escheator beyond Trent to take into
the king's hands all the lands which Ralph de Monte Hermerii and
Isabella, his wife, late the wife of John de Hastings, tenant in chief, held

in her dower of the lands late of the said John, she having married the said Ralph without licence; and to keep the same safely until further order, answering for the issues there at the exchequer.

(*f*) FROM: Rymer, II, i, 181 (12 August 1319)

The King, to all to whom this comes, greetings.

Know that, regarding the fine of 1,000 marks which our beloved and faithful Ralph de Monte Hermerii made to us, we have pardoned his transgression which he committed by entering into marriage with Isabella, who was the wife of the late John de Hastings, who held from us as a tenant in chief, and we have pardoned the transgression of that same Isabella, who married the aforesaid Ralph without having obtained our licence therefor.

We do not wish the aforesaid Ralph and Isabella to be molested or held to any threats or damages because of this matter.

Witnessed by the king at Gofford, Northumberland, the 12th day of August.

And it is ordered to William de Stoweford that the lands, tenements, goods and chattels of the aforesaid Ralph and Isabella, which on the occasion of the aforesaid transgression were taken into the king's hands and put into the custody of the aforesaid William by the king's commission, now be restored without any delay.

(*g*) FROM: *CPR*, 1317–21, 582

18 May 1321   Pardon, to Ralph de Monte Hermerii and Isabella, his wife, late the wife of John de Hastings, tenant in chief, of the 1,000 marks by which the said Ralph made fine for the trespass committed by the said Isabella in marrying him without licence.

61. An Unequal Marriage

FROM: *CPL* (1427–47), VIII, 601

3 Nones, May, 1436   To Roger Wentworth, donsel, lord of Parlyngton, in the diocese of York, and Margery, lady of Roos, his wife. Grant – at their recent petition – containing that they contracted marriage lawfully *per verba de presenti*, consummated it and had offspring, but could

not have the marriage solemnised before the church after the custom of
the country because, being unequal in nobility, they feared that scandals
might arise between their kinsmen and friends; and afterwards they had
the said marriage, thus consummated, solemnised within the bounds of
the parish church of Hemyngburgh in the said diocese, without banns,
and without the solemnisation wont by the custom of the country to be
made before the church, further offspring being born thereof; and
adding that they are moved by a scruple of conscience to doubt whether
anyone may hesitate as to the validity of the marriage thus contracted –
that the said marriage contracted between them and all in consequences
hold good as if it had not been clandestine, but had been proclaimed and
solemnised before the church, with banns and wonted solemnisations,
all the said offspring and likewise future offspring being hereby declared
legitimate.

62. Marriage without a Royal Licence

(a) FROM: Rymer, II, i, 101 (1316)

The King, to all to whom this comes, etc., Greetings.

Know that we lately conceded to Piers de Gaveston, then earl of
Cornwall and now dead, the marriage of Thomas Wake, son and heir of
John Wake, also dead, who held in chief from the Lord Edward,
formerly king of England, our father. Thomas is under age and is in our
custody and the disparagement of his marriage is involved in this.

And after the death of the said earl the same Thomas, being under
age, married elsewhere when we had obtained his marriage, and he did
so without obtaining a licence from us. We, wishing a special favour to
our aforesaid kinsman, granted him the marriage but the aforesaid
Thomas has done us an injury by marrying without our licence.

In which, etc.

Witnessed by the King at York, 9th day, October 1316.

(b) FROM: CPR, 1317–21, 251–2

9 December 1318   Pardon to Thomas Wake, son and heir of John
Wake, tenant in chief, for refusing whilst under age and in the king's
custody, a suitable marriage offered to him by the king, and afterwards,
when he had attained full age, for marrying elsewhere without licence.

For this pardon he has made a fine of £1,000, whereof the king assigned 1,000 marks to be paid, as satisfaction, to Thomas de Multon of Egremond, and directed the remaining 500 marks to be paid to himself.

63. Divorce (of the Earl of Arundel)

(a) FROM: *CPL* (1342–62), 164

2 Nones, December, 1344   To the archbishop of Canterbury and the bishop of Chichester; mandate, on petition of Richard, earl of Arundel, and Isabella, daughter of Hugh de Despenser – who at the respective ages of seven and eight, not by mutual consent, but by fear of their relatives, contracted espousals, and on coming to years of puberty expressly renounced them, but were forced by blows to cohabit, so that a son was born – to summon the said parties and by canonical procedure annul the marriage, they having constantly lived apart, and providing for their son, so that they may be free to intermarry with others.

(b) FROM: Ibid., 188

2 Nones, July, 1345   To the bishops of Hereford and Chichester. Mandate at the request of King Edward and Queen Philippa, to grant a dispensation to Richard, earl of Arundel, and Eleanor, daughter of Henry, earl of Lancaster, to remain in the marriage which they contracted on Saturday in Sexagesima last. Richard had a son by Isabella de Despenser, who is related to the said Eleanor in the second, third and fourth degrees. A mandate was issued to the bishop of Chichester to grant a dispensation, but as it is now discovered that the parties are related also in the fourth degree of kindred on both sides, a further dispensation is necessary. They are to be separated for a time, and then absolved and dispensed. Three chaplaincies, as directed in the former mandate, are to be founded and endowed by them in Richard's castle of Arundel, wherein they intend to found others.

(c) FROM: Ibid., 254

2 Kalends, August, 1347   To the Archbishop of Canterbury and the bishops of London and Chichester. Mandate, on petition of Edmund de Arundel, to cite Richard, earl of Arundel, Isabella, daughter of Hugh

de Despenser, and Eleanor, wrongly called Joan de BelloMonte, touching the following matter: Earl Richard and Isabella married and begot Edmund, but Robert, bishop of Chichester, under pretext of papal letters, surreptitiously obtained, pronounced sentence of divorce between them, thus bastardising Edmund. Richard thereupon married Joan de BelloMonte, daughter of the uncle of Isabella. Papal commission was issued to William, cardinal of St Stephen's, to cite the said Richard, Isabella, and Joan, Edmund being then eighteen years old, Master Walter de Segrave and Geoffrey de Borgeys being proctors of Richard. After divers acts, it appeared that Joan should be called Eleanor, and that she was not daughter of Isabella's uncle, but daughter of Isabella's aunt. Edmund was by this time twenty years old, and the pope was petitioned to relax the impediment of age touching the taking of an oath, upon which the cardinal was commissioned to proceed in the cause, Edmund present, and Richard and Isabella by their proctors, Geoffrey de Burgeis and Simon de Sagio. Appeal was made against the citation of Richard, Isabella and Eleanor, and was heard before Imbert, cardinal of the Twelve Apostles, Edmund and Geoffrey being present, and Bartholomew de Bononia being proctor for Isabella. Cardinal Imbert supported the action of Cardinal William, and condemned the appellants in costs. Appeal against this was made by Earl Richard and Isabella, upon which the pope issued this mandate, viz. to cite them within twenty-three days, to appear in person or by their proctors at the papal court within sixty days.

64. Mythical Family History: The Earls of Warwick

FROM: John Rous, 'Historical Account of the Earls of Warwick', printed in Thomas Hearne, *Historia Vitae et Regni Ricardi II* (London 1727), 217–39 (this excerpt, 225–6)

. . . Dame Felice, daughter and heir to Sir Roland, for her beauty called Felice le Belle, or Felice the fair, by true inheritance was countess of Warwick, and lady and wife to the most victorious knight Sir Guy, to whom in wooing time she made great strangeness and caused him, for her sake, to put himself into many great dangers and perils. But when they were wedded together a little season, he departed from her, to his great heavyness, and never was he conversant with her to her understanding, and all that time she kept her clean and true lady and wife to him, devoted to Guy, and by way of alms, greatly helping them that were in poor estate.

Sir Guy of Warwick, flower and honour of knighthood, son to Sir Seyward, baron of Wallingford, and to his lady and wife Dame Sabyne, a Florentine, born in Italy, into this realm, as Dame Genches, St Martin's sister, born in Greekland, was married here and had in this land noble St Patrick, who converted Ireland to the Christian faith. This worthy knight Sir Guy, in his acts of war, ever considered what parties had wrong and thereto would he draw; by which doing his fame spread so far that he was called the worthiest knight living in his days. The Dame Felice, his special lady, applied to his will and was married to him.

This noble warrior Sir Guy, after his marriage, considering what he had done for a woman's sake, his wife, thought to bestow the other part of his life for Guy's sake, and departed from his wife in pilgrimage, and in a pilgrim's weed, and did many great battles, of the which the last was at Winchester, by the warning of an angel, where he had the victory of a mighty giant called Sir Colybround, and from thence he went unknown, saving to the king only, to Warwick, receiving, as a pilgrim, of his own lady and wife, his abiding at Gibcliff, and his livery by his page daily from the countess of Warwick, and two days before his death an angel informed him of his passage out of this life, and of his lady's that day a fortnight after him, and at Gibcliff they were both buried. For there could no man remove them from thence, until his sworn brother Sir Tirrye come, with whom he was translated without let . . .

65. Noble Family as Warriors: The Scropes (1386)

FROM: Sir Harris Nicolas, *The Scrope and Grosvenor Controversy* (London, 1832), II, 377, 323–4

Sir Richard Waldegrave, aged forty-eight, armed twenty-five years, deposed that the arms Azure, a bend Or, belonged to the Scropes, who were reputed to be of ancient lineage, as he had heard, in the lifetime of the earl of Northampton. He saw Sir Richard so armed in the expedition of the late king before Paris, and at the same time Sir Henry Scrope with his banner, on which were the said arms with a white label. And also beyond the Great Sea he saw Sir William Scrope so armed, with a label, in the company of the earl of Hereford at Satalia in Turkey, at a treaty which was concluded between the king of Cyprus and 'le Takka', lord of Satalia, when the king of Cyprus became lord of Satalia. At Balyngham Hill the banner of Sir Henry was displayed; and in the expedition into Caux, when the lord of Lancaster was commander-in-chief. Sir William Scrope, son of the said Sir Richard, was so armed, with a label. The deponent could not say which of the ancestors of Sir Richard first bore the arms, but since this dispute he had heard that his ancestors came direct from the Conquest; and, before this challenge, he had been informed that they were of ancient lineage; but he certainly never heard of any challenge or interruption offered by Sir Robert Grosvenor, or his ancestors, to the bearing of the arms in question.

Nicholas Sabraham, Esquire, aged sixty and upwards, armed thirty-nine years, said that the arms Azure, a bend Or, were the arms of Sir Richard Scrope, for he had seen the arms of Scrope on banner and coat-armour in the expedition of Sir Edward Balliol in Scotland, also on a banner in the company of the earl of Northampton, when he rode by torchlight out of Lochmaben as far as Peebles, and had in his company Sir Henry Scrope with his banner. The deponent also said that in the assemblage from all Christian countries at the instance of the king of Cyprus, when he meditated his expedition to Alexandria in ships and galleys, one Sir Stephen Scrope was present, armed in the arms of Scrope . . . and immediately on landing, received in those arms the order of knighthood from the king of Cyprus. He further said that he was armed in Prussia, In Hungary, at Constantinople, 'a la bras' of St George and at Messembre, at which latter place there is a church, and therein lies one of the Scropes buried, and beneath him there are depicted on the wall the arms of Scrope . . . The deponent saw Sir Henry Scrope armed in France with a banner in the company of the earl of Northampton, and Sir William Scrope, elder brother of the said Sir Richard, in the same company, armed in the entire arms, or with differences, at the battle of Crecy, at the siege of Calais, in Normandy, in Brittany, in Gascony, and in Spain, and beyond the Great Sea in many places and at many chivalrous exploits . . . He had often heard his ancestors say that the said Sir Richard and his ancestors had a right to the said arms, they having used them from beyond the time of memory, as he learned from old men, lords, knights and squires in his country, now no more . . .

66. Private Devotions

FROM: *A Collection of Ordinances and Regulations for the Government of the Royal Household* (London, 1790), 37

A compendious recitation compiled by the order, rules and constructions of the house of the right excellent princess, Cecill, late mother unto the right noble prince, King Edward the Fourth.

Me seemeth it is requisite to understand the order of her own person concerning God and the world.

She uses to rise at seven of the clock, and has ready her chaplain to say with her matins of the day, and matins of our lady; and when she is fully ready she has a low mass in her chamber, and after mass she takes something to recreate nature; and she goes to the chapel hearing the divine service, and two low masses; from thence to dinner the time whereof she hath a lecture of holy matter, either Hilton of contemplative and active life: Bonaventure de infancia, Salvatoris legenda aurea, St Maud, St Katherine of Sienna, or the Revelations of St Bridget.

After dinner she gives audience to all such as have any matter to show unto her by the space of one hour; and then sleeps one quarter of an hour; and after she has slept she continues in prayer unto the first peal of evensong; then she drinks wine or ale at her pleasure. Forthwith her chaplain is ready to say with her both evensongs; and after the last peal she goes to the chapel and hears evensong by note; from thence to supper, and in the time of supper she recites the lecture that was had at dinner to those that be in her presence.

After supper she disposes herself to be familiar with her gentlewomen, to the occasion of honest mirth; and one hour before her going to bed she takes a cup of wine, and after that goes to her privy closet, and takes her leave of God for all night, making end of her prayers for that day, and by 8 of the clock is in bed. I trust to our Lord's mercy that this noble princess thus divides the hours to his high pleasure.

67. Family Involvement with the Church: The Beauchamps

FROM: *CPL* (1362–1404)

(*a*) p. 31: 3 Kalends September, 1363:
To John Bellocampo, knight, and Elisabeth, his wife, of the diocese of Worcester. Indult to enter, once a year, with six honest matrons, the monasteries of Denney, in the diocese of Ely, in which their daughter Elisabeth is a nun, and Newcastle in that of London.

(*b*) p. 36: 4 Kalends December, 1363:

To John Bellocampo, knight, and Elisabeth, his wife, of the diocese of Worcester. Indult to choose their confessor, who may also give leave to religious of mendicant orders to eat flesh-meat at the table of the said knight on lawful days.

(*c*) p. 40: 7 Ides May, 1364:

To the bishop of Worcester. Mandate, after consideration of the circumstances touching the fitness of John de Bellocampo, scholar, of illegitimate birth, to dispense him to be ordained and to hold two benefices.

(*d*) p. 5: 4 Kalends December, 1363:

To Thomas de BelloCampo, earl of Warwick. The pope has received with joy his letters, in which he offered himself and a large company of knights to serve the Church; but as the pope hopes to make peace with his enemies, there is no need at present for their services, which he is ready to accept when they are required. He hopes to see the earl at the apostolic see, and will grant his requests as far as possible.

(*e*) 9: 8 Ides May, 1364:

To Amadeus, count of Savoy. Requesting safe-conduct through his territory for Thomas de BelloCampo, earl of Warwick, and his English companions on their way to the Holy Land.

(*f*) p. 10: 2 Kalends July, 1364:

To Thomas, earl of Warwick. Exhorting him to carry out his purpose
of joining the crusade, and commending him to Peter, patriarch of
Constantinople, papal legate.

(*g*) p. 39: 5 Ides May, 1364:

Relaxation of three years and three quadragenes to penitents who on the
feasts of the Blessed Virgin visit the church of St Mary Warwick, in
which the ancestors of Thomas de Bello Campo, earl of Warwick,
founded a college for a dean and seven canons; and one year and 40 days
to those who visit and give alms for the repair of the same on the other
principal feasts of the year.

68. Into a Monastery (1343)

FROM: PRO, Inquisitions Post Mortem, C 135/66, no. 37

Inquisition made at Oxford before Robert FitzElys, escheator of the lord
king in the county of Oxford, 18th day of May, year of the reign of King
Edward III after the Conquest, 16, and of his reign in the kingdom of
France, 3.

This inquisition was taken according to the tenor of writs of the lord
king. By oath of Henry de Benwelles, John Jordan, Thomas Debenhalle,
Thomas de Stapenhull, Roger de Stoke, Walter de Lewe, Simon de
Lewe, John De Lewe, Richard Saunders, William Wells, Thomas
Frankeleyn, and Thomas Page: who say that Robert de Isle, who was a
servant of religion, is dead and he held nothing of land or tenements of
the lord king in chief, nor of any other lord within this bailiwick on the
day on which he died. And they say that John de Isle, son of the aforesaid Robert, is his nearest heir, and is aged 24 years. And they say that
the aforesaid Robert, for a long while before he assumed the habit of
religion, conceded to Alice, daughter of Robert de Insula, Elizabeth
Peverel, Richard de Baoicis, William de Ruston, Edmund de Benhale,
and Henry Ewenny the manor of Heyford Warin with its appurtenances in the aforesaid county of Oxford, for the term of their lives,
done by fine in the court of the lord king, and levied before John de
Stonore and his companions, justices of the lord king at Westminster,

three weeks from the day of St Michael, in the year of the present king, 13. And they say that the aforesaid manor is held of the duke of Cornwall by service of one-fifth of a knight's fee. And they say that the aforesaid manor is worth, per annum, in all and singular profits, £30.

To which things the aforesaid jurors bear witness.

Given in the day and place aforesaid.

69. Vow of Chastity

FROM: *CPL* (1305–42), p. 544

6 Ides of July, 1338   To the bishop of Lincoln. Mandate to warn and compel, by spiritual penalties, Alesya de Lascy, countess of Lincoln, widow, aged above 60, who on her husband's death made a vow of chastity and received in token thereof a habit and ring, to observe the same, she having been ravished by Hugh Freyn, knight, and having afterwards consented to live with him in matrimony until his death. Those who attempt to make her break her vow are to be visited with ecclesiastical censure.

70. Bequests to Relatives: The Will of Ralph, Lord Neville (11 March, 1388)

FROM: T. Madox, *Formulare Anglicanum* (London, 1702), 427–30

Item, to Ralph, my son and heir, 2 beds of the best silk, 6 beds with curtains, 12 beds with tapestries: 1 set of green hangings with my arms: 1 blue hanging with a cover and a bed of the same material: 6 dozen dishes: 4 dozen saucers: 8 two-quart pots, 4 gallon pots, 24 drinking cups, 4 dozen spoons, 8 flat dishes, 6 basins with 2 ewers, 1 drinking cup with a silver cover and 6 cups with covers, of which 1 is gold and 5 are gilded; all my animals for plowing, carting and wagon-pulling at my manors of Holton, Snap, Dighton, Middleham, Raby, Brauncepath and Claveryng: all my corn belonging to the said manors, either growing or in the granary or in sheaves: 200 calves: 200 steers and bullocks: 2,000 sheep, of which 1,000 are in the bishopric of Durham and 1,000 in the county of York: 2 sets of chapel vestments, 1 being black with my arms, and 1 white and red: 4 best altar clothes.

Item, to Thomas, my son: 24 silver dishes, 12 saucers, 2 basins and 2 ewers, 6 silver pieces, 2 of which are with covers and 4 without: 1 cup with a gold cover: 1 bed of pale silk, coloured red and black: 300 marks in silver or in the equivalent value in my goods and cattle.

Item, to Lord William Neville, my brother: 1 bed in green powdered material, with falcons thereon, and 1 set of tapestries: 12 silver dishes.

Item, to Lady Euphemia de Heslarton, my sister: 1 cup with a gilt cover and 2 pair of gold bears.

Item, to Lady Eleanor, my sister, a minoress: 100 marks for the building work on the House of the St Clares without Algate, London.

Item, to Elizabeth, my sister, a minoress in the same place, 40 marks.

Item, I give and bequeath to the said Elizabeth and the aforesaid house of St Clare, London, 15 marks annually from the revenues of my household in London for the term of life of the said Elizabeth.

Item, to Alesia Deyncourt, my daughter: 12 dishes, 6 saucers, and 2 two-quart pots of silver.

Item, to Lady Matilda le Scrope, my daughter: 12 dishes, 12 silver saucers, and 1 cup with a gilt cover.

Item, to Eleanore de Lumley, my daughter: 2 canopied beds of Norfolk with curtains, 12 dishes, 6 saucers, and 2 pots, 2 two-quart pots, 2 basins with lavers, 40 calves and 20 heifers for 4 years.

Item, to Lord Richard LeScrope: 2 basins with lavers of silver and 1 large chalice and a cooking pan.

Item, to Lady Elizabeth de Neville, wife of Lord William Neville, my brother: 1 silver cup with a gilt cover.

Item, to the lord archbishop of York, my brother: 1 set of red velvet vestments . . .

Item, to Lord Robert Neville of Hornby: 2 basins, 2 ewers, and 1 silver cup with a gilt cover . . .

Item, to the said Alice Deyncourt, my sister: 1 bed with red needle-point or another bed from the same place if someone else gets the first one . . .

Item, I leave for the marriage of Elizabeth, my daughter, if she is alive and unmarried, 1,000 marks . . .

71. Family Foundation and Bequests: The Montagues and Bisham Priory

(a) FROM: *CChR* (1327–41), IV, 471

3 February, 1339   Inspeximus of a charter in favour of the prior and convent of Bustlesham dated at Westminster, 22 April, 11 Edward III [1327], and confirmation of the same, notwithstanding an ordinance lately made by the king and certain of his council for the revocation of all charters and letters of quittance of tallages, taxation, customs and other divers liberties made by the king or his progenitors to any person whatever. Noticing that certain chantries and other works of piety have been there established to pray for the health of the king and his consort and their children during life and for their souls after death and for those of their progenitors and heirs and also for the soul of William de Monte Acuto, earl of Salisbury, the founder, and desiring to provide for the security of the prior and convent therein, the king ratifies hereby the said grants and confirmations, and grants that the prior and convent shall enjoy the said liberties and quittances, notwithstanding the said ordinance; and also that they shall have return of all the king's writs and summons of the exchequer and attachments of all pleas in the manor of Bustleham Montague, where the priory is situated, in the usual form; and that they shall have there infangenthef and outfangenthef in the manor of Bustlesham and all liberties thereto belonging without impediment; and that they shall have free warren in all their demesne lands of the same manor, and in all other demesne lands which they now have or which may be granted to them; and that the prior and convent shall be quit of the taking and prise of wool, victuals and other goods for the king's use, even if a subsidy thereof be granted to the king by the clergy or commonalty of the realm, which quittance shall apply to the subsidy of wools granted in the 12th year in parliament at Westminster, and to the ordinance for levying the same made in the great council assembled at Northampton by the prelates, magnates and commonalty there present.

(b) FROM: *TV*, 101 (21 November 1378)

Philippa de Mortimer, countess of March, at Plumstead, November 21 1378.

My body to be buried in the conventual church of the Holy Trinity in the priory of Bustlesham Montagu. I bequeath to the said church of Bustlesham all the furniture of my chapel, vestments, books, chalices, etc., to the use of the altar of St Anne, before which my body shall be buried, in the second arch, near the body of my honoured lord and father, on whom God have mercy, excepting my best vestment with three capes which I devise to the abbey of Wigmore, and my white vestment which I bequeath to the house of Lyngbrok. To the said altar of St Anne, a table of the best gold, which I bought of John Raulyn; also for the use of the said altar two basins of silver, enamelled with the arms of Mortimer and Montague . . .

(c) FROM: Chichele, II, 14–15 (24 November 1414)

[from the will of Elizabeth Montague, countess of Salisbury]:

. . . First I humbly commend my soul to God and his blessed mother and to all the saints, requiring mercy for all my sins, and that part which I leave at death I choose to be buried by Holy Church for my body in the conventual church of Bisham Montague. Also, I will that where I die, there vespers and the requiem mass are to be said in the morning, and each priest who is at the said service is to have 12d. Item, then I will that my body be carried to Bisham, reposing on the way at certain places as is arranged at the discretion of my executors, and in each place I will that a requiem mass be done as directed in the evening and in the morning before my departure. And that I will that there be distributed on the way of my coming to Bisham, for masses and other costs, £20 or more or less as needs be done at the discretion of my said executors, beyond what I devise, especially to the houses of Bruton and the friars at Ilchester.

I will that in coming to Bisham that 24 poor be dressed, each one in a tunic with a russet hood, and each one carrying two wax torches at my dirge and the requiem mass at my burial. I will that there be given to each of the 24 said poor men 20d in money. I will that my hearse be covered entirely with a black drape. I will that 5 large wax candles be around my hearse, each of 20 pounds of wax.

Item, I will that there be distributed, on the day of my interment, among 1,000 poor people, 25 marks: to each of them, 4d.

Item, I will and ordain £12 10s 0d be spent for singing 3,000 masses after my death, in all haste that can be well done for my soul and for all Christians, and I will that 20s be paid to those who dispense the pennies paid for the said masses.

Item, I devise to the prior of Bisham, the day of my dirge and the next day, for services, 14s 4d, and to each canon there who is a priest, 6s 8d, and to others, 3s 4d. Item, I devise to each priest coming to my interment for the dirge and to sing mass in the morning, 12d.

Item, I devise £20 to buy russet cloth for 100 poor men and women: to each of them, a tunic with a hood.

Item, I devise £12 to two honest priests to sing masses daily and the trental of St Gregory, for an entire year, for my soul and for all Christians.

Item, I devise to 80 poor and bed-ridden men and women, £26 13s 4d: to each of them, 6s 8d.

Item, I devise to the prior of Bisham and his convent: to have, hold and sustain a canon priest and a secular priest at my altar and tomb, perpetually. This is to be done in the left part of the choir of the church, next to the tomb of my lord husband, and they to pray for my soul and others, and 400 marks is to be delivered for this purpose.

Item, I devise and ordain for the expenses of my burial, £40 and more, if needed, by the discretion of my executors. I will and ordain £20 for the purchase of black cloth for all my household on the day of my interment.

Item, I devise and ordain 100 marks to make and repair an altar and a new tomb for me and my son in the left part of the choir of the church at Bisham, next to my lord my husband.

Item, I devise and ordain that a chalice of silver with a set of black vestments, and another set of black vestments, to be given to my said altar for the use of the said canon and priest in the perpetual chantry ...

72. Dispensations for an Ecclesiastical Career: George Neville

(a) FROM: *CPL* (1447–55), 2

7 July 1447   To George Neville, son of Richard, earl of Salisbury, a canon of York. Dispensation to him (who is of royal lineage and in his fifteenth year, and holds a canonry of York with the prebend of Massam and of Salisbury with the prebend of Cheristoke, value not exceeding £120 and £30 sterling respectively) to receive and to hold for life any two benefices with cure or otherwise incompatible, even if parish churches or their perpetual vicarages, or elective dignities, major or principal, etc., and to resign them, simply or for exchange, as often as he pleases, and hold instead for life two other incompatible benefices, notwithstanding his defect of age and any constitutions, etc., to the contrary; provided that the cure of souls be not neglected.

(b) FROM: Ibid., 717

25 June 1454   To George Neville, archdeacon of Durham:
Dispensation to him, who is in deacon's orders, is a legitimate son of the
earl of Salisbury, chancellor of England, and has completed his twenty-
first year, to be, as soon as he has completed his twenty-second year,
promoted to the order of priest.

73. The Gift of Books
   (by Humphrey, Duke of Gloucester)

FROM: A. R. Myers, *English Historical Documents* (London, 1969),
IV, 893

To all the faithful in Christ, present and to come, it shall openly appear
that on 25th November, 1439, the University of Oxford established
and ordained, firstly, that for the firm and perpetual custody of the very
large and munificent gift of 129 volumes by the most serene prince and
lord the most renowned lord Humfrey, the son, brother, and uncle of
kings, the duke of Gloucester, earl of Pembroke, and great chamberlain
of England to our university, given by his very great liberality, and for
the custody of whatever volumes may be given in future by the same most
serene prince, a new register should be made, to be placed in a chest
with five locks, in which register shall be entered *seriatim*, openly and
expressly, all the books of the statutes of the university, and all the
names of the volumes now given, with a note of all their contents, and
also with the first word of the second folio of each book, so that it may
appear clearly to all if any of the said volumes or the contents of the
same, however rare or unknown, shall be lost, taken away, pulled out,
cut away, or extracted.

Also the aforesaid university established and ordained that none of
the aforesaid volumes or books or contents of them shall ever be sold or
given away or exchanged, or pledged, or handed or passed to anyone to
copy by quires nor carried out of the common library of the university,
except for the purpose of being bound or repaired, in which case it shall
be bound and repaired as quickly as possible, and carried back to the
library as fast as possible. Provided however, that if the aforesaid prince
shall by his own special letters wish any of the said volumes to be lent to
him for a certain time, then under indenture between his serenity and
the said university, the said volume shall at once and by way of a loan be
released by the university for a prescribed and limited period.

74. An Inventory of a Peer's Books

FROM: C. L. Kingsford, 'Two Forfeitures in the Year of Agincourt', *Archaeologia*, LXX, 71–100 (these selections are from pp. 93–4, taken from PRO, Exchequer, K. R. Account, 513/24, and p. 99, PRO, Exchequer, L.T.R., roll 6, mm. 9–10)

[The goods of Henry, Lord Lescrope of Masham, include . . .]

4 large antiphonaries, whence the first begins in the second folio, 'dree', the second in the second folio 'cum Dol patre', the third in the second folio 'chorus', the fourth in the second folio 'et bus'.

3 small antiphonaries, whence one begins in the second folio 'aspiciens', of the use of York, the second in the second folio 'letemur', the third in the second folio, 'ut letemur'.

1 martyrology of the use of York, in the second folio 'indoti'.

1 missal, in the second folio, 'fundus'.

1 old missal, in the second folio, 'exita'.

1 missal of the use of Bangor, in the second folio, 'clama'.

1 book called 'gospeller', in the second folio, 'ut', and 1 other, in the second folio, 'in medio'.

1 large legend, in the second folio, 'Iam'.

1 large legend of the saints, in the second folio, 'cuius'.

1 whole legend, in the second folio, 'conventus'.

6 graduals, whence the first begins in the second folio, 'dicto', the second in the second folio, 'fundatur', the third in the second folio, 'Gilius', the fourth in the second folio, 'venerit', the fifth in the second folio, 'niger', the sixth in the second folio, 'tes'.

1 collect, in the second folio, 'credo'.

3 ordinals, when the first begins in the second folio, 'similiter', the second in the second folio, 'beate', the third in the second folio, 'vel sic'.

2 journalia for mass of the Blessed Mary, whence the first begins in the second folio, 'Cum', the second in the second folio, 'Pasche'.

1 invitatorum, in the second folio, 'et folio'.

4 large processionals.

14 small processionals.

1 manual, in the second folio, 'pugnas'.

1 book of the life of St Brigid.

1 book for mass and matins, of St John of Bridlington.

1 book called 'Genesis', written in French.

1 bible.
1 book called Bede 'de gestis Anglie'.
1 book called 'de Sermonibus Dominicalibus'.

75. A Noble Author

FROM: The Duke of Suffolk, 'In praise of Margaret the Queen',
printed in R. H. Robbins (ed.), *Secular Lyrics of the XIVth and
XVth Centuries* (Oxford, 1956), 186–7

My heart is set, and all my whole intent,
To serve this flower in my most humble wise
As faithfully as can be thought or meant,
Without feigning or sloth in my service;
For know it well, it is a paradise
To see this flower when it begins to spread,
With colours freshly renewed, white and red.

And for the faith I owe unto this flower,
I must of reason do my observance
To my flowers all, both now and evermore,
Since fortune wills that it should be my chance
If that I could do service of pleasance;
Thus am I set and shall be til I starve
And for one flower, all others for to serve.

So would God that my simple cunning
Were sufficient this goodly flower to praise;
For now to me there is no thing so rich
That it were able to over-praise this flower.
O noble Chaucer, thy day is past
Of poetry named as the worthiest,
And of making in all other days the best –

Now thou are gone, thy help I may not have;
Wherefore to God I pray right specially,
Since thou are dead and buried in thy grave,
That on thy soul he wishes to have mercy;
And to the monk of Bury now speak I,
For thy cunning is such, and also thy grace,
After Chaucer, to occupy his place . . .

76. A Noble Author

FROM: Earl Rivers' Prologue to Dictes and Sayings of the Philosophers . . . in W. J. B. Crotch (ed.), *Caxton's Prologues* (Early English Text Society, O.S., 176 [1928], 111–12)

Where it is so that every human creature that by the sufferance of our Lord God is born and ordained to be subject and thrall unto the storms of fortune, And so in divers and sundry ways man is perplexed with worldly adversities, Of the which I, Anthony Wydeville, Earl Rivers, Lord Scales, etc., have largely and in many different manners had my part,

And of them relieved by the infinite grace and goodness of our said Lord through the help of the Mediatrice of Mercy, and gratitude has compelled me to set this down as I know and understand, and driven by reason and conscience as far as my wretchedness suffices to render singular lovings and thanks, and exhorts me to dispose my recovered life to his service in following his laws and commandments, and in satisfaction and recompense of my iniquities and faults previously done, therefore I seek and execute the works that might be most acceptable to Him, and so far as my frailties would suffer me, I rest in that will and purpose.

During that season I understood the Jubilee and pardon to be at the holy Apostle St James in Spain, which was the year of grace 1473. Then I determined me to take that voyage and shipped from Southampton in the month of July the said year, and so sailed from thence until I came into the Spanish Sea, there lacking sight of all lands, the wind being good and the weather fair.

Then for a recreation and a passing of time I had delight to read some good history. And among others there was that season in my company a worshipful gentleman called Louis de Bretaylles, who greatly delighted in all virtuous and honest things, and he said that he had there a book which he trusted I should like right well. He brought it to me, which book I have never seen before, and it is called the sayings or 'dictes' of the Philosophers . . .

Notes

INTRODUCTION

1 Marc Bloch, *Feudal Society*, trans. L. A. Manyon (Chicago, 1961), 283.
2 There is a general treatment of this in Otto Forest de Battaglia, 'The Nobility of Europe in the Middle Ages', *Comparative Studies in Society and History* (1962–3), V, 60–75.
3 McFarlane, *Nobility*, xxiii–xxiv, for a discussion of the qualifications which recent scholarship has placed upon Bloch's general formulation.
4 The parliamentary peerage is treated, biographically, in G. E. Cokayne, *The Complete Peerage*, Hon. Vicary Gibbs (ed.) (London, 1910–59), 13 volumes. That great reference work is also supplemented by L. O. Pike, *A Constitutional History of the House of Lords* (London, 1894), and J. E. Powell and Keith Wallis, *The House of Lords in the Middle Ages* (London, 1968).
5 There are a few attempts to treat the peerage's vital statistics with some historical concern: T. H. Hollingsworth, 'A Demographic Study of the British Ducal Families', *Population in History*, D. V. Glass and D. E. C. Eversley (eds) (London, 1965), 354–78, and 'The Demography of the British Peerage', Supplement to *Population Studies* (November 1964), XVIII (2): J. T. Rosenthal, 'Mediaeval Longevity and the Secular Peerage, 1350–1500', *Population Studies* (July 1973), XXVII (2), 287–93.
6 Homer, *Odyssey*, trans. Robert Fitzgerald (New York, 1963), VI, 105.
7 The other side of the coin held that no peasant could ever look at all noble. The famous description of the ugly (and probably negroid) churl in *Aucassin and Nicolette*, trans. P. Matarasso (Harmondsworth, 1971), 45, reveals the loathing of (white) genteel folk. For a general treatment, Beatrice White, 'Poet and Peasant', *The Reign of Richard II*, F. R. H. DuBoulay and C. Barron (eds) (London, 1971), 58–74.
8 Gottfried von Strassburg, *Tristan*, trans. A. T. Halto (Harmondsworth, 1960), 78–82.
9 These lines are taken from Bertran de Born's 'How I Like the Gay Time of Spring', *Medieval Age*, Angel Flores (ed.) (New York, 1963), 186–7.
10 Shakespeare, 1 Henry IV, II, iii, 49–57.

I

1 Men summoned to parliament by individual writs is the universe covered by G. E. Cokayne in *The Complete Peerage* (London, 1910–59). McFarlane, *Nobility*, is less precise and sometimes talks of the gentry, particularly the great captains (e.g. Sir Robert Knollys, Sir John Fastolf, etc.) along with the parliamentary peers. T. H. Hollingsworth, 'Demography of the British Peerage', Supplement to *Population Studies* (November, 1964), XVIII (2), used parliamentary peerage (plus wives and children) as the criterion for inclusion.
2 This 'evolutionary process, is briefly described in: D. L. Keir, *The Constitutional History of Modern Britain, 1485–1937* (London, 2nd edn, 1943), 41; J. E. A. Joliffe, *The Constitutional History of Medieval England* (London, 3rd edn, 1954), 436–40; L. O. Pike, *A Constitutional History of the House of Lords* (London, 1894), Chs VI and VII.

3 From the Paston Letters as quoted by McFarlane, *Nobility*, p. 124.
4 E. F. Jacob, *The Fifteenth Century* (Oxford, 1961), 326; McFarlane, *Nobility*, 276. I make no systematic distinction in this book between the different ranks of peers when I treat them in aggregate. Many of the distinctions between a baron and a duke were quantitative, but some reflect a degree of real difference. Another large area I have skirted concerns the degree to which peers were summoned because they held 'baronies' from the king. Since the modern conclusion is that tenure and peerage were not organically related, I have avoided a problem which is treated in *RDP*, I, 389–448; J. E. Powell and Keith Wallis, *The House of Lords in the Middle Ages* (London, 1968), 222–7, and I. J. Sanders, *Feudal Military Service in England* (Oxford, 1956).
5 Jacob, op. cit., 323.
6 William Stubbs, *The Constitutional History of England* (Oxford, 3rd edn, 1887), II, 192.
7 Keir, op. cit., 41.
8 The lists of summonses are printed in *RDP*, vols III and IV.
9 These figures are from C. H. Parry, *The Parliaments and Councils of England* (London, 1839), lv–lviii. Parry's statistics have been refined by F. M. Powicke and E. B. Fryde, *Handbook of British Chronology* (London, 2nd edn, 1961), 492–534. G. O. Sayles offers his own list for the fourteenth century, *The King's Parliament of England* (New York, 1974), 138–41.
10 McFarlane, *Nobility*, 142–67 on 'replacement rates'.
11 On the suspicion Richard aroused, and his efforts to allay the dire interpretations placed on his acts and words, see A. Tuck, *Richard II and the English Nobility* (London, 1973), 75, 167, 210, 220.
12 Powell and Wallis, op. cit., talk of the 'haphazard' way in which writs were issued, and examples of the practice are discussed on pp. 230, 309–11, 314–15, 317, 360, 370, etc. See R. W. Southern, *The Making of the Middle Ages* (New Haven, 1953), 12–13, for the rise of a permanent nobility, one of the 'quiet revolutions' of history.
13 Lords Bavent, FitzHenry, and Ripar (Rivers) as well.
14 Others included Clavering, Somery, Brewes, Nicholas Segrave, Thomas Verdun, and Tyeys.
15 Also, John de la Warre, Lord Beaumont, St Amand, and John Le Straunge of Knokyn.
16 The summonses to the parliament of 2 Henry IV are in *RDP*, IV, 773–4.
17 For restraints which governed the descent of new peerages see Cokayne, op. cit., IV, appendix H, 726–31, and VII, appendix A, 718–33. Sayles, op. cit., 126, for limitations upon the king's freedom.
18 N. Denholm-Young (ed. and trans.), *Vita Edwardi Secundi* (London, 1957), 1.
19 *RDP*, V, 18.
20 Ibid., 27.
21 Powell and Wallis, op. cit., 325–8, for the new creations of 1337.
22 *CPR*, 1334–8, 409–10.
23 G. A. Holmes, *The Estates of the Higher Nobility in Fourteenth-Century England* (Cambridge, 1957), 26–8.
24 *Rot. Parl.*, IV, 400.
25 As quoted in Faith Thompson, *A Short History of Parliament* (University of Minnesota, 1953), 32.

26 Cokayne, op. cit., vol. VIII, appendix A, 721–48 on 'The Ducal Title in the British Isles', and T. H. Hollingsworth, 'A Demographic Study of British Ducal Families', in *Population in History*, D. V. Glass and D. E. C. Eversley (eds) (London, 1965), 354–78.
27 *Rot. Parl.*, III, 488.
28 *RDP*, V, 235.
29 *Rot. Parl.*, III, 210.
30 Ibid., IV, 267.
31 For the surrender of peerages, Cokayne, op. cit., vol. III, appendix A, 589–91.
32 Tuck, op. cit., 101, 128, and A. Goodman, *The Loyal Conspiracy* (London, 1971), 87–94.
33 *RDP*, V, 381–2. Not only were the felons to lose their lives and goods, but none were to aid them lest they too 'upon pain of death and forfeiture of their goods and livelihood and of all that they may forfeit unto us, that they nor any of them in any wise from henceforth help, assist, favour or succour . . . the condemned parties'.
34 H. Ellis, *Original Letters illustrative of English History*, 2nd series, 4 volumes (London, 1827), I, 48.
35 V. J. Scattergood, *Politics and Poetry in the Fifteenth Century* (London, 1972), 185. This particular poem refers to the duke of Buckingham, killed at the Battle of St Albans.
36 Thomas Wright (ed.), *The Political Songs of England* (London, Camden Society, 1839), VI, 258–9.
37 Charles Bemont, *Simon de Montfort*, trans. E. F. Jacob (Oxford, 1930), 256–7, and C. H. Knowles, *Simon de Montfort, 1265–1965* (London, Historical Association, 1965), pamphlet G. 60.
38 For Arundel, see Tuck, op. cit., 189, and for Scrope, Scattergood, op. cit., 120–1.
39 Thomas Wright (ed.), *Political Poems and Songs*, Rolls series (London 1859–61), II, 256–7.
40 For the overwhelming verdict on Thomas as a person, see J. R. Maddicott, *Thomas of Lancaster, 1307–22* (London, 1970), 318–34.

II

1 M. Gluckman, 'Rituals of Rebellion in South-East Africa', *Order and Rebellion in Tribal Africa* (London, 1963), 110–36, and *Custom and Conflict in Africa* (New York, 1964). This insight has become trite through overuse, but it is a good check on mechanistic or unilinear explanations.
2 The 'ascending' and 'descending' theses of government are expounded by W. Ullman, *A History of Political Thought: The Middle Ages* (Harmondsworth, 1965).
3 Troilus and Cressida, I iii. The literature on the proper order of the world is voluminous. See V. J. Scattergood, *Politics and Poetry in the Fifteenth Century* (London, 1972), 272–3; J. Huizinga, *The Waning of the Middle Ages* (Harmondsworth, 1955 edition), especially Ch. III, 'The Hierarchic Conception of Society', and A. Ferguson, *The Indian Summer of English Chivalry* (Durham, 1960).
4 Maude Clarke, *Medieval Representation and Consent* (London, 1936), 197–9, and J. J. Bagley and P. B. Rowley (eds), *A Documentary History of England, 1066–1540* (Harmondsworth, 1966), I, 163–87.
5 Bagley and Rowley, op. cit., 164–5.
6 S. B. Chrimes, *English Constitutional Ideas in the Fifteenth Century* (Cambridge, 1936), 165–91.

7   F. J. Furnivall (ed.), *The Babees Book & The Bokes of Nurture* (London, Early English Text Society, 1868), O.S. 32, for a good collection of pamphlets on this subject.

8   I dealt with this, though I suspect with limited success, in 'The King's "Wicked Advisers" and Medieval Baronial Rebellions', *Political Science Quarterly* (1967), 595–618.

9   Charles Bemont, *Simon de Montfort*, trans. E. F. Jacob (Oxford, 1930), 154–5.

10 E. Barker, *The Dominican Order and Convocation* (Oxford, 1913): William Stubbs, *The Constitutional History of England* (Oxford, 3rd edn, 1887), II, 171–4; C. H. McIlwain, *Constitutionalism, Ancient and Modern* (Ithaca, 1947); G. O. Sayles, *The King's Parliament of England* (New York, 1974), 90; H. M. Cam, 'The Theory and Practice of Representation in Medieval England', reprinted in E. B. Fryde and E. Miller (eds), *Historical Studies of the English Parliament* (Cambridge, 1970), I, 262–78.

11 H. G. Richardson, 'The Commons and Medieval Politics', *Transactions of the Royal Historical Society*, 4th series (1946), XXVIII, 25–7; S. B. Chrimes, op. cit., 105, for the first use of the term, 'lords temporal', in 1385; L. O. Pike, *A Constitutional History of the House of Lords* (London, 1894), 260–5.

12 M. McKisack, *The Fourteenth Century* (Oxford, 1959), 173, quoting from Birchington: '*omnium Parium Regni terrae Angliae praejudicium manifestum ac perniciosum exemplum*'.

13 R. A. Griffiths, 'The Trial of Eleanor Cobham: An Episode on the Fall of Duke Humphrey of Gloucester', *Bulletin of the John Rylands Library* (1969), 381–99, and Scattergood, op. cit., 153: 'of glowcestre I was duchesse, /of all men I was magnifyed./As lucifer fell downe for pride,/So fell I from felicitie'.

14 *Rot. Parl.*, III, 459. The following number of lay peers were summoned to the early parliaments of Henry IV: in 1 Henry IV, to the Westminster Parliament, 50 (*RDP*, IV, 769); in 1 Henry IV, to the York Parliament, 35 (*RDP*, IV, 771); in 2 Henry IV, 47 (*RDP*, IV, 774); and in 3 Henry IV, 42 (*RDP*, IV, 777).

15 W. H. Dunham, *The Fane Fragment of the 1461 Lords' Journal* (New Haven, 1935), appendix B, 'Table of Attendances at 1461 Parliament', 93–6.

16 Charles Johnson (trans.), *Dialogue of the Exchequer* (London, 1950), 70.

17 *PPC*, VI, 187–8.

18 Ibid., 181–2.

19 J. E. Powell and Keith Wallis, *The House of Lords in the Middle Ages* (London, 1968), *passim*, for a comment on the various numbers summoned to different parliaments.

20 *PPC*, VI, 248; ibid., 65–6.

21 *RDP*, III, 224.

22 Dunham, op. cit., p. 19, 'Item this day there come up from the lower house a notable nomber of the substans of the same house. And in the parliament chamber without the barr, had communicacioun with my Lords . . .'

23 *Rot. Parl.*, III, 486.

24 Pike, op. cit., 284, and 258–64 for miscellaneous privileges enjoyed by peers.

25 *CPR*, 1461–7, 560, 576.

III

1   G. A. Holmes, *The Estates of the Higher Nobility in Fourteenth-Century England* (Cambridge, 1957), 4. The *Modus* assumes an earl to have an annual income of £400, a baron of 400 marks, while Edward III was more generous yet with his new earls.
2   H. L. Gray, 'Incomes from Land in England, 1436', *English Historical Review* (1934), XLIX, 611.
3   Ibid., 607–39, and T. B. Pugh and C. D. Ross, 'The English Baronage and the Income Tax of 1436', *Bulletin of the Institute of Historical Research* (1953), XXVI, 1–28.
4   T. B. Pugh, 'The Magnates, Knights and Gentry', in S. B. Chrimes, C. D. Ross, and R. A. Griffiths (eds), *Fifteenth-Century England, 1399–1509* (Manchester, 1972), 91–3.
5   McFarlane, *Nobility*, 59, also 61–82.
6   *Romeo and Juliet*, I, iii, 22–5. There is a description of the procedures which led to an IPM by E. R. Stevenson, 'The Escheator', in W. A. Morris and J. R. Strayer (eds), *The English Government at Work, 1327–36* (Cambridge, Mass., 1974), II, 109–67. Some of the problems of the IPM are treated in R. H. Hunnisett, 'The Reliability of Inquisitions as Historical Evidence', *The Study of Medieval Records: Essays in Honour of Kathleen Major*, D. A. Bullough and R. L. Storey (eds) (Oxford, 1971), 206–37. J. C. Holt has noted some duplications of terminology that make it seem possible that IPMs were either faked or patched up by royal clerks: *Economic History Review*, 2nd series (1973), XXVI, 695–6 (in a review of vol. XV of the *Inquisitions Post Mortem, 1–7 Richard II*).
7   The details of this quarrel are set out in R. I. Jack, 'Entail and Descent: The Hastings Inheritance, 1370 to 1436', *Bulletin of the Institute of Historical Research* (1965), XXXVIII, 1–19. Also, R. Jeffs, 'The Poynings-Percy Dispute', *BIHR* (1960), XXXIII, 148–64.
8   McFarlane, *Nobility*, 203. McFarlane's essay, 'The Beauchamps and the Staffords', 187–202, explores two detailed case studies of this phenomenon.
9   J. M. W. Bean, *The Decline of English Feudalism, 1215–1540* (Manchester, 1968), 41–2, and T. F. T. Plucknett, *The Legislation of Edward I* (Oxford, 1949), 116–18.
10 R. L. Storey, 'The Wardens of the Marches of England toward Scotland, 1377–1489', *English Historical Review* (1957), LXXII, 593–615.
11 *CCR*, 1429–1436, 150–1 (for 12 May 1432).
12 Bean, op. cit., 104–79; M. McKisack, *The Fourteenth Century* (Oxford, 1959), 261–2; and McFarlane, *Nobility*, 62–79 *passim*, 73, 'Thanks to the freedom conferred by the use, every conceivable alternative to straight inheritance had its devotees'.
13 Chichele, 543.
14 G. E. Cokayne, *The Complete Peerage* (London, 1910–59), VII, appendix A and appendix E.
15 *CCR*, 1296–1302, 54; *CFR*, 1272–1307, 399; *Calendar of Inquisitions Post Mortem*, V, no. 534. For land settled on a nephew, *CChR*, 1327–41, charter of 4 November 1330, and *CPR*, 1327–30, 500.
16 The treatment of traitors' widows is discussed in C. D. Ross, 'Forfeiture for treason in the Reign of Richard II', *English Historical Review* (1956), LXXI, 560–75. Margaret Badlesmere, forced to enter the Minories in London, had to subsist on 2s per day in 1322. This, however, was unusually harsh and most widows fared better.

17 British Museum: Egerton MS. 2822 (for 1462–3), Add. MS. 34,213 (for 1465–6), and Add. MSS. 22,644–5 (for 1472–3).
18 *CCR*, 1374–7, 448. Also, 189–90.
19 J. M. W. Bean, *The Estates of the Percy Family, 1416–1537* (Oxford, 1958), 7–10, and Holmes, op. cit., 7–8.
20 *CPR*, 1396–9, 285.
21 *CCR*, 1454–61, 415–16.
22 Bean, *Estates of the Percy Family*, 69–77.
23 *CCR*, 1413–1422, 150.
24 *Rot. Parl.*, VI, 57 (and also *Rymer*, IV, ii, 119).
25 *Rot. Parl.*, VI, 315.
26 E. Lamond (ed.), *Walter of Henley's Husbandry* (London, 1890), 35. D. Oschinsky, *Walter of Henley and other Treatises on Estate Management* (Oxford, 1971) for a discussion of the popularity of such works.
27 M. M. Postan, 'Medieval Agrarian Society in Its Prime: England', *Cambridge Economic History of Europe* (Cambridge, 2nd edn, 1965), I, 548–632, and especially 581–600. Also Holmes, op. cit., 92–3, 115–20.
28 C. D. Ross, 'The Estates and Finances of Richard Beauchamp, Earl of Warwick', Dugdale Society, Occasional Papers, 12 (Oxford, 1956); J. F. Baldwin, 'The Household Administration of Henry Lacy and Thomas of Lancaster', *English Historical Review* (1927), XLII, 180–200; N. Denholm-Young, *Seignorial Administration in England* (Oxford, 1937) are all good summaries of the baronial administrative structure.
29 McFarlane, *Nobility*, 3–4.
30 Holmes, op. cit., 90.
31 M. M. Postan, 'The Fifteenth Century', *Economic History Review* (1938–9), 160–7. For various views concerning the decline of manorial revenues over this period, see Holmes, op. cit., 126–8 (for a statement by the Lancastrian auditor on the causes of falling revenues in the 1388 accounts); McFarlane, *Nobility*, 58–9 (for the suggestion that the decline was more than balanced by the survivors' tendencies to accumulate new lands); Bean, *Estates of the Percy Family*, 12–42, 107–8 (and, on 107, 'It is clearly wrong to claim that the increasing pressure of debt forced the Percies to engage in a struggle for the profits of political power').
32 L. F. Salzman (ed.), *The Ministers' Accounts of the Manor of Petworth, 1347–1353*, Sussex Record Society (1955), LV, 44–51.
33 Gray, op. cit., 627: 'a manor which yielded an income of £20 to £39 in the fifteenth century was a goodly one'.
34 McFarlane, *Nobility*, 15–16: 'Rarely did they owe their ruin to the inability of their members to manage their own affairs'.

IV

1 J. Fortescue, *The Governance of England*, Charles Plummer (ed.) (Oxford, 1885), 128, 119. Plummer's discussion of bastard feudalism is still a good concise introduction.
2 From *PL*, II, 132, quoted in Fortescue, op. cit., 23.
3 *SR*, I, 106, and T. F. T. Plucknett, *Legislation of Edward I* (Oxford, 1949), 102–8.
4 *A Collection of Ordinances and Regulations for the Governance of the Royal Household* (London, 1790), 38.
5 McFarlane, *Nobility*, 140. For other examples, J. R. Maddicott, *Thomas of Lancaster*, 60–3: 'Family ties of this kind must have contributed a great deal to the vigour of the retinue' (60).

6   G. A. Holmes, *Estates of the Higher Nobility in Fourteenth-Century England* (Cambridge, 1957), 76–7.
7   Quoted by Holmes, op. cit., 75 (and on p. 124 in French).
8   *PL*, I, 442 (Letter no. 329, between 1454 and 1459).
9   From *John of Gaunt's Register*, E. C. Lodge and R. Somerville (eds), Camden Society, 3rd series, vols LVI and LVII (1937).
10 Reginald Pecock, *The Repressor of over much blaming of the clergy*, C. Babington (ed.), Rolls Series, vol. XIX (London, 1860), II, 306.
11 V. J. Scattergood, *Politics and Poetry in the Fifteenth Century* (London, 1972), 311–13.
12 *CPR*, 1452–61, 143–4. The king's council 'fully licenced all suche persones as he wolde calle to his counsail frely without any impediment to entende unto him' as a concession.
13 McFarlane, *Nobility*, 47.
14 *PL*, I, no. 184 (an indenture of 18 December 1452).
15 T. F. Tout, *Chapters in the Administrative History of Medieval England*, 6 volumes (Manchester, 1920–33), V, 289–440 (written by Margaret Sharp). For Gaunt, the earlier registers are available as well: *John of Gaunt's Register*, S. Armitage-Smith (ed.), Camden Society, 3rd series, XX and XXI (1911).
16 Printed in J. F. Baldwin, *The Household Administration of Henry Lacy and Thomas of Lancaster*, *EHR* (1927), XLII, 196–200. N. Denholm-Young, *Seignorial Administration in England* (Oxford, 1937), 7–8, for a brief description of a thirteenth-century hierarchy of accountants and officials.
17 B. Lyon, *From Fief to Indenture* (Cambridge, Mass., 1957).
18 *Gaunt's Register* (1937), no. 584.
19 Quoted in Denholm-Young, op. cit., 167, from Bodl. Lib., manuscripts, Dugdale, 18, fo. 83v.
20 W. H. Dunham, *Lord Hastings' Indentured Retainers, 1461–83* (New Haven, 1955), 123, 128, 129 respectively.
21 N. B. Lewis, 'The Organisation of Indentured Retainers in Fourteenth-Century England', in R. W. Southern (ed.), *Essays in Medieval History* (London, 1968), 212.
22 *PL*, I, no. 373.
23 Wm Langland, *The Book Concerning Piers the Plowman*, R. Attwater (ed.) (London, 1957), 29.
24 *Rot. Parl.*, II, 166.
25 *SR*, I, 264. Also, for the laws of 1468, ibid., II, 426–9.
26 R. L. Storey, 'Liveries and Commissions of the Peace, 1388–1390', *The Reign of Richard II*, 131–52.
27 *Rot. Parl.*, IV, 364.
28 This is treated in J. R. Lander, 'Bonds, Coercion, and Fear: Henry VII and the Peerage', in J. G. Rowe and W. H. Stockdale, *Florilegium Historiale, Essays Presented to W. K. Ferguson* (Toronto, 1971), 325–67.
29 *PPC*, IV, 36–7.
30 R. L. Storey, *The End of the House of Lancaster* (London, 1968), 88–92.
31 Compare the famous dictum, 'The Wars of the Roses were to a large extent a quarrel between Welsh Marcher Lords, who were also great English Nobles, closely related to the English throne', in G. M. Trevelyan, *History of England* (New York, 2nd edn, 1955), I, 339.
32 J. T. Rosenthal, 'Feuds and Private Peace Making: A Fifteenth-Century Example', *Nottingham Mediaeval Studies* (1970), XIV, 84–90.
33 *Rot. Parl.*, V, 409 (no. 29).

34 See G. R. Elton, 'The Body of the Whole Realm', *Studies in Tudor and Stuart Politics and Government* (Cambridge, 1974), 19 ff. (esp. 45 ff.), for a similar interpretation.

35 K. B. McFarlane, 'Parliament and "Bastard Feudalism"', *Essays in Medieval History*, R. W. Southern (ed.) (London, 1968), 263. The whole essay is the major treatment of the issue, 240–63.

v

1   I. S. Leadam and J. F. Baldwin (eds), *Select Cases before the King's Council, 1243–1482*, Selden Society (1918), XXXV, cx.

2   H. Trevor-Roper, *Men and Events* (New York, 1957), 31–2.

3   *TV*, 95–6.

4   A long, complicated, and repetitious marriage contract between Lord Botreaux's daughter and John Stafford is printed in *Collectanea Genealogica* (London, 1881–5), IV, 249–55. It covers such details as who shall provide 'mete, drynk, and horse mete' at the wedding banquet. There is a briefer agreement between the involved parents in *CCR*, 1381–5, 249–50.

5   PCC, 30 Vox.

6   McFarlane, *Nobility*, 136–7.

7   *PL*, I, 121–2 (no. 91).

8   *TV*, 140–5.

9   *TV*, 110–13.

10 Chichele, 393.

11 M. T. Martin (ed.), *The Percy Cartulary*, Surtees Society (1911), XCVII. The extant private cartularies are listed in G. R. C. Davis, *Medieval Cartularies of Great Britain* (London, 1958).

12 L. T. Smith (ed.), *Expeditions to Prussia and the Holy Land*, Camden Society, new series (1894), LII, 116–18.

13 R. H. Scaife (ed.), *The Register of the Guild of Corpus Christi in the City of York*, Surtees Society (1872), LVII.

14 Chichele, 22.

15 E. J. Arnould, *Le Livre de Seyntz Medicines* (Oxford, 1940), 244.

16 *CPR*, 1334–8, 545.

17 Chichele, 178.

18 Chichele, 95.

19 *CPR*, 1334–8, 270.

20 McFarlane, *Nobility*, 228–47, 'The Education of the Nobility in Later Medieval England'.

21 Marc Bloch, *The Historian's Craft* (New York, 1953), 164 for the use of this atrocious phrase.

22 PCC, Whittleseye 116b.

23 PCC, 7 Holgrave.

24 *Historical Manuscripts Commission, 9th Report*, pt I, appendix, 217: all local children were to come and 'frely be taught without exaccion of any Scolehire'.

25 R. Weiss, *Humanism in England during the Fifteenth Century* (Oxford, 2nd edn, 1957); R. J. Mitchell, *John Tiptoft, 1427–70* (London, 1938).

26 W. A. and F. Baillie-Grohman (eds), *Edward II, Duke of York: The Master of Game* (London, 1909).

INDEX

Abergavenny, Lord George of 59
Admiral, office of 53–4
Alms 93, 152
Amadeus of Savoy 182
Anglo-Saxon Chronicle 39, 75
Annuities 76, 80, 154–6
Aristocracy 17–19, 20, 22, 38, 42–4, 165; class consciousness of 45, 47; income and wealth of 56–7; service of 52–4
Aristotle 122
Arthur, son of Henry VII 96
Arundel Castle 76
Arundel, earls of, see FitzAlan
Arundel manor, Sussex 148–9
Assessment of 1436 57, 65
Audley, Nicholas 104

Badlesmere, Bartholomew 104
Bardolf family 92; Thomas 104
Barnet, battle of 55
Basset of Drayton, Ralph 104
Bastard feudalism 39, 44, 74–6, 80
Bavent, Roger 38, 104
Baynard, Robert 26, 104
Beauchamp family 58, 65, 92, 97, 182–3; Guy, earl of Warwick (d. 1315) 25, 103; Guy, mythical earl of Warwick 178–9; John of Kidderminster (d. 1388) 31; John of Powicke (d. 1475) 31, 127; John of Somerset 104; Richard, earl of Warwick (d. 1439) 33, 57, 129, 163; Roger of Bletsoe 62; Thomas, earl of Warwick (d. 1401) 67–8, 142–4; Walter, Lord St Amand (d. 1457), 127; William 65
Beaufort family 32, 34, 78; Edmund, duke of Somerset (d. 1455) 49, 127; Henry, bishop of Winchester 34, 91; John, earl of Somerset (d. 1410) 28, 32, 34, 91; Thomas, duke of Exeter (d. 1426) 34
Beaumont, family of 32–3; Henry 104; Joan 178; John, viscount (d. 1460), 77, 107, 129

Becket, Thomas 118–9
Bedford, duke of, see Plantagenet, Neville
Benet, William 126
Berdeswell, William 154–5
Beverley Abbey 95
Bisham Abbey (Brustlesham), Berkshire 95, 186–8
Bloch, Marc 18
Blount, James 158; Walter, Lord Mountjoy 163
Bohun family 58, 62; Humphrey, earl of Hereford (d. 1322) 25, 103; William, earl of Northampton (d. 1360) 77
Bois, William 61
Bonds of behaviour 82–3, 162–4
Bonville, William (d. 1461) 83, 164–7
Books 94, 189–92
Boroughbridge, battle of 36–7, 67
Bosworth, battle of 67, 81
Boteler, Ralph, Lord Sudeley (d. 1473) 129
Botetourt, John 104
Botiller of Wemme, William 104
Botreaux, William 31
Bourchier, family of 35–6, 63; Bartholomew (d. 1409) 28; Elizabeth 28; Henry, earl of Essex 33, 129; Thomas, archbishop of Canterbury 96; Lord Bourchier, see Robbesart, Stafford
Bramham Moor, battle of 68
Brewes, William 104
Briouge, family of 62
Brooke, Edward, Lord Cobham 49
Brun, Maurice 26, 104
Buckingham, duke of, see Stafford
Burghersh, Bartholomew 38, 62
Burke, Edmund 43
Burnel, Edward 26, 29, 104

Cambridge, earl of, see Plantagenet
Cambridge University 98
Camoys, family of 29

201